Second-Language Acquisition in Childhood:

Volume 1. Preschool Children
Second Edition

BARRY McLAUGHLIN
Adlai Stevenson College
University of California, Santa Cruz

LEA LAWRENCE ERLBAUM ASSOCIATES, PUBLISHERS
1984   Hillsdale, New Jersey   London

Lawrence Erlbaum Associates, Inc., Publishers
365 Broadway
Hillsdale, New Jersey 07642

Library of Congress Cataloging in Publication Data

McLaughlin, Barry.
    Second-language acquisition in childhood.

    (Child psychology)
    Bibliography: p.
    Includes indexes.
    Contents: v. 1.   Preschool children.
    1. Language acquisition.   2. Language and languages—
Study and teaching.   I. Title.   II. Series.
P118.M39   1984   401'.9   83-20749
ISBN 0-8058-0095-6 (v. 1)

Printed in the United States of America
10 9 8 7 6 5

SECOND-LANGUAGE ACQUISITION IN CHILDHOOD:
VOLUME 1. PRESCHOOL CHILDREN
SECOND EDITION

CHILD PSYCHOLOGY

A series of books edited by **David S. Palermo**

To Quinn and Christopher,
who provided the inspiration for this book.

Contents

Preface

This book is a comprehensive treatment of the literature on second language acquisition in childhood. There is increasing interest in this area and a number of collections of readings have appeared, dealing with various aspects of the topic. There is, however, no general overview of the field for the interested professional reader. The present book is intended to fill this gap.

Like many people, I became interested in how children acquire a second language through my own children. We lived in Germany for three years when our children were very young, and I was impressed with how they could make sense out of English and German and could produce the two languages in their speech. I began to read the professional literature on bilingualism and second-language acquisition and was struck by the sense of excitement that permeated the field. It seemed to me that the excitement that marked research on first-language acquisition in the 1960s had spread to the field of second-language acquisition. There were important breakthroughs on a number of fronts. New and stimulating ideas were providing researchers with a wide range of hypotheses for empirical scrutiny. Moreover, I found some surprises in the older literature. The problem was that the literature, old and new, was relatively inaccessible to the nonspecialist. There was a definite need to make the findings available to educators, psychologists, and psycholinguists.

My first attempt in this direction was an article that appeared in the *Psychological Bulletin* (McLaughlin, 1977) in which I itemized some misconceptions about second-language acquisition that have been perpetuated in popular (and sometimes professional) literature. A more detailed treatment of these issues was presented in the first edition of this work. This edition updates the discussion and restricts it to the preschool period. I have decided that the question of the acquisition of a second language during the school years deserves a volume in itself. The present volume is concerned with untutored, naturalistic learning of oral skills in a second language. The second volume deals with second-language learning in the classroom, where the child has to learn both to speak the language and to read and write it.

I have tried to be sensitive to recent developments. Because of the research boom in second-language acquisition, this edition (though written only 5 years after the first appeared) has a much greater data base. Consequently, much of the book required re-writing and there are over 200 new references. At that, I have only been able to cover some (to my mind the most important) of the many new studies that have appeared in what is an extremely vigorous line of research.

I have attempted in this book to view second-language acquisition in terms of contemporary models of language acquisition. Gone are the behavioristic models of yesterday, and slowly departing from the scene are models based on formal linguistic theory. Psycholinguists today want to account both for what the child acquiring a language *can* do and what the child *does* do. For this reason there is increasing attention given to the development of process models of language. In Chapter 2 I discuss these models and throughout the book I view language acquisition, at least in general terms, from this perspective.

Chapter 3 compares second-language acquisition in children and adults and discusses the critical period notion. Chapters 4 and 5 are concerned with simultaneous and successive acquisition of a second language. I attempt in these chapters to summarize what is known about the developmental processes involved in simultaneous and successive second-language acquisition, to examine the effect of interference between languages, and to discuss the topic of code switching—or how the bilingual alternates languages.

Chapter 6 takes up the question of individual differences in language learning, and Chapter 7 discusses the effects of early bilingualism on language development and intellectual and cognitive functioning. Both of these chapters are new, Chapter 7 being an expanded version of McLaughlin (in press). In Chapter 8 I spell out the limits of our knowledge in the area of second-language acquisition and draw some tentative conclusions suggested by research.

It may be somewhat foolhardy to attempt to write a book about a field as dynamic as that of second-language acquisition. There is so much activity in this area at present that it is difficult to keep abreast of the literature, and I apologize for any oversights. I have tried to reflect what I believe is the trend in this field of research—away from simplistic statements favoring one extreme position or the other, to a more complex description of the language learning process. Second-language learning in children involves both biological and social-psychological factors; it is influenced by transfer from the child's first language and by the developmental constraints of the target second language; it is systematic in some respects yet there is room for individual variation; it may have negative or positive consequences, depending on a number of intervening variables. This complexity may be frustrating, but it is a sign of a maturing field.

I am indebted to the Alexander von Humboldt Foundation for the financial support that made writing the first edition of this book possible. Dr. Suitbert Ertel of the Institut für Psychologie, Göttingen, provided encouragement and research facilities. My thinking in writing the second edition has been influenced by conversations with Ann Peters, Lily Wong Fillmore, Marilyn Vihman, and Kenji Hakuta, whose work figures prominently in Chapter 6 and Chapter 7. Above all, I wish to thank my wife, Sigrid, for translating numerous articles and for her comments on various drafts of the manuscript.

Barry McLaughlin
Santa Cruz, June 1983

Acknowledgments

The preparation of this book has been aided by the cooperation of a number of sources. The figures and tables used have been made available through the courtesy and permission of their original authors and publishers and are listed below in order of appearance.

For Table 1.1:
  From Macnamara, J. The bilingual's linguistic performance: A psychological overview. *Journal of Social Issues,* 1967, *23,* 58–77, page 59, Figure 1. (Copyright 1967 by the Society for the Psychological Study of Social Issues. Reprinted by permission of author and the Society for the Psychological Study of Social Issues.)

For Figure 3.1:
  From Fromkin, V., Krashen, S., Curtiss, S., Rigler, D., & Rigler, M. The development of language in Genie: A case of language acquisition beyond the critical period. *Brain and Language,* 1974, *1,* 81–107, p. 99, Figure 1. (Copyright 1974 by Academic Press. Reprinted by permission of V. Fromkin and the Academic Press.)

For Table 4.3:
  From Clark, E. V. What's in a word? On the child's acquisition of semantics in his first language. In T. E. Moore (Ed.), *Cognitive development and the acquisition of language.* New York: Academic Press, 1973, p. 87, Table 9. (Copyright 1973 by Academic Press. Reprinted by permission of the author and the Academic Press.)

For Table 5.1:
  From Milon, J. P. The development of negation in English by a second language learner. *TESOL Quarterly,* 1974, *8,* 137–143, p. 140, Table 4. (Copyright 1974 by Teachers of English to Speakers of Other Languages, Washington, D.C. Reprinted by permission of the author and publisher.)

For Table 5.2:
  From Ervin-Tripp, S. Is second language learning like the first? *TESOL Quarterly,* 1974, *8,* 111–127, p. 119, Table 2. (Copyright 1974 by Teachers of English to Speakers of Other Languages, Washington, D.C. Reprinted by permission of the author and publisher.)

For Table 5.4:
  From Ervin-Tripp, S. Is Second language learning like the first? *TESOL Quarterly,* 1974, *8,* 111–127, p. 116, Table 1. (Copyright 1974 by Teachers of English to Speakers of Other Languages, Washington, D.C. Reprinted by permission of the author and publisher.)

For Table 5.6:
  From Dulay, H. C., & Burt, M. K. Goofing: An indication of children's second language learning strategies. *Language Learning,* 1972, *22,* 235–252, pp. 245–246, Tables 1–4. (Copyright 1972 by *Language Learning.* Reprinted by permission of H. Douglas Brown, Editor, *Language Learning.*)

For Table 7.1:
  From Ianco-Worrall, A. D. Bilingualism and cognitive development. *Child Development,* 1972, *43,* 1390–1400, p. 1395, Table 1. (Copyright 1972 by the Society for Research in Child Development, Inc. Reprinted by permission of the author and University of Chicago Press.)

SECOND-LANGUAGE ACQUISITION IN CHILDHOOD:
VOLUME 1. PRESCHOOL CHILDREN
SECOND EDITION

1 Bilingualism in Society

INTRODUCTION

For most societies of the world, linguistic diversity is the norm—not the exception. Bilingualism is present in practically every country of the world, at all levels of society and in all age groups (Grosjean, 1982). This is sometimes difficult for Americans to appreciate. We have become accustomed to the notion that the world is becoming more homogeneous, that there is a linguistic convergence, with English gradually becoming the universal language. It is no doubt true that English is used widely as a medium of communication in scientific and technical domains, but this does not mean that English is replacing indigenous languages. If anything, the spread of English as a universal technical language is one reason why an increasing number of people in the world are bi- or multilingual. English (or French or Russian) may be learned as an international language, but national and ethnic languages are maintained in communicating with one's countrymen.

A similar phenomenon seems to occur on the national level. It often happens that central governments attempt to enforce national homogeneity by the imposition of a standard national language. The result is usually an increase in bilingualism, with large segments of the population speaking both the standard tongue and the local language or dialect. When the government attempts to do away with local languages and dialects, it meets with resistance and an upsurge of ethnic feelings on the part of the people affected.

Even in the United States, there is resistance to the imposition of a single standard language. Various ethnic groups strive to maintain their identity

1

by raising their children bilingually (Fishman, 1980). Many American children hear Japanese, Spanish, Italian, or French in the home and in school. In fact, it is estimated that 28 million Americans come from homes where a language other than English is spoken (Waggoner, 1978) and that 15 million Americans speak a language other than English on a regular basis (Grosjean, 1982).

Bilingualism As a Social Problem

Bilingualism is a social problem precisely because language is so intimately a part of one's identity. The distrust shown by many people and governments toward bilingual individuals stems largely from the feeling that they are not loyal citizens because they can speak another language. Their loyalties are in question because they hold dual linguistic (and cultural) allegiance. The Basques in Spain and the Ukrainians in the Soviet Union are examples of people who have suffered for this reason.

In spite of the efforts of governments and the distrust of their fellow citizens, there seems to be an increase in feelings of ethnic identity, especially among linguistic minorities in Europe. The Scots, the Bretons, the Basques, and the Catalans, among others, have been striving for increasing autonomy and for the bilingual education of their children. For the most part, these efforts have been resisted by the central government, but this resistance often has served to stimulate ethnic feelings.

The more activist ethnic groups are but a small fraction of the total number of multiethnic and multilinguistic communities in Europe: the Catalans, Basques, and Galicians in Spain; the Bretons and Provençals in France; the Welsh, Scots, and Irish in Great Britain; the Flemings and Walloons in Belgium; the Valoise, Piedmontese, and Germans in Italy; the Frisians in Holland; the Italians, Hungarians, Slovenes, Croatians, Albanians, and Macedonians in Yugoslavia; the Laps in Scandinavia; the Germans, Poles, and Slovaks in Czechoslovakia; the Finns, Estonians, Latvians, Lithuanians, and Ukrainians in the Soviet Union, and so forth. This same linguistic diversity is represented even more dramatically in countries of Africa, Latin America, and Asia. India, for example, has 13 major languages aside from Hindi and a large number of minor languages. Even in the Arab countries, which share a common language, classical Arabic coexists with the vernacular variety spoken by the people of Egypt, Syria, or Iraq (Macnamara, 1967a).

In many countries where two or more languages or dialects are spoken, a second language is necessary to serve as a common medium of communication or instruction. Examples include Russian in the Soviet Union, English or French in many countries of Africa, Bahasa Indonesian in Indonesia, and Pilipino in the Philippines. In some cases, a national language is established from one that has not been spoken for centuries or only by a small group; for example, Hebrew in Israel or Swahili in Tanzania. Some countries have two or more official languages—for example, Canada, Switzerland, Finland, Wales, Belgium, and Sri Lanka.

In the United States monolingualism traditionally has been the norm. Bilingualism was regarded as a social stigma and a liability (Fishman, 1966). Immigrant parents, and even American Indians (Casagrande, 1948), sometimes have attempted to raise their children in English rather than in their native tongue, so that the children would become assimilated into the larger social context as soon as possible. Bilinguals did not fit into the American scene because they were carrying extra linguistic baggage. This made them seem foreign and hence suspect.

Although such ethnic groups as Mexican–Americans and Indians currently are attempting to maintain their native languages as part of their cultural identity, it is difficult for the individual to belong to two communities at once. There are often cultural, religious, and moral differences that lead to strain and identity conflict. To be accepted in two communities means having to shift back and forth in language, behavior, and attitudes. This can be an enormous burden for the individual and can drain one emotionally (Ulibarri, 1972). Bilinguals usually opt for one of their two worlds and risk being rejected in the other (Child, 1943).

The same is often true of bilinguals in other societies. The language minority may be looked down upon by the "standard" majority. There may be stereotyping and even hostility. Bilinguals may find that they are disadvantaged economically when compared to their monolingual counterparts. Even in countries where linguistic diversity is officially tolerated, there may be subtle (or not so subtle) forms of discrimination exercised against members of linguistic minorities.

This hostility toward bilingualism has nothing to do with language as such. The hostility is directed not at language but at culture. The bilingual represents an alien way of thinking and alien values. Often, too, the bilingual is a member of a minority group whose interests threaten the economic interests of the majority. Language becomes a convenient way of separating "them" and "us." But language itself is not the critical factor.

What matters are the attitudes of members of the minority and majority communities. When the attitudes are favorable and relations are friendly, bilingualism need not have negative consequences for the individual or for a group. Some countries, such as Switzerland, seem to have achieved a remarkable degree of harmony between people speaking different languages. In America, on the other hand, the experience of assimilating waves of immigrants led to negative attitudes toward those who speak with an accent. The official school doctrine has been that language diversity is undesirable (Kobrick, 1972). The school has been the means of separating immigrant children from their cultural past and of assimilating them into the dominant culture. This view of the school's purpose seems to be changing, however, at least on the official level. Minority group demands for recognition of their cultural values and the passage in 1967 of the Bilingual Education Act, Title VII of the Elementary and Secondary Education Act, have led to an increasing number of bilingual education programs, especially at the kindergarten and early elementary levels.

It remains to be seen whether such programs will succeed in changing the attitudes of the American people. In the public mind, English is the language of technology and industrial progress; bilingualism is associated with the culture of poverty and academic failure. If, however, bilingual education programs give Indians, Mexican–Americans, Puerto Ricans, and other groups a sense of their historical and cultural roots, these minority group cultures may make a compensatory rehumanizing contribution to our industrial mass culture (Christian & Sharp, 1972; Fishman, 1980).

We are, however, a long way from realizing these objectives. There is still a strong residue of xenophobia and isolationism in this country. Prejudice against the foreign and the alien is still widespread. This need not mean the consequences for the bilingual individual are necessarily negative. As we shall see subsequently, general statements about the effect of bilingualism on the individual are difficult to support empirically. There are important social and individual difference variables. The experience of a poor Chicano who acquires English as a second language is different from that of an upper-class white child who learns French or German in a kindergarten where these languages are spoken. The child's own sense of self-identity and confidence also play an important part in determining the effect of bilingualism on development. These social and individual differences make predictions impossible. One person may suffer throughout life because of a feeling of anomie and a sense of not belonging (Zedlitz, 1963); another may experience no such feelings and may view bilingualism as an asset to personal adjustment and intellectual development (Elwert, 1960).

Bilingualism as a Psycholinguistic Problem

Research with adult bilinguals. Bilingualism represents an interesting problem for psycholinguistic investigation. How is it that a person can separate two languages in storage and production? How does a bilingual individual think? Are cognitive processes in bilingual subjects different from cognitive processes in monolingual subjects?

For the most part, psycholinguists have investigated these problems using the *experimental method.* That is, they have examined the way in which bilinguals process information under tightly controlled laboratory conditions.

For example, Dornic (1979) reported on a number of studies in which he found that processing speed increased according to the experience the subject had with a language. This was true for both comprehension and production. In the comprehension studies, subjects had to follow short directions telling them to check off a series of items defined by position, value, shape, or color. Even with the simplest form of this test, speed of response was found to be slower in the language with which the bilinguals had relatively less experience. In the production test, subjects were asked to name pictures of common objects in either of their two languages. Again, the speed with which subjects could perform such a task depended on their experience with the two languages.

In these studies, Dornic followed the conventions for experimental research. He carried out his research in a laboratory setting, where subjects could be tested individually without interruption. Each subject received the same instructions and each was tested following the same procedures. Objective measurement techniques were used to determine comprehension (reaction time) and production (naming latencies).

Like Dornic's research, most psycholinguistic investigations of bilingual information processing have been carried out with adult subjects. This research follows the conventions of experimental investigations, and is concerned principally with memory and information processing. Very little research of this nature has been conducted with bilingual children. Instead, researchers studying children have tended to use two other research paradigms: the case-study method and elicitation techniques. These methods are used with adults, but they predominate in the child literature.

Research with bilingual children. In the past 20 years considerable attention has been given to the question of how language develops. Progress has been made in tracing the stages through which children pass in their language development (Brown, 1973a) and in identifying those processes that operate in the child's language acquisition system (Ervin-Tripp, 1970b). Careful observation of children learning to talk has revealed certain sets of semantic relations that are reflected in early one- and two-word utterances (Bloom, 1973; Bowerman, 1973; Brown, 1973a). Some insights have been acquired about how children learn relational concepts and concepts of space and time (E. V. Clark, 1973; H. H. Clark, 1970, 1973). Researchers have also begun to explore parent–child interaction patterns and how these affect language development (Wells, 1981).

Yet there remains a great deal that is not known about language development in children. In part, this is because it is so difficult to study children. One cannot analyze a child's speech in the way a psycholinguist analyzes an adult's. The researcher can ask adults why they use certain forms and whether specific forms are correct or incorrect. With a young child, this is impossible. Furthermore, a child's language is developing and does not remain constant; the child's grammar is continually changing.

The best that can be done is either to observe the child's speech or attempt in various ways to elicit language from the child. The first technique has been the most widely employed and shall be referred to here as the *case–study method.* Most of the important recent findings about children's language development have come through the use of this method. Investigators have spent many hours with a few children, recording carefully their utterances over an extended period of time. In this way information has been gained about the stages through which children progress in phonological, syntactic, and semantic development. There are difficulties with such observational procedures: observers may see only what they want to see and may tend to record data consistent with their hypothesis more readily than data opposed to it. There is also the problem of interpreting the child's meaning, especially in early utterances. When a child says *Milk,* for example, does that mean that the child wants milk, or that an object seen is white like milk, or that milk is in a bottle, or that the child is hungry, or what? The context helps, but one is never entirely sure that one's interpretation is correct. This becomes a critical issue in attempting to infer knowledge of semantic relations in young children on the basis of their utterances (Brown, 1973a).

Because of the danger of observational bias inherent in the case–study method, this approach has been complemented by *elicitation methods.* The purpose of these methods is to determine in a more systematic manner whether children can understand and produce specific grammatical constructions. Quite ingenious methods have been devised to elicit constructions from children. For example, Bellugi (1971) was interested in how children construct *wh-* questions. She used a puppet to elicit different types of questions from young children:

Adult: Adam, ask the old lady (puppet) what she'll do next.
Adam: Old lady, what will you do now?
Adult: Adam, ask the old lady why she can't sit down.
Adam: Old lady, why you can't sit down.

DeVilliers and DeVilliers (1972) used a procedure that required young children to take the role of a puppet they had seen correcting the utterances of another puppet who sometimes spoke correctly with respect to word order (*Fill the cup*) and sometimes incorrectly (*Cup the fill*). Only children who were quite advanced in their language development were able to make judgments of appropriate word order correctly. A final example of a technique successfully employed with young children is the elicited imitation technique (Slobin & Welsh, 1973). Here the child's task is simply to repeat sentences or strings of words uttered by a model:

Adult: Mozart who cried came to my party.
Child: Mozart cried and he came to my party.

Adult: The owl who eats candy runs fast.
Child: Owl eat the candy and he run fast.

Adult: The boy the book hit was crying.
Child: Boy the book was crying.

For the most part, studies of bilingualism in children have used the case–study method. They are subject, consequently, to the difficulties of all case studies: lack of adequate control, selective sampling procedures, lack of measurement reliability, and observer bias. This is not to say that the case–study literature is of little value; indeed, its value is great. Some studies were anecdotal and impressionistic, but others were very well conducted. Most of the studies to be discussed in this book fall into this second category. Without these case studies we would know very little about early bilingualism.

From a specifically psycholinguistic point of view, there are at least three critical issues of interest in the study of bilingualism in children. The first of these concerns the *developmental sequence* followed by the child simultaneously acquiring two languages or acquiring a second language once a first language has been established. Does the bilingual child follow the same developmental sequence in acquiring two languages as the monolingual child does? What happens if the developmental sequence for the two languages is not the same? Does the child acquiring a second language once the first has been established progress through the same stages of development as a native speaker of that language? Do children recapitulate the stages of their first language when learning a second language? Or is language development completely different in such cases?

A second issue concerns *interference between languages*. What effect does acquiring two languages simultaneously have on the acquisition of each? Are bilingual children retarded in their language development when compared to monolingual children? What types of mistakes appear in the utterances of children acquiring a second language? What is the evidence for phonological, syntactic, and semantic interference in the speech of children who experience a bilingual presentation or who acquire a second language subsequent to the establishment of their first language?

The third issue concerns *code switching*. Here I refer to the child's ability to move from one linguistic code or language to another. The term also is used to refer to types of speech within a single language: formal versus informal codes, intimate versus public codes, colloquial and vulgar codes. Are special processes involved in the bilingual's ability to switch languages? Under what conditions is switching difficult? What determines the language to be used in specific situations?

What Is Bilingualism?

At this point it is probably a good idea to attempt to tighten up some concepts bandied about until now. First of all, there is the question of what is meant by *bilingualism*. What degree of proficiency must a person possess in two languages to be considered a bilingual? The answer, of course, depends in part on the age of the individual. A bilingual adult is expected to possess a greater facility with two languages than a bilingual child. But suppose an adult has simply a reading knowledge of a second language. Is this person bilingual?

Some authors regard a person as bilingual who knows some words in another language (whether the individual can say the words or not). At the other extreme is the definition of bilingualism that equates it with native-like control of two languages (Bloomfield, 1935). This, however, begs the question of what is meant by native-like and seems to set too high a standard. The appropriate degree of knowledge of two languages seems to lie somewhere between the criterion set by the maximists and that of the minimists. The easiest way out is probably to lean toward the minimist side and allow the label of bilingual to be attached to anyone who possesses a mere smattering of knowledge of a second language in whatever medium. Macnamara (1967a), for example, regarded as a bilingual anyone who possessed, even to a minimal degree, at least one of the language skills listed in the matrix in Table 1.1. Any attempt to set a more definite criterion seems arbitrary.

Nonetheless, throughout this book, *bilingualism* refers to the ability "to produce complete and meaningful utterances in the other language [Haugen, 1956, p. 6]." Arbitrary and unspecific as such a definition is, it does not allow the term *bilingual* to be applied to an individual who knows

TABLE 1.1
Matrix of Language Skills[a]

Encoding		Decoding	
Speaking	Writing	Listening	Reading
Semantics	Semantics	Semantics	Semantics
Syntactics	Syntactics	Syntactics	Syntactics
Lexicon	Lexicon	Lexicon	Lexicon
Phonemes	Graphemes	Phonemes	Graphemes

[a]From Macnamara (1967b).

merely one or two words of a second language. In fact, there is no particular advantage to setting arbitrary limits for a definition of bilingualism, since what matters is the extent of the individual's knowledge of the two languages (Jakobovits, 1970). Bilingualism is best described in terms of degree rather than as an all-or-none dichotomy (DeAvila & Duncan, 1980). In this way the notion of bilingualism lends itself to quantitative assessment.

Such an approach is more realistic, because it avoids the implication that a bilingual is a person who is equally proficient in two languages. It often happens that a child's two languages are limited to different situations. One language may be used with playmates and another with parents. The child may use one in school and a different language at home. As a result, the child may become more fluent in certain areas in one language than in another. In general it is usually fairly difficult for the bilingual to maintain linguistic *balance*—to attain the same level of fluency in all spheres in both languages.

Some authors have distinguished between different types of bilingualism. The most common distinction is that between *compound* and *coordinate* bilingualism (Ervin & Osgood, 1954; Haugen, 1956; Weinrcich, 1953). The distinction refers essentially to the semantic aspect of language. Compound bilinguals are defined as those who attribute identical meanings to corresponding words and expressions in their two languages. This fusion of meaning is thought to result from learning a foreign language through vocabulary training in a school situation (i.e., in terms of meanings established by one's first language) or from acquiring two languages in a home where both are spoken interchangeably by the same people and in the same situations. Coordinate bilinguals are defined as those who derive different or partially different meanings from words in the two languages. The distinction in meaning is thought to arise from learning the two languages in different situations where the languages are rarely interchanged. In spite of the existence of at least 27 tests for measuring compound versus coordinate bilingualism (Jakobovits, 1970), the distinction has not been validated experimentally and is difficult to maintain in practice (Diller, 1970; Kirstein & de Vincenz, 1974). Hence I avoid speaking of bilingualism in these terms.

Nor are cases of *diglossia* treated here, either in Ferguson's (1959) original sense of separate language codes (standard and vernacular) that serve different functions within a single society, or in the sense in which the term is used by other authors (Fishman, 1964, 1970; Gumperz, 1962) to refer to separate dialects, registers, or functionally differentiated language varieties of whatever kind. Although admittedly the distinction between language and dialect is often blurred, I use language in this book to refer to standard language types such as standard English, Spanish, French, and so forth.

The use of the terms *native tongue, mother tongue, foreign language,* and *primary language* are avoided. Instead I speak of *first* and *second languages.* By first language is meant that language which is chronologically first, even though it may belong to a brief stage of the child's development and subsequently may be forgotten and never used. Thus it can happen that a second language—one that is acquired after a first language—becomes the individual's main and even only language in daily discourse. Although there are drawbacks to the chronological distinction between first and second languages (Halliday, McIntosh, & Stevens, 1964), it seems better to differentiate on this basis rather than on the basis of facility in a language (Lado, 1964), since facility may change with time or place.

Strictly speaking, one cannot use the terms *first* and *second languages* in the case of a child who is exposed from birth to bilingual language presentation. In such cases I speak of *bilingual children* and avoid the distinction between first and second languages. Thus children who hear one language from their mother and another from their father or one language from their parents and another from their nurse or playmates and who acquire both languages to the extent that they speak both are referred to simply as bilingual children. Acquisition of the two languages in such cases is *simultaneous.*

A different situation occurs when one language is established first and a second is learned subsequently. Here the first language-second language distinction is valid, and learning can be said to be *successive.* The question arises, however, of deciding when a first language can be said to be "established." For the present purposes, I arbitrarily set the cutoff point at three years. The child who is introduced to a second language before three years of age is said to be *simultaneously* acquiring two languages. The child who is introduced to a second language after three is said to be *successively* acquiring two languages.

It should be noted, however, that the distinction between simultaneous acquisition of two languages and successive acquisition of a second language is not always easy to make. Children differ considerably in the rate at which they acquire a first language. Hence a cutoff point based on linguistic and cognitive developmental criteria is preferable to one based on chronological age (Vihman & McLaughlin, 1982). Here, however, one confronts the intractable problem of what it means to say that a child (or chimp, for that matter) possesses a language (Limber, 1977; Palermo & Molfese, 1972). It seems the better part of wisdom to avoid this quagmire and stay with the three-year criterion.

A final point needs to be made about the phrase "second-language learning." Some authors distinguish *second-language acquisition* and *second-language learning.* For Krashen (1981), in particular, this distinction is critical theoretically. Second-language acquisition refers to the subconscious acquisition of a second language in a natural environment. Second-language learning refers to conscious learning in a formal classroom situation with feedback, error correction, rule learning, and an artificial linguistic environment that introduces one aspect of the grammar at a time. It is extremely difficult, however, to distinguish "acquisition" from "learning" in specific cases (McLaughlin, 1978). Reliance on the situational context is not satisfactory because one can "acquire" language in a classroom setting focused largely on formal rules (Krashen, 1981), just as one can "learn" rules in informal situations from native informants. The conscious–subconscious distinction is not satisfactory because it is often impossible in a given instance to know to what extent learners are consciously aware of what they are learning.

Because the learning-acquisition distinction is nebulous in practice, I have avoided its use. In this book the terms "learning" and "acquisition" are used interchangeably. As was noted in the Preface, this volume is concerned almost exclusively with naturalistic, untutored second-language learning; whereas the second volume will be concerned with second-language learning in the classroom.

2 First-Language Acquisition

I do not attempt in this chapter the rather Gargantuan task of surveying what is known about the child's acquisition of a first language. The amount of information that has accumulated, especially in the last two decades, is formidable. Furthermore, excellent accounts of first-language acquisition exist elsewhere (especially Brown, 1973a; Lindfors, 1980). The aim is a more modest one: to provide background and perspective for the discussion that follows in subsequent chapters of the child's acquisition of a second language.

This chapter has four sections. First, I examine different ways of looking at the language acquisition process and at the skills that the child is thought to bring to this task. Then I turn to a consideration of just what it is that the child must accomplish in order to acquire a language. A discussion of the linguistic environment of the child language learner follows. Finally, a brief overview is presented of the developmental stages characteristic of first-language acquisition.

THE CHILD'S LINGUISTIC CAPACITIES

Descriptions of the language development process and of the child's linguistic capabilities differ depending on the epistemological stance one adopts. Usually a distinction is drawn between the rationalist and the empiricist positions. The rationalist regards cognitive abilities as given. Experience does not teach directly; it activates an innate capacity. We know the world as we do, because we are biologically structured to know it in this

way. We acquire language as we do, because we are preprogrammed to acquire it in this manner. Indeed, only humans can acquire language, because
only the human species is so constituted. Language is a species-specific, innate ability.

The empiricist is skeptical of explanatory attempts that depend on the existence of nonobservable, innate characteristics. It is true that humans are
born with a specific biological structure and certain cognitive and linguistic
capacities. These are, however, by no means as general and as predetermining as the rationalist would have it. Innate capacities are few and relatively
simple, such as the ability to form associations. The essential characteristic
of the human species is plasticity, the capacity to learn from experience. The
child has no special ability for language; language acquisition simply
reflects a general capacity to learn.

The rationalist does not, of course, deny that the child learns from experience. Obviously, children learn to speak a certain language, because
they hear others around them speaking it. On this score the difference between the two positions is one of degree, as it is on the question of the role
of innate structures in the learning process. But the two positions differ
radically on the question of the child's capacity for language. The rationalists believe in the species specificity and uniformity of language acquisition. The empiricists deny that language acquisition is different from
any other type of learning.

Models of Language Acquisition in Children

In contemporary psycholinguistic theories of language acquisition, the rationalist position usually is advocated by those who follow Noam Chomsky
and approach language from a transformational grammar point of view.
The empiricist position is associated with B. F. Skinner and other
behaviorists for whom language is a response to the stimulus characteristics
of the environment. Many workers in the field, however, prefer to side-step
this debate entirely. For them, a different model—one that views language
in process terms—is superior to that of either behaviorism or transformational grammar. Let us briefly consider each of these three models.

The behaviorist model.   Traditional American, behaviorist psychology
has taken a cavalier attitude toward language acquisition. Languages were
thought to be learned like anything else. One need not study language learning as such; it was enough to study general principles of behavior. When B.
F. Skinner wrote his *magnum opus* on language, *Verbal behavior* (1957), he
did not draw on an extended program of research with human subjects performing various linguistic tasks. Instead, his book was an unabashed ex-
trapolation from laboratory research with nonverbal organisms.

In Skinner's system, language is a function of *reinforcement*. The parent teaches the child to talk by reinforcing verbal behavior. The child learns to name things correctly because of reinforcement for doing so. Initially, learning involves a slow and laborious process of successive approximations, but subsequently less tedious procedures for evoking the correct response are possible as the child learns to respond to such generalized reinforcers as signs of approval or praise from parents and other members of the verbal community.

Grammar is acquired like other verbal responses. The child learns a framework within which to place lexical items. When a 2½-year-old girl says, *When you untry to do it,* she does not yet have all of the morphemes in their appropriate order within the grammatical frame. In time she will learn the correct order in the same way she learns other behavioral patterns. Such learning, like all learning, occurs gradually; eventually most errors will be corrected through selective reinforcement from the verbal community.

Skinner's theory was subjected to rigorous examination by Chomsky (1959), who argued eloquently that the theory was erroneous in its assumptions, untestable, subjective, and cluttered with vague and poorly defined concepts. Reinforcement could not possibly handle the explanatory load Skinner assigned it; grammars could not possibly be learned by fitting words into grammatical frames. How would Skinner, for example, explain why *is* can be substituted for *can be* in the sentence, *Marking papers can be a nuisance* but not in the sentence, *Struggling artists can be a nuisance,* although the two sentences have the same frame? Behaviorist theory, as represented in Skinner's book, was irredeemably naive from a linguistic point of view.

For linguists, other applications of behaviorist principles were equally oversimplified. To attempt to explain language acquisition in terms of such behaviorist concepts as imitation (Miller & Dollard, 1941), sign learning and secondary reinforcement (Mowrer, 1960), or response hierarchies and stimulus control (Staats, 1968) was just whistling in the dark. Behaviorist mechanisms did not and could not in principle apply to the acquisition of language.

The difficulty is that the associationistic model assumes that the organism possesses a finite repertoire of behaviors, any one of which may, on occasion, be triggered by specific stimulus parameters. The probability of such an occurrence depends on the organism's history of reinforcement and may be represented by a construct such as habit strength or associative connection. This model runs into trouble when it is applied to language, because in acquiring a language a speaker internalizes a finite set of rules that are, however, sufficient to provide him with a repertoire of infinitely many linguistic responses (Garrett & Fodor, 1968). The stimulus–response, associationistic theory is insufficient because it requires that the speaker select from a pre-existing response repertoire one of a finite number of responses on the basis of some previously established association. Such a model is incapable in principle of accounting for indefinitely diversified responses.

By the time linguists and psycholinguists had finished storming the behaviorist castle, traditional psychological thinking about the nature of language development had been modified appreciably. The older behaviorist models seemed to be definitely inappropriate. Much more sophisticated and complex models were indicated. Some steps in this direction have been made, but the new formulations were attacked as sharply as the old (McLaughlin 1971). More important, the behaviorist tradition generated relatively little empirical research on the problem of language. This is telling, since the behaviorists had steadfastly maintained that language must be susceptible to empirical scrutiny. Yet over the last two decades, linguistic theory has proved to be a far richer source of hypotheses on language than has behavioral theory.

Furthermore, the language acquisition process did not seem to correspond to the pattern the behaviorists expected. Chomsky seemed to be right about the secondary importance of reinforcement. Careful observation of young children showed that parents rarely corrected errors in pronunciation or grammar. In fact, the grounds on which an utterance is approved or disapproved usually are not linguistic at all (Brown, 1973a). If a young boy says *I ranned faster than him,* his father is more likely to pat him on the back than correct his syntax.

Nor did imitation, another favorite behaviorist mechanism, seem to play a very important role in language acquisition. The child's language is simply too strange. The child has never heard *two foots* or *I comed,* yet such constructions are quite common and persistent. It seems as though the child is going through an active process of testing, discarding, and refining grammatical rule systems. Moreover, this happens even if the child cannot speak at all but simply hears other speaking (Lenneberg, 1962). This seemed to exclude any account of language development that gives a central role to imitation.

As more information accumulated about children's language, it became quite apparent that the child's linguistic behavior is much more complex than was supposed. One of the reasons for postulating innate mechanisms was that the speech input to which the child is exposed did not seem to be a rich enough source for induction of the rules of grammar. Furthermore, the facts of grammar were not explicable simply on the basis of surface structure. It seemed necessary to postulate some sort of deep structure to account for how we understand ambiguous sentences such as the famous, *They are eating apples.* Transformational grammar appeared to offer a more powerful approach to language than did traditional psychological theory.

The transformational grammar approach.   Chomsky and his followers argued that languages cannot be acquired by application of step-by-step inductive operations. What the child seems to do is formulate a theory of grammar on the basis of limited (and often faulty) data. That all children do this regardless of intelligence, motivation, or emotional state seems to leave little doubt that the human organism is biologically preprogrammed to acquire language. Furthermore, children acquire language in a remarkably short period of time. In a few years they have constructed a grammar on the basis of which they can distinguish sentences from nonsentences. This task is so complex as to suggest the presence of built-in biological structures and genetically programmed maturational processes.

The task of linguistic analysis is to account for how it is that the child produces and understands an indefinite number of new sentences, distinguishes sentences from nonsentences, and interprets ill-formed sentences. According to Chomsky (1957) the grammar of a language can be thought of as a hierarchy—a *deep* or base *structure* component, which produces a set of deep structures; a set of *transformations,* which operates on the deep structure; and a set of *surface structures,* which are the result of the transformations. In addition, there is a semantic component and a phonological component (Figure 2.1). The transformational rules make it possible for the speaker to generate sentences or phrases or clause segments of sentences. No sentences (not even the simple, active, declarative sentences of English) can be generated without the application of at least a limited number of obligatory transformational rules (e.g., rules for subject–verb concord). The meaning of the sentence is a function of the deep structure and the meanings of the individual words (the semantic component of the sentence).

It is possible for two sentences to have different surface structures and the same (or roughly the same) deep structure, as in: *The man threw the ball* and *The ball was thrown by the man.* The difference is that in one case transformational rules have converted the deep structure into an active sentence, and in the other case into a passive sentence. Similarly, it is possible, by applying appropriate transformations to the deep structure, to produce interrogative sentences, negative sentences, and so forth.

Chomsky argued that children cannot help constructing a particular kind of transformational grammar any more than they can control their perception of solid objects or their attention to line and angle. The way children acquire a language reflects not so much experience as the general capacity for knowledge. Experience will affect language development, but its ultimate form will be a function of those language universals that exist in the human mind.

The data from which the child works are the utterances of speakers. Language is acquired by developing and *testing hypotheses* about regularities in the corpus to which the child is exposed. Language acquisi-

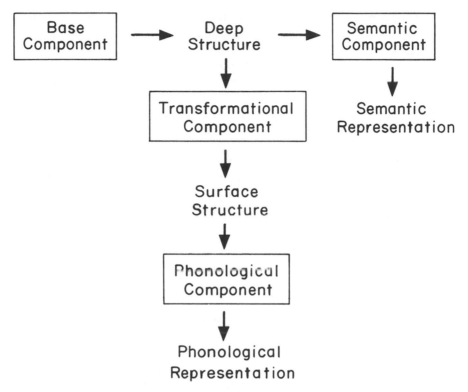

FIG. 2.1   The organization of transformational grammar (the boxes represent systems of rules that determine the structures or representations).

tion is a process of implicit theory construction whereby children formulate hypotheses about the rules governing the linguistic structure of sentences they hear, test these hypotheses against new evidence they acquire, eliminate those hypotheses that are contrary to the evidence, and evaluate those that are not eliminated by a simplicity principle that selects the simplest as the best hypothesis concerning the rules underlying the linguistic corpus (Katz, 1966). The rule system that children develop enables them to generate an infinite variety of sentences, most of which they have never heard from anyone else.

This view of the language acquisition process has been persuasively challenged, however, by Martin Braine (1971a), who pointed out that a hypothesis-testing model is too inefficient to account for the way in which a child acquires a language. Experimental research with concept formation has demonstrated that both positive information and negative information (information as to what is and what is not an instance of what is to be learned) are necessary for efficient learning. This means that children must be able to distinguish what is from what is not a sentence in order to learn which of their hypotheses about the grammar are correct and which are incorrect. Yet, as we have seen, observation of parental interaction with children indicates that parents rarely correct incorrect grammar. They are much more concerned with meaning and truthfulness than with syntax. Furthermore, when children are presented with negative information, they resist using it. Braine cited the following dialogue with his 2½-year-old daughter (Braine, 1971a):

> Child: Want other one spoon, Daddy.
> Father: You mean, you want the other spoon.
> C: Yes, I want other one spoon, please Daddy.
> F: Can you say "the other spoon"?
> C: Other . . . one . . . spoon.
> F: Say "other."
> C: Other.
> F: "Spoon."
> C: Spoon.
> F: "Other . . . spoon."
>   C: Other . . . spoon. Now give me other one spoon [pp. 160–161]?

Those who have had experience attempting to correct the grammar of 2- and 3-year-old children can testify that this is the usual outcome. Braine's contention, then, was that children usually do not receive negative information about syntax and that they often do not utilize it when it is given.

In addition, Braine noted experimental research on artificial languages that indicates that learners (both children and adults) are capable of acquiring grammar-like relations merely from exposure to sentences. That is, they learn merely on the basis of exposure to positive instances (even when these positive instances are accompanied, as they are in real-life situations, by unsystematic errors). Braine argued that the evidence suggests that the acquisition process requires a model based not on hypothesis formation but on *discovery procedures*. In his formulation, such a model requires a scanner that receives input sentences and a memory component that accumulates the features of sentences noticed by the scanner. A detailed account of the mode of operation of this model can be found in Braine (1971a); in its essential characteristics the model is similar to computer-based processing models developed for the acquisition and comprehension of natural language (Kelley, 1967; Schank, 1972; Winograd, 1972).

Process models.   This brings us to the third approach to language acquisition—process or strategy analysis. Process models differ from traditional behaviorist models in that they are essentially cognitive models of language. They are mainly concerned not with external, stimulus–response events but with internal, cognitive processes. The model attempts to delineate how language is processed cognitively and how it is manifested behaviorally.

Process models differ from a transformational grammar model in that they are concerned with language behavior occurring in real time; linguistic models, however, such as a transformational grammar approach, are essentially static: emphasis is placed on characterizing what it is that people must know to comprehend and produce grammatical and meaningful utterances. The linguist aims at accounting for the speaker's competence in a language; process models are concerned not only with what it is that people *know* to comprehend and produce sentences but also with what it is that people *do* in such comprehension and production (Bock, 1982; Clark & Clark, 1977). This means that attention must be given both to linguistically relevant criteria (such as judgments of grammaticality, paraphrase equivalence, and structural parallelism) and to behaviorally relevant criteria (such as processing time, mistakes in repetition, and mistakes in recall) (Ervin–Tripp, 1970b).

Clark and Haviland (1974) have characterized process models as explanatory attempts that accommodate the following information:

- The moment-to-moment changes in the mental state of the speaker or listener.
- The speaker or listener's knowledge of the language, as represented in the rules required for changing from one mental state to another.
- The speaker or listener's processing capacity, as found in the limitations on what rules can be applied, how many can be applied at one time, and how long each rule takes.
- The time required to say or understand an utterance.

Thus such models attempt to accommodate both competence and performance simultaneously.

One reason why process models are becoming increasingly popular among psycholinguists is that they account for language phenomena left unexplained by a static linguistic description. For example, implied requests such as *Could you open the door?* are rarely interpreted as questioning the listener's ability physically to open the door. In most situations, both the speaker and the listener understand that the speaker is conveying a request. One explanation for why this is possible posits that the listener goes through an inferential process, utilizing knowledge of the situation to infer what it is that the speaker means (Gordon & Lakoff, 1971). Since knowledge of the situation changes from moment to moment, a satisfactory account of implied requests requires a dynamic model that makes reference to the construction of knowledge states, the alteration of such states, and how it is that the speaker or listener is able to consult these knowledge states. And the model must be able to do all this in real time (Clark & Haviland, 1974).

A number of other linguistic phenomena require similar situational analyses. The sentence *John says the Dodgers* does not make much sense unless it is seen as occurring in the context of the question *Who won the ball game yesterday?* The study of language is the study of the communicative act and not simply the study of the way in which speakers generate grammatical utterances (although this is an important aspect of language use).

This is the perspective I take to language development throughout this book. I view it in terms of the child's processing capacities and in terms of the strategies the child employs in learning to communicate with others. One advantage of such an approach is that it accentuates the similarities between language acquisition and other types of learning. Children process linguistic data in a manner analogous to the way in which they process sensory information—by registering properties of the input and accumulating them in memory.

At the present time, however, no processing model exists that can account for all relevant linguistic and behavioral phenomena. As Ervin–Tripp (1970b) pointed out, filling in the details of such a model will take many years. Present models are usually developed to explain a limited domain in terms of a series of hypothesized mental states, a collection of rules for changing from one mental state to another, and sequentially ordered processes (e.g., Bates & MacWhinney, 1982; Bock, 1982; Clark & Chase, 1972). More complete models must account for the whole range of tasks that children face as they begin to acquire language, including phonological, semantic, and syntactic processes. Before considering what such models would involve, some comments are in order about children's processing capacities.

Language and Cognitive Development

From the present perspective, the old debate between rationalists and empiricists about innate capacity for language acquisition appears misdirected. Children's cognitive and learning capacities are much more general and predetermining than the empiricists would have it. They are born with certain innate abilities that structure and determine the way they learn. They are not, on the other hand, born with an innate set of ideas, as the rationalists would have it, but with a processing mechanism that enables them to discover linguistic patterns just as they discover perceptual patterns in the world of senses. Both processes are part of general cognitive development. The categories that an individual develops—linguistic and perceptual—are the result of an innate set of cognitive inference procedures.

In Braine's (1971a) model, for example, the scanner is thought to be preset to notice certain features of the input and ignore others. The form of the grammar that the learner is capable of acquiring is therefore predetermined by the range of properties to which the scanner responds. The model allows for the possibility of universal properties of natural languages, not because there are innate linguistic categories, but because language acquisition is governed by a particular sort of processing mechanism.

It follows, then, that what linguists propose to be universals of language are simply products of universal cognitive processes. For example, the noun/verb distinction in language is the result of the cognitive strategy of distinguishing between objects and the relations between objects. Transformations themselves are cognitive operations that are reflected not only in language but in visual perception as well (Bever, 1970).

The priority of general cognitive processes has been stressed by a number of authors (Bates & MacWhinney, 1982; Macnamara, 1972; Sinclair-deZwart, 1973; Slobin, 1979). The exact nature of the cognitive prerequisites for language is still debated, although there is general agreement that the language acquisition process involves the assimilation of information into existing cognitive structures and that these cognitive structures set limits on the child's language development.

Processing limitations. There is evidence, for example, that the length of a child's imitations of an adult model's utterances remains about the same, regardless of the length of the adult model's utterances, and that the length of the imitation is about the same as the length of the child's spontaneous utterances (Brown & Fraser, 1963). There seems to be some processing limitation that restricts the length of utterances children can program. As the child grows older, this limitation is gradually overcome and sentences become longer.

Further evidence for this processing limitation comes from Bloom's (1970) finding that deletions seem to occur in the negative sentences of children. Since negative sentences are usually one word longer than positive sentences, the hypothesis of a length limitation leads one to expect that the addition of a negative element would require that some other constituent of the sentence be dropped. This is what Bloom found. Her daughter said *Daddy like coffee,* immediately followed by *Lois no coffee.* The introduction of the negative *no* seemed to cause the deletion of the verb *like.* Presumably, the child could not process the sentence *Lois no like coffee* at this time.

Why is it that the length of the child's utterances is limited? One answer is that there is a processing restriction imposed by the limitations of operative memory. Brown and Fraser (1963) observed that simple digit-span memory and chronological age are systematically related, with a progressive increase in digit-span memory continuing until adulthood. This pattern replicates the systematic increase in length of utterance (Brown & Fraser, 1963; McCarthy, 1946) and suggests that the two processes are related, utterance length being dependent on the child's memory span.

Most authors feel that children's speech is limited by performance constraints but disagree as to their source. The memory span hypothesis seems questionable, since as Olson (1973) pointed out, when more appropriate indices of children's memory capacities are used, such as pictorial materials, children do not perform worse on memory tasks than adults (Brown & Scott, 1971). Olson argued that the capacity for immediate memory was ontogenetically invariant and that the performance deficits found in younger children are due to their failure to organize, plan, monitor, and integrate their information processing and memory as efficiently as do older children and adults. Indeed there is evidence that when children as young as 3 or 4 years of age are taught to do so, they can employ many of the strategies they will later use routinely in memory tasks (Flavell, 1970). Olson proposed that the child's initial utterances are single-word utterances, because the child finds that with the help of extralinguistic factors a single word can convey a meaning that an adult expresses in a sentence. As children escape from their egocentric world and have to cope with other persons and points of view, they cannot rely on extralinguistic cues in the immediate situation, and so their utterances become longer.

According to this view, cognitive limitations to the child's language development are indeed based on the limitations of operative memory, though not on the limitations of immediate memory span. Children have fewer automatic processes in long-term memory: they have less experiential knowledge, a smaller lexicon, and fewer retrieval devices (Chi, 1976; Dempster, 1978). In contrast, adult performance involves the ability to plan and organize output, the ability to monitor and assess the state of this planning and the readiness to perform, the ability to integrate in real time the flow of information through immediate memory and to retrieve information from long-term memory (Olson, 1973). In addition, adults have a conceptual repertoire and previous learning experience at their disposal. These obvious differences in cognitive abilities mean that the experience of the child learning a language is different from that of an adult. In Chapter 3 I discuss the question of how different these experiences are.

Processing capabilities.   Susan Ervin–Tripp (1970b) singled out three kinds of linguistic performance that provide information about children's language processing capabilities. The first of these is *imitation*. When children are given the task of imitating the sentences of an adult model, they must, at a minimum, be capable of perceiving the model's speech, storing it in immediate memory, and organizing output. They must also be capable of performing the appropriate motor behavior to make the necessary speech sounds.

A second type of performance is comprehension or *interpretation*. What is involved here is revealed through such tasks as answering and acting upon sentences and paraphrasing their meaning. The processing capacities involved in imitation are needed here as well: speech perception, storage in short-term memory, and organization of output. In addition, long-term storage may occur, although many characteristics of surface structure are apparently not stored (Bransford & Franks, 1972). Furthermore, lexical and syntactic processing at some minimal level are necessary for the child to perform the interpretative task.

The third type of performance is the *production* of meaningful utterances. All of the processing capacities involved in interpretation seem to be necessary here, as well as the organization and motor output processes of imitation. Yet production seems to involve different processing than either interpretation or imitation. Studies of children's language development indicate that production usually lags behind comprehension, most likely because the child must learn to organize sentence output, especially in terms of word order and syntax. Similarly, expert linguists can mimic greetings and common expressions in other languages without being able to understand or produce more complicated intelligible utterances in those languages, which also suggests that production differs from interpretation.

Table 2.1 summarizes the minimal processing capacities children must possess in order to perform linguistic tasks. In addition, it seems that the child, like the adult, must possess certain heuristic devices to minimize the amount of effort required to process linguistic information (Ervin–Tripp, 1970b). Like the adult, the child learns to process language with great rapidity.

This outline of the child's linguistic capacities is of course very rudimentary. It leaves out of consideration how it is that the child performs more

TABLE 2.1
Minimal Processing Capacities for Performing
Linguistic Tasks

Perceptual Level:
    Ability to organize perceptually strings of sounds

Memory Level:
    Immediate memory storage capacity
    Long-term memory storage capacity

Information Processing Level
    Phonological processing capacities
    Lexical processing capacities
    Syntactic processing capacities

Output Level
    Organizational capacities
    Appropriate motor behavior

---

complicated linguistic tasks. How is it, for example, that the child learns to comprehend implied requests such as his mother's request that he shut the door, expressed in the sentence *Michael, you left the door open.* Such requests are understood by children very early. When a child says *I'm hungry,* she is herself using such a strategy. It would seem that to understand and generate such requests, the child must be able to make inferences about various levels of meaning, literal and implied.

Furthermore, these comments on the child's linguistic capacities are rudimentary because they are based on a consideration of general tasks that the child performs such as imitation, interpretation, and production and not on a consideration of more specific tasks that require more specific linguistic skills.

THE CHILD'S LINGUISTIC TASKS

What are the specific tasks that a child faces in acquiring a language? For one thing, the child has to master the sound system and must attach sounds to their referents. Then there is the task of developing the lexicon and a system of meanings that matches the meanings used by other speakers in the child's environment. The syntactic system must also be acquired and, finally, all of these systems must be used appropriately in social interaction.

Phonological Tasks

From the age of two weeks, children are capable of distinguishing the human voice from other sounds. One-month-old infants can discriminate between consonant sounds, such as [ba] and [pa] (Eimas, Siqueland, Jusczyk, & Vigorito, 1971). Speech perception seems to depend on interaction with the environment, since the children of deaf parents are not able to discover sound patterns merely through exposure to television or radio. The recurrence of sound patterns at times of significance to the child such as feeding, being held, and being stimulated visually, appears to mark off particular sounds for attention (Ervin–Tripp, 1973a).

Experimental research indicates that certain sound features are more salient in unanalyzed input and are more likely to be preserved in imitation and recall (Ervin–Tripp, 1970b):

- In English, peak pitch, what is stressed or not stressed, and terminal fall or non-fall.
- Timing and length of stressed syllables.
- Approximate quality of stressed vowels, especially unrounded vowels.
- Approximate location of marked features such as friction and nasal consonants.

During the babbling period (the second 6 months) the infant vocalizes an increasing variety of sounds in increasingly complex combinations. These sounds appear to include a large number that the infant does not use in producing meaningful utterances. Infants select out certain sounds from their corpora and use these in intended vocalizations (Jakobson, 1941). There seems to be considerable uniformity among infants exposed to different languages in the first sounds they produce: the front consonants, *p* or *m,* and the back vowel, *a,* preceding the back consonants, *k* and *g,* and the front vowels, *i* and *u.*

In addition to the phonemic structure of the language—its sound units—the child must learn its phonological structure—the *rules for combining sounds* into pronounceable sequences in the language and for relating such sequences to the surface structure of sentences. Somehow the child must come to realize that although *trown* is not a word in English, it could be; whereas *lrown* is not and could not be an English word. The reason for this is that there is a phonological rule in English that allows the *tr* combination but not the *lr* combination.

Other phonological rules relate to the stress words receive in sentences. In English, for example, the main stress falls on *black* when the speaker is referring to a *blackboard.* When referring to a board that is black, however, the speaker is more likely to say *the black board,* stressing *board.* The rule in such cases is that the main stress falls on the first vowel of a noun but elsewhere in constituents of other kinds, such as noun phrases (Chomsky & Halle, 1968). It seems that such rules are only gradually mastered by children, but little is known of their developmental course.

Aside from distinguishing sound units and learning phonological rules, the child must learn to *attach sounds to their referents.* This, as was noted, requires the co-occurrence of speech with referential events. A child cannot acquire the linguistically important features of speech unless a significant portion of the sounds heard make reference to concrete objects, relations, and events to which the child already attends. Note that attaching sounds to their referents is a more complex process than simply learning the names of things (as behaviorists usually assume in their theories of meaning). The child stores such words as *want, allgone,* and *more,* which refer not to observable objects but to one's own inner states and relationships between objects and events (Ervin–Tripp, 1973a).

An adequate model of sound processing, then, must account for how the child learns and stores sound discriminations, how sound units are selected out and produced, how phonological rules are learned and stored, and how sound units are related to lexical items (Clark & Clark, 1977). Aside from perceptual, storage, and retrieval processes, the model must be able to provide some account of the rule-acquisition process and of the various heuristics the child uses to discover phonological rules.

Semantic Tasks

Somehow the child has to develop a *dictionary of meanings.* Perhaps the first entries in this dictionary are whole sentences of one, two, or three words. In time, though, the dictionary becomes a dictionary of words, each of which is given its particular meaning. The word *dog,* for example, has a certain matrix of phonological features, a set of syntactic markers that define it as a common noun, and a collection of semantic features including perhaps (physical object), (living), (small), and (animal).

As children grow older, they modify and elaborate the semantic features attached to the words in the dictionary. There is some disagreement as to how this is done (E. Clark, 1973). One suggestion, for example, is that the child goes from the concrete to the abstract (Anglin, 1970). Initially, there is awareness only of the specific, concrete features of words. As the child's semantic knowledge increases with age, generalizations are made over more abstract categories. At first children know *rose, tulip, oak,* and *elm.* Subsequently, they group the pairs together under *flower* and *tree.* Then they become able to group all words together under *plants* and, ultimately, under *living things.* One problem with this hypothesis is that children do not inevitably acquire such subordinate terms as *oak* or *elm* before they acquire the superordinate one—*tree.* In fact, the reverse is usually the case.

A somewhat different hypothesis is that there are certain universal, primitive features that are common to all languages and that reflect the basic dispositions of the cognitive and perceptual nature of the human organism (Bierwisch, 1967). The child does not have to learn the primitive features but simply the rules for combining primitives into lexical items. Although the primitives are given as part of biological endowment, the rules differ from language to language. This theory is consistent with much recent thinking about the priority of nonlinguistic to linguistic processes; but it suffers from the important defect of being untestable, in that the primitives have not been identified and the rules for combining them into lexical items have not been specified.

A third hypothesis has been called semantic features acquisition (E. Clark, 1973). The assumption here is that when children first begin to use identifiable words, they do not know their full adult meanings. They have only some of the features or components of meaning that are present in the adult's lexicon. As children acquire semantic knowledge, they add more features of meaning to the lexical entry for individual words until the combination of features corresponds to that of the adult. However, since the young child does not yet possess the full combination of features, the child's referential categories will often differ considerably from those of adults for the same word. If, for example, the meaning of *dog* is defined by the features (physical object), (living), (small), and (animal), the child will give this word an extension an adult would not. The child's category *dog* might include cats, mice, guinea pigs, and other small animals. As other features are added to the definition, the child will gradually narrow down this initial, very general meaning.

Finally, there is the argument that what are learned are not features, but prototypes of common categories (Rosch, 1973). According to this view, children define a category by means of concrete "clear cases," rather than in terms of abstract criterial attributes. This helps to account for why children do not categorize words according to the same principles of abstraction used by adults. Children operate instead on the basis of an internal structure of a category determined by what are perceived to be the best examples of the category.

Unfortunately, we are still far from understanding the complexities of the process of lexical development. It does seem safe to say that learning to understand and use words appropriately is not an all-or-none process. Furthermore, it seems clear that children are aided both by their own understanding of the contexts in which words are used and by the attempts of adults to render more salient the relevant aspects of the context to which the child should pay attention (Bridges, Sinha, & Walkerdine, 1981).

In addition to building up a dictionary of lexical meanings, the child acquires a set of *semantic relations*. Observers of children's language have noted that early sentences seem to be confined to a relatively restricted and universally shared set of semantic relations. These seem to reflect the way in which the human mind processes nonlinguistic experiences common to all children. Brown (1973a) has listed the following basic semantic relations:

- Agent and action: *Car go, Mommy push*
- Action and object: *See sock, Pick glove*
- Agent and object: *Eve lunch, Mommy sandwich*
- Action and location: *Sit chair*
- Entity and location: *Baby table*
- Possessor and possession: *Daddy chair*
- Entity and attribute: *Yellow block, Little dog*
- Demonstrative and entity: *Here truck, Here sock*

Other authors have slightly different lists (Ervin–Tripp, 1973a; Schlesinger, 1971); one problem with codification is that it is not always clear from what the child says which underlying semantic relations are being expressed.

Note that semantic relations are not the same as grammatical relations such as subject, predicate, and direct object. Instead, they refer to a set of semantic intentions that the child attempts to communicate through linguistic means. Initially, the child's communication efforts may be quite simple: utterances such as *Mommy eat, Baby go, Mommy shoe* are understood by family members in spite of their fragmentary nature. As the child comes into contact with more people and attempts to become more intelligible in a wider variety of situations, these semantic relations must be given more adequate expression in well-formed utterances.

In short, there are at least two tasks involved in semantic development. The first of these is building up the lexicon. An adequate model must account for how and why certain features are initially chosen to characterize lexical items, how meanings are stored and are related to each other in the semantic system, and how they are retrieved (Kuczaj, 1982). Second, there is the question of semantic relations: how and in what order are they acquired, what is the role of nonlinguistic experiences, and how are semantic relations given normative (i.e., grammatical) expression.

Syntactic Tasks

Possibly the most important cue for the child in learning to express semantic relations grammatically is *word order* (Braine, 1971a). For example, to recognize that an item acted upon normally follows an action word in English, the child must be able to store such specific instances as *Eat your dinner, Mary rolled the ball.* The semantic relationship between action and object is then matched with the order action–object. Such order processing heuristics are an integral part of syntactic development in all languages, although in inflected languages morphological features probably have a greater role.

The child's dependence on order regularities in a noninflected language such as English will lead to misinterpretations of certain types of sentences. For example, the young child will usually understand the sentence *The boy is chased by the dog* to refer to a picture of a boy chasing a dog. In such cases, the child operates on the basis of a rule that specifies that the sequence Noun–Verb–Noun means Agent–Action–Object.

As the child begins to pay more attention to syntactic information, a *grammar* develops based on the rules discovered in the corpus to which the child is exposed. The child's grammar differs from that of an adult, though there is little agreement on its exact form (see Bloom, 1970; Bowerman, 1973; McNeill, 1966). In several cases, fairly detailed developmental analyses have been made of grammatical constructions.

For example, Klima and Bellugi (1966) found that it was possible to distinguish three phases in the child's development of *negative sentences.* First, the negative word occurs outside of the sentence nucleus in such utterances as:

No wipe finger,
Wear mitten no,

No singing song,
Not a teddy bear.

The only negative forms at this stage are the words *no* and *not*. In the second stage, about 2 to 4 months later, more negative forms occur, especially monomorphic verbs such as *can't* and *don't*. The negative may occur before the predicate:

He no bite you,
I can't catch you.

Or it may be outside the sentence nucleus as it is during the first stage:

No pinch me.
Touch the snow no.

In the third stage, which occurs from 2 to 6 months later, the adult pattern appears:

You don't want some supper,
Ask me if I not make mistake,
I not hurt him.

The development of *questions,* like the development of negative constructions, proceeds from the simple to the more complex. Initially rising intonation and the use of *wh* words are the only interrogative devices:

No ear?
See hole?
What doing?

In the second stage, the child asks such questions as:

Where my mittens?
What me think?
Why you smiling?

This stage seems to be characterized by the prefixing of question words to otherwise complete sentences. In the third stage, the auxiliary system emerges, and the modal *do* is inflected for tense:

Where the other Joe will drive?
What he can ride in?

What did you doed?
Why you caught it?

Note that even in the third stage the child has not learned all the rules characteristic of the adult grammar. The child says *Why he don't know how to pretend?* whereas the adult would say *Why doesn't he know how to pretend?* The child has not yet learned the inversion rule for *wh*-questions, although *yes–no* questions are inverted at this time.

These and other more complex syntactic tasks are possible, because the child is able to retain information and retrieve it in acquiring grammatical rules. In process terms, children can do this because they possess a language acquisition system with storage capacity in short- and long-term memory, selection and organizational capacity, heuristic features allowing short cuts, and perceptual capacities. In addition, some sort of "interpretation template" (Ervin–Tripp, 1973a) seems necessary to provide interpretation of utterances according to their syntactic and semantic properties, so that formal similarities can be discovered. An adequate model, then, has the following minimal components:

- Selective retention of features in short-term memory, especially order of acoustical input.
- Phonological and semantic selection and reorganization for retention in long-term memory.
- Interpretation templates for identifying structures according to the formal and semantic features of sequences.
- Successive processing by alternative heuristics, allowing shortcuts for frequent phrases, for instances where non-linguistic determinants are strong, and so on.
- Formal feature generation to identify abstract classes and provide marking of the lexicon [Ervin–Tripp, 1973a, p. 285].

This is by no means a complete list—the system needs devices for organizing and regulating output, for example. But this should give some picture of what a satisfactory process model would look like.

Communicative Competence

In addition to specifically linguistic tasks, an adequate process model must account for how it is that the speaker utilizes nonlinguistic information in speech to achieve full communicative competence. Communicative competence refers to the relationship between grammatical competence, or knowledge of the rules of the grammar, and sociolinguistic competence, or knowledge of the rules of language use (Canale & Swain, 1980). For example, we saw earlier in this chapter that implied requests such as *Could you open the door?* require a knowledge of the situation in order for the listener to be able to infer what it is that the speaker means. Similarly, when the salesman at the door asks the child *Is your mother home?* he intends the child to understand that he would like to speak with her. Somehow, the child must learn how to process such requests. Apparently children do, since they use similar strategies in their own speech (*My glass is empty, My car is broken,* and so forth).

Another important aspect of communicative competence is learning to use various styles or *codes* of speaking to different people under differing circumstances. The child must master the features of various levels of linguistic structure and must learn the rules for switching levels. There are at least three levels that seem present in all societies: formal or polite, collo-quial, and slang or vulgar (Hymes, 1964).

The child in American society has to learn a formal code for dealing with teachers, ministers, and other "formidable strangers" (Gleason, 1973). For instance, it seems that many children develop a characteristic style in talking to adult strangers that is marked by pauses between words, careful enuncia-tion, and a flat, affectless tone (Gleason, 1973). Another stylistic variant that children use is the *-in* versus *-ing* ending for the present participle. Fischer (1958) reported that his observation of the speech of 24 children revealed that the choice of *-in* and *-ing* variants was related to the sex, class, personality (aggressive/cooperative), and mood (tense/relaxed) of the speaker. As children grew more relaxed in an interview, for example, *-in* forms became more frequent.

The child uses the colloquial and slang codes in interaction with peers and siblings. Gleason (1973) reported that children's peer-group language was different from the language they addressed to adults. It involved a rich use of expressive words, very frequent use of first names, no terms of endear-ment, and a striking amount of echoing behavior. In American society, the child often employs the informal code with parents as well, while in other societies this is not necessarily the case (Ervin–Tripp, 1973b; Lambert, 1967).

Observers of children's language have also noted that children switch codes when speaking to younger children. Children as young as 2 years of age demonstrate lexical, phonological, and paralinguistic changes when they speak to infants (Ervin–Tripp, 1973b). This may, however, be a form of stereotyped, role-playing behavior in young children. Gleason (1973) found age differences in ability to use a baby-talk style in her sample of 4- to 8-year-old children. The older children controlled the basic features of baby talk—short, repetitive sentences uttered in a kind of singing style—but the younger children had not learned this particular linguistic code.

Situationally determined linguistic behavior—as represented by such phenomena as implied requests and code switching—clearly involves complex cognitive abilities. To attempt to outline the prerequisite capacities would be presumptuous. Similarly, the abstract process model required to explain adequately such linguistic behavior will be much more complicated than anything presently on the drawing board. Little empirical data have been gathered, for example, about what features of the nonlinguistic environment trigger code switching in specific situations.

THE LINGUISTIC ENVIRONMENT

Interest in the linguistic environment of the child is relatively recent in child language research. For years focus had been exclusively on the internal processes of the child. This emphasis was part of the Chomskyan heritage: Chomsky had argued that the child possesses at birth a language sensing mechanism—or what he called the Language Acquisition Device (LAD). According to this view the contents of LAD are unknown—it is the proverbial black box as applied to language learning. Something is known about what goes into the black box and about what comes out. The output is assumed by Chomsky to be the adult competence in a language that is formally described by a grammar of that language. What goes in—the input—is the content of sentences heard by children from parents, other adults, other children, television, and so forth.

Chomsky argued that this input is basically "meager and degenerate," characterized by false starts, hesitations, slips of the tongue, unfinished and ungrammatical utterances. That children can work from this meager and degenerate input to adult competence indicated for Chomsky that input is not a major factor in language acquisition—and hence is uninteresting; instead it is the internal processes of LAD that matter in language development.

It turned out, however, that Chomsky was wrong in his claim that language input to the child is "meager and degenerate." It has now been well documented that the great majority of utterances addressed to children are well-formed by any criterion. It seems that Chomsky and his followers had gone too far in denying the importance of factors external to the child.

Rather than being "meager and degenerate," the linguistic environment of the child appears to be quite well suited to facilitate language development (Cross, 1978; Snow & Ferguson, 1977). Recent research on mother–child communication suggests that mothers and other caretakers have a special way of talking to the child in early conversational interactions—a language convention that persists over generations and has been called *caretaker speech*. There are three general characteristics of this particular style of speech. First of all, there is a special lexicon, a special set of words, that characterizes caretaker speech. The lexicon contains names for body parts, basic qualities, kin terms, names for some animals and games. There are also intonational variations—speech has a higher overall pitch, there is often a rising intonation at the end of sentences, there are more instances of emphatic stress, and speech is slower and more precise than speech to adults. Finally, there are grammatical modifications—much greater use of nouns and pronouns, more third person constructions, fewer verbs, modifiers, conjunctions, and prepositions in speech addressed to young children than in speech addressed to older children or adults.

Speech addressed to young children learning the first language also contains more repetitions and is more likely to be about the here and now. Caretakers direct the child's attention to what the child is seeing and doing, to features of immediate environment. They name objects for the child, ask rhetorical questions, repeat and expand the child's utterances. Parental speech to young children has been described as a set of language lessons. Parents prod and prompt the child, ask questions of the child, and answer their own questions:

What's that?
It's a ball, isn't it?
Ball. Ball.
Can you say ball?

In short, investigators have found that the speech of adults to young children is in many ways well suited to gain and hold the child's attention and to make meaning apparent. Nonetheless, although it is clear that caretaker speech facilitates language development in a general manner, it is not clear how and why this is the case and which aspects of caretaker speech make a difference. This is certainly the next step for research in this area (there is some information—e.g., Cross, 1978; Furrow, Nelson, & Benedict, 1979; Hoff–Ginsberg & Shatz, 1982). At this point, it seems safe to say that *both* internal and external factors are important for language development in children.

It should also be noted that the type of linguistic environment that has been described in the literature on caretaker speech is not necessarily the environment that all children experience. This discussion has been limited to "mainstream" children—to children growing up in middle-class and upper-middle-class families. These are the children studied in most of the research to date on first language development. We know less of language development in "non-mainstream" families—in working-class families. Presumably many of the same processes are involved in language learning regardless of the child's socioeconomic background, but there is increasing evidence that the input to the child in some working-class families differs greatly from the middle-class pattern (Heath, 1983). These differences in the linguistic environment to which the child is exposed affect the child's approach to language. This is a topic that deserves fuller treatment and, because such differences relate to individual differences in language learning, further discussion of this issue will be postponed until Chapter 6.

THE DEVELOPMENT OF THE CHILD'S LANGUAGE

I have tried to indicate what linguistic capacities the acquisition of language requires, to outline the characteristics of an abstract process model that would satisfactorily account for the child's linguistic knowledge and behavior, and to describe the linguistic environment within which language acquisition occurs. Because the discussion to this point has been chronologically loose, this chapter ends with a brief review of the child's linguistic development. Again, not everything can be said; I attempt simply to provide a backdrop for subsequent discussion of second-language development.

The Early Stage

One way of looking at the child's early language development, consistent with the viewpoint adopted in this chapter, is to focus on the strategies employed in acquiring a language. An analysis in these terms has been presented by John Macnamara (1972) in his discussion of the cognitive basis of language acquisition in infants.

Macnamara began with the proposition that infants acquire their language by first determining nonlinguistically the *meaning* a speaker intends to communicate to them. They do this by developing a set of cognitive strategies that function as short cuts in relating acoustical input to a speaker's intention. For example, once they are able to distinguish an object held before them from the rest of the environment, children adopt the strategy of taking the word heard as the name for that object, and not the name for a property or subproperty of the object. Thus when the child sees a red, round object and hears *ball,* she names the object *ball.* This strategy generally works well, although there are occasionally mistakes—for example, when an oven is always referred to as *hot.*

The child learns the names for colors, shapes, and sizes only after having learned the names for many objects. Similarly, the child does not learn the names for states or activities until having firmly grasped the names for at least some entities that exemplify such states and activities. A constant problem at this stage is learning what the semantic features of words are. The child may, for example, regard certain objects as *toys* and certain other objects as a *truck* and a *train*. The truck or train is not a *toy;* nor are the toys assigned the name *truck* or *train*. Somehow, however, hierarchical categories develop (Horton & Markman, 1980), and the child learns to assign words their appropriate semantic features so that overextensions, such as referring to the television repairman as *Daddy,* become less common.

Subsequently, the child—in hearing others speak—adopts the strategy of taking the main lexical items in the sentences heard, determining the referents for these items, and using this knowledge of the referents to decide what the semantic intentions of the speaker are. For example, the child hearing the sentence *Give John the book* relies on the knowledge that books are objects that can be given to people, but that people cannot be given to books. In this way the child uses nonlinguistic knowledge of the referents of lexical items to arrive at the notions of agent–action, of direct and indirect object, and so forth.

In the scheme Macnamara proposed, *syntactic development* always has reference to meaning. Syntax is learned by noting the syntactic devices such as word order, prepositions, number affixes, and the like that correlate with semantic structures. Such a strategy eventually yields all of the main syntactic devices of the language. There are, of course, complications. The child will hear such sentences as *John hit the ball* and *John walked home.* Both have the same surface structure, but the verb in one case is transitive and in the other, intransitive. To resolve this particular problem, the child must come to realize at some cognitive level that the effect of *hit* on *ball* is not the same as that of *walk* on *home.* This is done by recourse to meaning.

But in other cases, syntactic riddles cannot be solved by semantic means. The rule of subject verb concord, for example, seems to be purely syntactic. When interpreting the sentences *The boys strike the girl* and *The girl is struck by the boys,* the child must be able to conclude that they mean roughly the same thing, although the voice of the verb is different in the two sentences. Macnamara argued that the evidence from such examples indicates that the child is capable of detecting syntactic regularities in language, regardless of whether they are tied in some way to meaning.

Nonetheless, the evidence does strongly support the priority of semantics in the initial stages of speech development. The child's first utterances are single words, expressing a variety of semantic relations. *Milk* means *This is milk, I want milk, I want more milk,* etc. (Bloom, 1973). The child is at this stage syntactically innocent. At the two-word stage, a few syntactic features appear, but for the most part speech continues to depend primarily on semantics (Bloom, 1970).

At this point "mapping lessons" (Clark & Clark, 1977) provide children with clues for mapping ideas onto language. One of the features of the caretaker style is that adults usually speak about objects, actions, and events that are immediately accessible to the children they are talking to.

This focus on the "here and now" assists the child to make use of contextual clues as to what the words might mean. For instance, young children can understand such indirect requests as, *Can you shut the door?* just by knowing the word *door* and using knowledge of context—the fact that the door is open and the speaker is looking at it (Shatz, 1979). The parent's use of language about the "here and now" provides children with a limited setting in which to start working out how meanings map onto language.

In time, increasingly more reliance is placed on syntax to convey meaning. Semantics alone does not do the trick. Children have to express what they mean to adults other than their parents and to playmates. Moreover, they discover that they can convey variations in inner states through language. Language then becomes a powerful tool, the subtle nuances of which must be mastered if it is to be used at all effectively.

Once words are combined, the complexity of the child's language increases. Children begin to employ noun phrases, differentiating nouns from their modifiers. At first all modifiers seem to belong to a single class, although they express a variety of semantic relations, including possession and attribution (Brown & Bellugi, 1964). At a later stage, the child produces such sentences as *That's a your pencil* and *That a blue flower.* Speech at this point is marked with articles, which occur before other modifiers, and demonstrative pronouns, which occur before articles and modifiers. As the process of differentiation continues, possessive pronouns form a separate class, because—unlike other modifiers—they do not occur after articles. Such phrases as *a your pencil* drop out of the child's speech.

As we have seen, *word order* is particularly important in the syntactic development of the English-speaking child. At first there are no inflections at all in the child's speech, and the full weight of syntactic structure falls on word order. This seems to be true of some inflected languages such as Russian and German, although evidence from languages with simple inflectional systems and no standard order such as Garo, Hungarian, and Turkish suggests that inflections are learned simultaneously with (or even prior to) word order.

Inflections appear to be learned according to a pattern in which inflectional classes whose referents are concrete develop first. Slobin (1966a) examined studies of Russian inflectional development (which is much richer than English) and concluded that plural inflections of nouns and imperative marking of the verb develop first (about the time when the child passes from the two- to the three-word stage). Then come classes based on relational criteria such as the tense and person markings of the verb. Third, and much later, are conditional markings of verbs, followed by nouns marked for various abstract categories of quality and action. Finally, very late, are gender markings for nouns and adjectives.

Case studies of early *phonemic and phonological development* (Burling, 1959; Leopold, 1947; Moskowitz, 1970; Velten, 1943) reveal no consistent pattern. This may be because children themselves are not consistent. There does seem to be evidence that phonemic development consists of the acquisition of a set of contrasts or distinctive features (Jakobson, 1941) rather than disparate sounds. There is a small number of contrasts that distinguish all the phonemes in English: the voiceless-voiced contrast (/p/ versus /b/), the alveoloar-labial contrast (/d/ versus /b/), the continuant-stop contrast (/s/ versus /t/), and a number of others. These contrasts seem to develop in a particular order (Velten, 1943), although probably not in the order predicted by Jakobson's theory (see Table 2.2). Moreover, although the theory predicts that contrasts are added to the phonemic system in a unified fashion, this is rarely reported. The more usual finding is that a contrast appears first in a single pair of phonemes; only after some time does the contrast generalize to other phoneme pairs.

Analysis in terms of distinctive features or contrasts has been helpful, however, in clarifying the developmental course of the phonemic system. The following are some tentative generalizations (from Ervin–Tripp, 1966):

- The vowel consonant contrasts are probably learned earliest.
- The continuant-stop contrast is quite early.
- Affricatives (*ch, j*) and liquids (*l, r*) usually appear later than stops and nasals.
- Contrasts between low and high vowels (/a/ versus /i/) precede contrasts between front and back vowels (/i/ versus /u/).
- Oral vowels precede nasal vowels.
- Consonant clusters or blends are usually late.
- Consonant contrasts usually appear earlier in initial than in medial or final position.

Studies concerned with the development of phonological rules in children (e.g., Ingram, 1974; Menn, 1979; Moskowitz, 1970) have been directed at

TABLE 2.2
Jakobson's Predictions Concerning the Order of Acquisition of
Consonant Contrasts

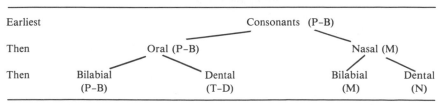

Earliest		Consonants (P–B)		
Then	Oral (P–B)		Nasal (M)	
Then	Bilabial (P–B)	Dental (T–D)	Bilabial (M)	Dental (N)

From Jakobson (1960).

discovering the systematic nature of this process. Ingram (1974) argued that the child initially develops a phonological system that is a mental representation of the adult system to which the child is exposed, but that does not necessarily bear a simple relationship to the adult system. That is, the child's phonological development involves the application of strategies that the child uses to organize and systematize phonological information. For example:

- Cluster reduction: simplifying consonant clusters into a single sound—as when *screw* is pronounced *gru* or *clock dak*.
- Reduplication: the child compensates for the inability to represent appropriately or produce the second syllable of a word by repeating the first syllable—*dada* for *daddy*.
- Weak syllable deletion: dropping the unstressed initial syllable in two-syllable words—as when *away* is pronounced *way;* or dropping the unstressed syllable in three-syllable words—pronouncing *pyjama dama*.

Such strategies reflect a simplification process whereby the diversity of the sound system is organized according to a limited number of rules, and a generalization process whereby these rules are applied to the child's own speech productions.

Middle Stages

By the age of 3 or so, the child has usually reached the final stage in the development of negatives and questions. Utterances can be relatively complex but still contain syntactic errors. Some examples:

Can't it be a bigger truck?
Did you broke that part?
What you have in your mouth?
Does turtles crawl?

Obviously at this stage children have not yet mastered all of the inflectional rules of the language. An auxiliary system has developed, however; and the child uses it in declaratives, negatives, and questions.

In addition, complex sentence forms, including relative clauses and conjunctions, appear:

I want this doll because she's big.
You have two things that turn around.

The child can also form complex sentences with *wh-* adverbial constructions:

I show you when I'm done.
I show you where we went.

Moreover, the child has begun to use complement verbs such as *want, think, hope, see,* etc. (Limber, 1973):

I want to go home.
I see you sit down.

The child at this stage is going through the process of *rule discovery.* This is not to imply, of course, that the child can conceptualize and formulate the various grammatical rules acquired. Yet the fact that the speech of the child is characterized by consistent patterns that are extended to new instances is evidence that the child's speech is governed by rules. Children speaking English do not use all possible word orders. By this stage, they have learned to use one word order for declarative sentences and another for questions. Similarly, the child generalizes knowledge of morphological rules to new instances. This is one reason why such utterances as *He comed* and *Two mouses* appear in the child's speech. Children do not simply imitate words or phrases they hear but use rules to generate new words and phrases.

Jean Berko (1958) studied this rule-discovery process in an experiment designed to test children's ability to extend their knowledge of morphological rules to new cases. She gave children nonsense words and pictures that corresponded to these words. The child's task was to form new combinations, using the nonsense words as a starting point. For example, she presented children with the picture of a *tor* and asked them to name a picture with two of these creatures. Young children were generally able to supply the correct ending /-z/. Similarly, the child was shown a picture of a man who is *ricking* and who did the same thing yesterday. When asked what it was that the man did yesterday, most young children were able to answer correctly that he *ricked.* They had more trouble, however, with such nouns as *gutch, kazh, and niz* and such verbs as *spow, mot,* and *bod.* Less than 50% of the preschool children in Berko's sample gave the correct plural form or past tense for these nonsense words (Table 2.3). Note that first-grade children were usually not significantly better.

Aside from syntactic and morphological development, it is clear that *semantic development* continues during the period from 3 to 6 years. By 3, most semantic overextensions seem to have disappeared. Children appear to

TABLE 2.3
Percent of Children Supplying
Correct Morphological Forms[a,b]

Plural of:	Percent correct preschool	Percent correct first grade
glass	75	99*
wug	76	97*
lun	68	92*
tor	73	90
cra	58	86*
gutch	28	38
kazh	25	36
niz	14	33
Past of:		
bing	60	85*
gling	63	80
rick	73	73
melt	72	74
spow	36	59
mot	32	33
bod	14	31*
ring	0	25*

[a]From Berko, 1958.
[b]Asterisk (*) signifies difference significant at $\alpha = .05$.

give most of the words in their vocabulary roughly the same set of semantic features that adults do. Of course, there may be occasions when the child overextends words without this being noticed by adults. Moreover, the set of features the child assigns words is not as elaborate as an adult's. The child's features appear to be derived predominantly from perceptual input—from visual, tactile, olfactory, or auditory sources (E. Clark, 1973). No one theory, however, seems adequate to account for how features are assigned or how the child's words come to meet adult semantic criteria (Clark & Clark, 1977). Nor is much known about how children learn the connotative meanings of words (Kuczaj, 1982).

Children from the ages of 3½ to 4 have been found to interpret the relational terms *more* and *less* as being identical in meaning. When presented with cardboard apple trees on which they could hang from one to six apples and asked to hang more/less apples on one tree than on the other, children at this age level usually understood *more* and *less* to mean the same thing. Questions that contained the word *less* were answered exactly the same way as those with *more* (Donaldson & Balfour, 1968). Similar findings were obtained in tasks where children had to distinguish the pairs, *same–different, big–wee (small), long–short, thick–thin, low–high, tall–short,* and *fat–thin*

(Donaldson & Wales, 1970). In each case, the child usually took the second word of the pair to mean the same as the first.

One way of interpreting these findings is to say that the meaning of the first word in the pair was overextended by the child to cover the second word as well, so that the second word is interpreted as being a synonym rather than an antonym of the first (E. Clark, 1973). This seems to be a fairly common phenomenon. Eve Clark (1974) has noted that it applies also to locative terms such as *in–on, in–under,* and *on–under.* Children younger than 3 seem first to interpret all three prepositions as meaning *In,* then *on* is acquired and takes priority to *under,* and finally all three are distinguished. The child seems to be following a strategy of applying the first learned meaning to both members of such pairs. Since *in* is learned prior to *on,* and *on* prior to *under,* the child's mistakes reflect this strategy. Similarly, since positive dimensional adjectives (*big, tall, fat*) are learned before negative ones (*small, short, thin*), the preference for positive members of relational pairs can also be explained in terms of this strategy (Clark, 1974)

Full communicative competence requires, as we have seen, not only mastery of the formal and semantic aspects of language but control of the various styles of speaking that characterize how different people talk to each other under differing circumstances. In role-playing doctor or postman, preschool children seem to be able to modify their speech accordingly. They also can shift codes when addressing authority figures. Moreover children learn appropriate conversational routines, repairs, and a broad range of speech acts suitable for such speech genres as playing a game, telling a story, role playing, arguing, or responding in class (Ervin-Tripp, 1981).

Later Stages

In her now classic monograph on *syntactic development* between the years 5 and 10, Carol Chomsky (1969) showed that a number of important syntactic structures are still being acquired during this period. She tested the child's linguistic knowledge by determining ability to interpret correctly sentences with complex syntactic structures where there were no contextual or semantic clues that might influence interpretation. For example, in English there is a rule for sentences of the form "NP₁ V NP₂ to infinitive verb," that assigns NP₂ as subject of the infinitive verb (*John told Bill to leave*). This Chomsky called the minimal distance principle (MDP). The verb *ask* can be used in a form that constitutes an exception to this rule: *John asked Bill what to do,* although this is not always the case: *John asked Bill to leave.* The verb *promise* always violates the MDP rule: *John promised Bill to go.*

Chomsky found, as predicted, that children had trouble interpreting *promise* sentences and even more difficulty with *ask* sentences. For example, in an experiment in which children were to act out sentences with dolls, protocols such as the following were obtained:

Q: Bozo promised Donald to do a somersault. Can you make him do it?
A: (making Donald do a somersault): I promised you you can do a tumblesault.
Q: Would you say that again?
A: I promised you you could do a tumblesault.

Similarly:

Q: Ask Joanne what to feed the doll.
A: The hot dog.
Q: Now I want you to *ask* Joanne something. Ask her what to feed the doll.
A: The piece of bread.
Q: Ask Joanne what *you* should feed the doll.
A: What should I feed the doll?

In another experiment, Chomsky showed children a doll with a blindfold over its eyes and asked them *Is the doll easy or difficult to see?* Up to the age of about 9 the children answered incorrectly with *Difficult.* Apparently, they interpreted the question as if it were asking whether the doll could see rather than whether someone could see the doll. Indeed, it seems that there are a number of reasons why children misinterpret such questions (Cambon & Sinclair, 1974).

Other evidence for syntactic development after the age of 6 comes from studies of the comprehension and production of passives in older children. Research suggests that children of 6 have considerable difficulty understanding passive sentences and even more difficulty producing them (Gaer, 1969). Only at the age of 7 did some children begin to produce passive sentences when describing pictures; but they required an example, and the acted-upon object had to be shown first in the picture (Turner & Rommetveit, 1967).

On the basis of her research, Paula Menyuk (1971) concluded that children from 5 to 7 years of age have not yet mastered the auxiliary *have,* participial completion, iteration, nominalization, pronominalization, and conjunction with *if* and *so.* In addition, other syntactic structures were only partially mastered. The evidence suggests that there is a consolidation of syntax that continues at least until the age of 12 or so. This process is for the most part gradual, but there may be sudden shifts (O'Donnell, Griffin, & Norris, 1967). Berko's (1958) research with the development of morphology also indicated that older children are still in the process of mastering the appropriate rules.

Furthermore, children continue to elaborate their speech acts (Clark & Clark, 1977). That is, they learn how to ask, order, forbid, permit, and promise (Grimm, 1975). They engage in complicated role-playing activities that involve a combination of stereotyped, imitated, and invented parts (Andersen, 1977). They learn how to speak to younger children and learn the nuances of a variety of speech codes for dealing with people in different social contexts (Gleason, 1973).

There is also *semantic development* after the age of 6. Obviously, vocabulary is expanded and the semantic features of words are elaborated. There is evidence that elementary school children have substantial sets of words in their vocabularies that have different meanings than they have in the vocabularies of adults (Asch & Nerlove, 1960). Werner and Kaplan (1964) found that younger children listed items in their dictionaries in terms of functional rather than semantic properties. A bottle was to drink out of, to pour out of, to drink milk from, and so on.

Bradshaw and Anderson (1968) studied children's use of adverbial modifiers using a paired-comparison procedure. Each of nine adjectives—*slightly, somewhat, rather, pretty, quite, decidedly, unusually, very,* and *extremely*—was compared with the other eight as modifiers of the word *large.* Reliable developmental differences were obtained, with 7-year-old children considering *slightly* and *somewhat* to be relatively neutral modifiers. *Slightly large,* for example, was thought by these children to be larger than *rather large* or *quite large.* By the age of 10, *slightly* and *somewhat* were at the lower end of the continuum, as they are in the adult's system. Similarly, *very* was considered equivalent to *extremely* by 7-year-old children, but later it shifted to the more neutral position it occupies in the adult scale.

There is also evidence that *phonological development* continues after the age of 6. Snow (1964) analyzed the sound substitutions of 6- to 8-year-old children on an articulation test and reported that a number of sounds have not been mastered by children in this age range. Menyuk (1971) and Carroll (1971) also noted that certain sounds were not mastered until after the child's 8th birthday.

In their review of research on language acquisition after the age of 5, Palermo and Molfese (1972) noted that in spite of the relatively small amount of research on language development in older children, it is clear that the 5-year-old child has some way to go before achieving adult mastery. Language development can by no means be said to be over when the child enters school. If nothing else, the gap between the child's language at this age and that of the adult—in all areas of linguistic knowledge and behavior—indicates that the learning process continues.

In concluding this chapter, there are several points worth emphasizing. First, of the various ways of conceptualizing the language acquisition process, the most satisfactory is one that takes both the linguistic knowledge and behavior of the child into account. Second, the acquisition of language is a dynamic process, reflecting the child's changing experiences with the linguistic and nonlinguistic environment. Third, full competence in the language requires more than mastery of phonology, syntax, and semantics; the child must also acquire competence in those communicative skills that facilitate interaction with others sharing the same linguistic and social environment. Finally, language development is a gradual process, reflecting the gradual expansion and exercise of the child's cognitive capacities.

3 Language Learning in Childhood and Adulthood

The notion that language acquisition is a gradual process is not universally accepted. Indeed, many authors are much more impressed by the speed with which a child acquires a language. This was one of Chomsky's (1959) main arguments against the behaviorist position: the child simply acquires a language too quickly for this to be explained in terms of reinforcement and successive approximation. He cited the example of the immigrant child who has no difficulty acquiring the language of the new country, whereas the child's parents—in spite of their strong desire and motivation to learn the language—struggle ineffectively with it and impose the phonology and syntax of their first language on the new one.

The child's language acquisition feats so impressed Chomsky and the transformational grammar school that they maintained that the only explanation possible was that children are preprogrammed to acquire language at a definite point in their development. The view that the child possesses a capacity for language that the adult has lost is widely shared (e.g., Andersson, 1969; Jakobovits, 1972; Wilkins, 1972) and has been formalized in what is known as the "critical period" hypothesis.

In this chapter I examine the evidence for and against this hypothesis. Then language learning in childhood and adulthood is discussed, first by comparing adult second-language learning to the learning of a first language in childhood, and then by comparing adult second-language learning to second-language learning in childhood. We shall see that there are differences of opinion as to how similar these processes are.

THE CRITICAL PERIOD HYPOTHESIS

The critical period for language learning is usually defined as lasting from about age 2 to puberty. Before the child reaches age 2, language acquisition is impossible because of maturational factors, and after puberty the natural acquisition of language is thought to be blocked by a loss of "cerebral plasticity" resulting from the completion of the development of cerebral dominance through lateralization of the language function. In addition to this biological argument, the ability of young children to acquire a language quickly and efficiently and without an accent is regarded as support for the critical period notion.

The Biological Argument

In discussing the acquisition of languages from a physiological point of view, Wilder Penfield (Penfield & Roberts, 1959) noted that there seemed to be considerable anecdotal and impressionistic evidence that children acquire languages with ease before the age of 9. After that, language learning seems to be much more difficult, as though the individual had become stiff and resistant. Penfield argued that this behavioral evidence has a physiological basis. The brain of the child is plastic, that of an adult rigid and set.

Penfield cited the evidence that children are able to relearn language skills after an injury or disease destroys the speech areas in the dominant left hemisphere, whereas this is often impossible for adults, depending on the severity of the illness. There are cases of children transferring speech dominance to the opposite hemisphere if lesions occur in the speech area, but this does not seem to happen with adults.

Penfield concluded that the brain has a plasticity in childhood (before the age of 9) that it subsequently loses. He felt that an adult cannot learn a language as a child does because the adult learns through structures that have lost their flexibility. The child, on the other hand, can acquire one or more languages with ease because the corticothalamic speech mechanism in the child is still in the process of development.

Lateralization of language function.   The critical period argument was most definitively advanced by Eric Lenneberg (1967) in his classic work, *Biological foundations of language.* Lenneberg argued that natural language acquisition by mere exposure can take place only during the critical period, which he set as occurring between the ages of 2 and puberty. The brain has not developed the capacities it needs for language acquisition earlier, and after puberty the brain has lost its cerebral plasticity because of the completion of the process of cerebral dominance, or the lateralization of the language function.

Of course, Lenneberg did not deny that language learning was possible after puberty. A person can learn to communicate in a foreign language at the age of 40; but automatic acquisition from exposure to a second language seems to disappear after puberty, and foreign accents cannot be overcome easily after this age. Lenneberg also noted that "language-learning blocks" rapidly increase after puberty.

Lenneberg reviewed the evidence for the phenomenon of cerebral dominance and concluded that in childhood the left hemisphere is ordinarily more directly involved in speech and language function than the right, though the right hemisphere is not passive with respect to verbal communication. As the child grows older, however, the two hemispheres become increasingly specialized for function, and eventually, with the completion of lateralization, the polarization of function between left and right takes place, displacing language entirely to the left and certain other functions predominantly to the right. If a lesion occurs in either hemisphere during childhood, this polarization cannot take place, and the language function—together with other functions—persists in the unharmed hemisphere.

Lenneberg cited two kinds of evidence in support of his argument that lateralization for language is complete by puberty: data from unilateral brain damage in children and data from hemispherectomies (or the removal of an entire hemisphere). The evidence from the effects of unilateral brain damage in children (Basser, 1962) suggests that injuries to the right hemisphere cause more language disturbance in children than in adults: of the 20 cases of speech disturbance reported by Basser, 7 were from right lesions or 35% (Table 3.1). In adults, right lesions cause speech disturbance in only about 3% of all cases (Russell & Espir, 1961), usually with left-handed patients. Lenneberg saw this as evidence that children are less lateralized than adults and, conversely, that adults are more lateralized than children.

The evidence from hemispherectomies also suggests that children are less lateralized than adults. Basser's (1962) survey of this literature revealed that in no cases of left hemispherectomy of children did speech disorders occur, except for three cases in which the children had aphasia before the opera-

TABLE 3.1
Lesions After Onset of Speech and
Before Age of 10[a]

Location of lesion	After injury speech was:	
	Normal	Disturbed
Left hemisphere	2	13
Right hemisphere	8	7

[a]From Basser, 1962.

tion. The children were apparently able to transfer the speech function to the less dominant hemisphere. In adults, however, complete transfer has not been reported after left hemispherectomies. Lenneberg concluded that the transfer of function, whereby language acquisition takes place in the less dominant right hemisphere, can occur only between the ages of 2 and about 13.

Some questions, however, have been raised about Lenneberg's account of the process of lateralization. Krashen (1973) reanalyzed Basser's data on unilateral brain damage in children and pointed out that in all cases of injury to the right hemisphere resulting in speech disturbance, the lesion was incurred before the age of 5. There was one exception in Basser's data where the child was injured at 10, but in this case no speech disturbance resulted. Similarly, all cases of left hemispherectomy with no resultant speech disturbance involved children younger than 5. This suggests that the completion of lateralization occurs much earlier than Lenneberg supposed, possibly by the age of 5.

Additional evidence for this position comes from dichotic listening research. In dichotic listening, subjects are presented with competing simultaneous auditory stimuli, one to each ear. Normally the right ear excels for verbal material, reflecting left hemispheric specialization (Figure 3.1). If lateralization is not complete until puberty, right ear superiority should not be established until that time. Tests with children from the ages of 4 to 9 revealed no significant changes in degree of lateralization (right ear advantage); nor were the children's scores different from those of adults tested under similar conditions (Berlin, Lowe–Bell, Hughes, & Berlin, 1972; Harshman & Krashen, 1972). This suggests that the development of lateralization may be complete as early as the age of 4.

The evidence, then, appears to call for a revision of the critical period hypothesis as originally put forth. If its biological basis is the lateralization of language function, then the critical period for language development would seem to occur between the ages of 2 and 4 or 5. A great deal of syntax is acquired during this time span but—as we saw in the previous chapter—by no means all syntax. Nor is phonological or semantic development complete by the age of 4 or 5. To assert that the child acquires language during this period of time seems to be too strong a claim.

Certainly the relationship between the presumed critical period and lateralization remains an open question. At present, the data on the developmental course of lateralization are inconsistent; some authors even argue that lateralization is essentially complete at birth (Krashen, 1975; Whitaker, Bub, & Leventer, 1981). In view of our lack of knowledge about when lateralization is complete, speculations about a critical period based on cerebral dominance seem premature. Furthermore, there are other considerations.

Left Hemisphere   Right Hemisphere

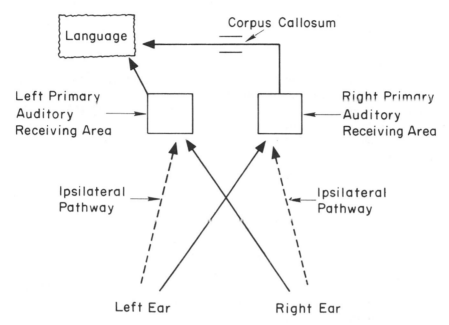

FIG. 3.1   Model of auditory processing in "normal" dichotic listening (Fromkin, Krashen, Curtiss, Rigler, & Rigler, 1974).

Functional localization.   According to Lenneberg, the development of lateralization in the cerebral cortex brings about specialization for function in the two hemispheres, with verbal functions located exclusively in the dominant hemisphere. Once this development process is over, the brain loses the cerebral plasticity it needs for language acquisition to occur easily and quickly.

Research with methods for monitoring the activity of different brain structures in human subjects has raised questions about the adequacy of a strict localization of function model. Generally speaking, localization of function for higher mental processes in the human cortex is not static and constant but variable during development and at subsequent stages (Luria, 1973). It would be surprising if this interhemispheric plasticity does not apply to at least some language functions as well.

In their studies of split-brain patients (patients whose cerebral commissures had been sectioned to prevent epileptic discharges from spreading from one hemisphere to the other), Sperry and his associates found that certain basic linguistic abilities are reflected equally in both the dominant and nondominant hemispheres. In these studies, (e.g., Gazzaniga, 1970; Sperry & Gazzaniga, 1967; Sperry, Gazzaniga, & Bogen, 1969) split-brain patients were tested for minor-hemisphere speech comprehension by being asked to retrieve unseen objects or carry out commands with the left hand. Since information from the fingers is projected on the contralateral hemisphere, such tests provide information about minor (right) hemispheric functioning. Similarly, a series of words was presented tachistoscopically to the minor hemisphere, and subjects had to indicate with the left hand when the written word matched a spoken word.

Split-brain research of this nature showed that although the verbal abilities of the minor hemisphere were clearly inferior to those of the dominant hemisphere, the minor hemisphere could comprehend spoken and written nouns, some phrases, and very simple sentences. Moreover, the minor hemisphere was aware of the semantic properties of nouns. There is also evidence from reaction-time studies with normal subjects (Moscovitch, 1973) that the minor hemisphere can perform adequately on verbal tasks that are relatively memory-free.

In short, though verbal abilities are functionally localized in the dominant hemisphere because of its greater competence for these behaviors, the evidence does not appear to support a strict lateralization model that would restrict all language functions to the dominant hemisphere. For this reason, Moscovitch (1976) proposed a functional localization model, according to which the minor hemisphere has at least latent verbal skills. These skills are usually not utilized, but they may be when there is damage to the dominant hemisphere or damage to or absence of interhemispheric pathways.

Certainly the question of the extent to which the components of language are functionally and neurologically asymmetrical remains open to debate (Albert & Obler, 1978). On the basis of what information we possess, however, it seems reasonable to conclude that the brain has more plasticity with respect to language function after childhood than Penfield or Lenneberg were willing to admit. In fact, most recent reviews of the biological evidence point to the conclusion that the aging of the brain during childhood does not diminish the ability to learn language and that no period of the life span is critical to such acquisition (Ekstrand, 1979; Kinsbourne, 1981; Walsh & Diller, 1981).

Genie.   It follows from a strict reading of the critical period hypothesis that language acquisition ex nihilo is impossible after puberty. If a child has for some reason not acquired a first language during that period, there is little chance that she will do so later. The study of feral children or other children raised in environments of extreme social isolation should throw light on the truth of this contention.

Unfortunately, such studies have rarely provided conclusive evidence for or against the critical period notion. Victor, the wild boy of Aveyron, for example, was 12 when he was found in the woods but was probably abandoned at the age of 4 or 5 (Itard, 1962). If this is so, his speech may have already developed and been effaced from his memory because of his isolation. His subsequent language learning may have been facilitated as a result of this previous experience. Similarly, not enough is known about the background or the extent of language development of other "wolf children" (Singh & Zingg, 1966) to shed light on the validity of the critical period notion. Studies of children reared within institutional settings or of children whose isolation is associated with congenital or acquired sensory loss usually do not bear upon the hypothesis, either because the children were isolated for short periods of time or because they emerged from their isolation at a relatively young age.

The case of Genie (Curtiss, 1977; Fromkin, Krashen, Curtiss, Rigler, & Rigler, 1974) is an exception to the general rule. Genie was 13 years and 9 months at the time of her discovery in Los Angeles in 1970; she had suffered physical and social isolation for most of her life. When found, she was unable to stand erect, could not chew solid or semisolid foods, and was incontinent and mute. From the age of 20 months, she had been isolated in a small, closed room. She was physically punished by her father if she made any noise. According to her mother, her father and brother never spoke to Genie, although they barked at her like dogs. The mother was forbidden to spend more than a few minutes with her during feeding. There was no radio or television in the house.

After she was found, Genie was kept in a hospital for almost a year before being given to a foster family. Medical examinations showed no signs of brain damage or neurological disease. Although Genie was functionally severely retarded, she was not autistic or pathologically disturbed. Within 4 weeks of her admission to the hospital, her behavior changed markedly—she was no longer apathetic and socially unresponsive, but responsive and alert. There was no evidence, then, of anything wrong with Genie other than what resulted from the extreme social and sensory isolation to which she had been subjected.

It was not known for certain whether Genie had spoken prior to her isolation. When she was admitted to the hospital, she could not talk and made few noises of any kind. Tests of linguistic competence were given to her almost weekly, beginning 11 months after she was found. When testing began, there were some signs of comprehension of individual words, but Genie had little if any comprehension of grammatical structures. Over a period of 2 years, she showed slow but steady development, learning to understand such grammatical structures as singular–plural contrasts, negative–affirmative distinctions, possessive constructions, modification, compound sentences with *and,* comparatives and superlatives, and a number of prepositions including *under, beside, over, next to,* and probably *in* and *on.*

Less progress was made in speech production than in comprehension, presumably because Genie did not learn the necessary neuromuscular controls over her vocal organs. The sounds she made showed considerable effort, revealing the difficulties she had regulating air flow and volume and controlling her laryngeal mechanisms. Her sound productions were monotonic and had a strange voice quality. Nonetheless, her phonological development did not deviate sharply from that of normal children, and she showed signs of intonation.

Genie learned to combine words in three- and four-word strings and could produce negative sentences, strings with locative nouns, noun phrases, possessives, and plurals. Her speech was rule-governed, with fixed word orders for sentence elements (SVO) and systematic ways of expressing syntactic and semantic relations. Her language development was slower than normals, but it seemed generally to parallel that of normal, English-speaking children. There were differences, however. Genie could deal with written language far more effectively than a child at her stage of language development. She acquired color words and numbers very early, had a 200-word vocabulary at the 2-word stage (compared to the normal child's 50 words), and could comprehend all *wh-* questions equally early (the normal child learns *why, how,* and *when* questions after *who, what* and *where*). This suggests that Genie's cognitive development exceeded her linguistic development.

In spite of these differences, there is little doubt that Genie has in fact acquired many language skills. What does this mean for the critical period hypothesis? The evidence from research with Genie suggests that children as old as 13 can acquire many language skills in spite of previous deprivation. In fact, Buddenhagen (1971) reported the establishment of language in an 18-year-old child who was mute, retarded, and mongoloid. At this point, what limited evidence we have does not compel belief in the notion that language capacity atrophies from disuse and cannot be restored after a "critical period."

Other Arguments for the Critical Period Hypothesis

Associated with the biological argument for the critical period are a number of other arguments based on impressionistic evidence that children acquire language more quickly and with greater ease than adults and that they do so without acquiring the accents that characterize languages learned by adults.

The argument from speed and efficiency of acquisition.   We have seen that Chomsky (1959) used the immigrant child argument in his famous polemic against Skinner and behaviorism. Penfield (Penfield & Roberts, 1959) also noted that the children of immigrant families typically acquire the new language in a brief period of time and can speak it easily and with little accent, regardless of whether they go to school or simply play in the street with other children. The same can rarely be said for their parents, who typically have enormous problems learning the language and usually never learn to speak it without an accent.

It is not clear, however, just why the child acquires a language so much more easily than an adult. Indeed, there is even some question of whether language acquisition is that easy for the child. Close observation of the speech development of children acquiring their first language suggests that the child must expend a great deal of effort, that there are many false starts and mistakes, and that the language acquisition process is by no means automatic (Cukovsky, 1965; Weir, 1962). Even for the 3-year-old child, the process of acquiring a second language requires an enormous amount of exposure and practice (Valette, 1964).

According to the critical period hypothesis, the child capitalizes on maturational processes that make the acquisition of language easy and quick. This is the reason for the speed and efficiency of the child's acquisition as compared to adult learning of second languages. One problem with the speed of acquisition argument, however, is that the child acquiring a first language has much more intensive and continuous exposure to the language than is ever possible for an adult learning a second language (Lee, 1973). Assuming that young children are exposed to a normal linguistic environment for at least 5 hours a day, they will have had, conservatively, 9,000 hours of exposure between the ages of 12 months and 6 years. In contrast, the Army Language School in California regarded 1,300 hours as sufficient for an adult to attain near-native competence in Vietnamese (Burke, 1974). The same argument applies to immigrant children, who typically have much more exposure to the language than do their parents.

The argument based on speed of acquisition may be criticized from another perspective. Many aspects of language do not develop phenomenally fast. Thurstone's analysis of seven primary abilities indicated that verbal comprehension reaches 80% of adult competence only at age 18 and word fluency at age 20. In contrast, number and memory factors reached 80% of adult level at 16, space and reasoning at 19, and perceptual factors at age 12 (Thurstone, 1955). In comparison with other mental capacities, then, language capacity does not seem to develop remarkably quickly.

Returning to the immigrant child example, one can ask just what is responsible for the superiority of children's language acquisition when compared to that of their parents. In addition to the possibility that the child has more exposure to a second language than adults do, it is also very likely that children are more highly motivated to acquire the language than their parents are. For the child, learning to communicate with peers in the classroom or playground is a life-and-death affair. This is often overlooked by those who attribute greater motivation to the parents. Often the parents learn enough of the language to get by in the new environment but—in spite of protestations to the contrary—are not highly motivated to learn much more. They frequently have friends and neighbors who speak the same native language and tend to restrict their social interaction to this circle. Or they may avoid social contact with other adults in the new country, something that the child cannot easily do. Children in the school or neighborhood environment are likely to be forced to interact constantly with peers who speak in their second language.

There are other considerations as well. Less is demanded of the child in achieving linguistic competence—constructions are simple, vocabulary relatively small—when compared with what is necessary for an adult to speak at an adult's level of competence. The child's attitude toward the new language is also likely to be different. It may well be that in the adult, the development of firm ego boundaries and a sense of cultural identity place constraints on language learning that are not found in the child (Schumann, 1975). These psychological and social factors—rather than neurological considerations—may be responsible for any superiority in second-language acquisition on the part of the child.

One inference frequently drawn from the critical period notion is that the younger children are when they begin to learn a second language in the classroom, the better (Andersson, 1973; Montessori, 1959). Strictly speaking, the critical period hypothesis does not make such a claim, because it is concerned only with differences between learning before and after puberty. Nonetheless, a number of authors have argued that the young child learns a second language quickly and without apparent effort. As children become older their language habits are thought to become more fixed. Some evidence for this view comes from a study by Ramsey and Wright (1974) in which they examined immigrants in Canada and found that the older the child was when introduced to English, the poorer the performance on various tests of English language skill. Children who arrived after the age of 6 tended to have lower scores on tests of language skills as their age of arrival increased. No relationships were found for younger children. There was considerable variance in the scores, however, and correlations were modest. In addition, a reassessment of the data from this study by Cummins (1981) showed that the disadvantages of older learners (over 6 years) were related to length of residence, not age on arrival.

Furthermore, other research leads to a quite different conclusion from that reached by Ramsey and Wright. Politzer and Weiss (1969), for example, found that in tests of auditory discrimination of French vowel sounds, older English-speaking children performed significantly better than younger children. This was also true for tests of pronunciation and for a recall test for vocabulary items. Politzer and Weiss argued that their results are not necessarily evidence against the critical period hypothesis, since the comparative inability of younger children to identify sounds and to transfer and recall vocabulary in terms of their first language gives them an advantage in learning a second language —without interference from their first language. This conclusion seems somewhat forced, however, and implies that younger children are superior to older children and adults in learning a second language because of their cognitive limitations. This view is at variance with the critical period hypothesis, which stipulates that the young child learns languages with ease because the child's brain is ideally programmed for linguistic input.

Further evidence against the notion that younger children are better second-language learners than older children comes from a study by Urs Bühler (1972) of Swiss school children learning French as a second language. Bühler reported that research on over 1,500 students who began French either in the fourth or fifth grade showed that the older children performed significantly better on various tests of French language skills on two separate testing occasions. Bühler found these results to be a compelling argument against the proposition that the earlier the child begins to learn a second language, the better.

Of course, it may be that the schools do not utilize the advantage younger children have in developmental psychological terms. Susan Ervin–Tripp (1974) reported, however, that even in a natural milieu where communication was emphasized and where the second language was heard most of the day, older children acquired the language faster than younger children. She found that older children in her sample of 4- to 9-year-old children were superior in their acquisition of morphology and syntax, although they had no more exposure to the second language than did younger children. She attributed this to more efficient memory heuristics and to a superior ability in problem solving and rule learning on the part of older children. In another study of natural second-language acquisition—as opposed to formal language learning through instruction—Snow and Hoefnagel-Höhle, 1978 found that in a sample of American children, adolescents, and adults learning Dutch in Holland, it was the adolescents who acquired the language most readily.

Krashen, Long, and Scarcella (1979) argued that older learners acquire the morphology and syntax of a second language faster than young children, but that child learners will ultimately attain higher proficiency. These authors endorsed a "younger-is-better" position, according to which child second-language learners are expected to be superior to adolescents and adults in terms of ultimate achievement. Two of the studies cited as evidence for this position were, however, misinterpreted. There is no evidence from the studies of Fathman (1975) or Snow and Hoefnagel–Höhle (1978) in support of the argument that ultimate proficiency in morphology and syntax is highest among informal learners who began acquisition as young children. It is true that young children made larger gains over time, but this was because older learners had reached "ceiling" levels of proficiency. In fact, the final measures of morphological and syntactic development taken (after a year) in the Snow and Hoefnagel–Höhle (1978) study showed that the adolescent group (12–15 years) maintained a slight advantage over the younger children (6–10 years). In the Fathman (1975) study of immigrant children who had been in the United States from one to three years, measures of morphology and syntax indicated that older children (11–15 years) continued to perform better than younger children (6–10 years).

Krashen and his associates also cited the research of Patkowski (1980) as evidence for their notion that "younger is better" in terms of ultimate attainment. In Patkowski's study transcripts of the speech of immigrants to the United States were rated for syntactic proficiency by two trained judges. Analysis revealed that those immigrants who had arrived before the age of 15 received higher syntactic ratings than those who arrived after the age of 15, even when amount of informal exposure and formal instruction was controlled. Patkowski argued that the optimal age for second language learning was from 12 to 15 years, a position that is consistent with the Snow & Hoefnagel–Höhle (1978) and Fathman (1975) results, but not with the notion that "younger is better," because there is no evidence that children younger than 12 ultimately outperform older children.

Patkowski (1980) interpreted his results as indicating that individuals who arrive before the age of 15 utilize a genetically based language acquisition system in learning a second language. An alternate explanation is that younger arrivals are more motivated, for economic and social reasons, to learn the second language. Furthermore, individuals who arrive in a new country as adults may be less motivated to learn a second language because of fear of losing their cultural-personal identities (Christophersen, 1973; Snow & Hoefnagel–Höhle, 1977).

One final point in this connection: if second languages are easier to learn before puberty, one would expect that after that age people who immigrate to a new country would be less likely to use the new language. Braine (1971a) reported, however, that a study of census data on the language use of immigrants to Israel showed that there was a drop in the use of the new language among those who immigrated after the age of 30; according to Lenneberg's critical period argument, however, the drop should come around the age of 13.

The evidence regarding accents.   In a discussion of second-language acquisition, Scovel (1969) cited Lenneberg's argument that cerebral lateralization is complete at puberty and saw this to be related to evidence that foreign accents appear at this time. He contended that the ability to master a second language without an accent before the age of about 12 was directly associated with the fact that lateralization has not yet become permanent at this time. The adult has lost the cerebral plasticity of the child, and all attempts to eliminate accents in adult speech are, on biological grounds, futile.

One difficulty with this argument is that a single exception constitutes a disproof of the hypothesis. Has there ever been a case of an individual who learned a second language after the critical period and was able to speak it without an accent? Scovel argued that this is biologically impossible. Even Penfield (Penfield & Roberts, 1959) did not go this far, however. He referred to the author Joseph Conrad, who learned English at the age of 15; according to an Englishman who knew him, Conrad spoke the language beautifully and without an accent.

The example is particularly instructive, since Scovel used Conrad as proof that an adult could *not* learn to speak a second language (or a third, since Conrad had learned French and Polish as a child) without an accent. He cited a biographer (Gerald, 1967), who maintained that Conrad had such a strong accent that he was prevented from lecturing in English. Perhaps Penfield's British informant was overly tolerant or perfected Conrad's accent in his memory. Or perhaps Conrad used his nonexistent accent as an excuse for not giving public lectures. At any rate, the example shows the difficulty of relying on subjective and impressionistic judgments of a speaker's accent.

Societies seem to vary considerably with respect to their sensitivity to foreign accents (Hill, 1970); and within a society such as our own, different individuals set different standards for accent-free speech. The linguist is far more likely to perceive an accent than the ordinary person. Must one meet the linguist's criteria or those of the ordinary person? The linguist is probably too precise; for the linguist, almost everyone has an accent, depending on the part of the country one comes from. The ordinary person is probably too imprecise; a foreigner could pass for a native speaker if the foreigner's accent approximated that of some dialect with which the listener was not familiar. Without an adequate definition of what it means to speak with an accent, it seems doubtful whether this question can be resolved.

Nonetheless, there is some empirical evidence that younger children have a biological predisposition that enables them to achieve fidelity in pronunciation. Asher and Garcia (1969) tested 71 Cuban immigrants—most of whom had been in the United States for about 5 years—and found that the younger the children were when they entered the country, the more closely their pronunciation approximated that of native English-speaking children. Oyama (1976) studied 60 Italian male immigrants and also found that the younger the person was when he entered the United States, the better his accent. Fathman (1975) also found that younger children were given better pronunciation ratings than were older children. There is some conflicting evidence, however, with older children testing better than younger children or no differences between older and younger children (Ekstrand, 1976, 1979; Ervin-Tripp, 1974; Snow & Hoefnagel-Höhle, 1978).

Even granting the argument based on accents does not prove the critical period hypothesis to be true. It is quite possible that the motor patterns involved in speech are directly correlated with neurophysiological mechanisms and that once the maturation of the brain is completed, plasticity in the production of speech sounds is lost. But the critical period hypothesis was applied to all aspects of language acquisition, not simply to the motor aspect.

In conclusion, it seems that the critical period hypothesis remains very much a hypothesis at the present time. The evidence for functional localization based on recent research seems to rule out a strict lateralization model. There appears to be more flexibility with regard to language functions that was believed possible a decade ago. Possibly there is a critical period for the neuromuscular patterns involved in speech, after which time it becomes much more difficult to acquire a new language without an accent. Walsh and Diller (1981) have proposed that it is not so much a question of a critical period as a developmental stage in which the learning of a second language is somewhat different from learning a second language at a later developmental stage. They argued that with proper instruction and an optimal natural environment, accents in a second language can be overcome to a reasonably large extent.

Whether this is the case, how in fact one should define the critical period hypothesis (Seliger, 1981), whether there are critical periods for other language skills (Seliger, 1978), what the length of the critical period is in each case, and how this relates to the process of lateralization cannot be answered with any certainty. As Hegel said of Schelling's philosophy, "this is a night where all cows are black." There does seem to be an emerging consensus, however, that the critical period hypothesis, as originally formulated, is not supported by available evidence (Ekstrand, 1979; Kinsbourne, 1981; Walsh & Diller, 1981). Many authors favor an approach based on social and cultural, rather than on biological factors (H. D. Brown, 1980a; Gardner, Smythe, Clement, & Gliksman, 1976; Snow-Hoefnagel-Höhle, 1978).

FIRST-LANGUAGE LEARNING IN CHILDREN AND SECOND-LANGUAGE LEARNING IN ADULTS

In addition to the question of whether children are biologically predisposed to acquire language, there is the question of how children's language learning differs from adult language learning. It is this question that I wish to focus on now, first by considering the arguments for and against viewing second-language learning in adults as a qualitatively different process from first-language acquisition in children then by looking at some experimental research that bears on this issue.

The Debate over Differences in Kind

Does an adult learning a second language with formal instructions learn that language in the same way that a child acquires a first language in the natural environment? There is considerable debate in the literature over this issue, although all authors admit that there are differences between the language learning of an adult and the language acquisition of a child. The focus of debate is whether such differences constitute differences in kind, whether there is a qualitative difference in the two processes, whether the processes are radically different. I consider first the arguments of those who believe that there are qualitative differences between second-language learning in adults and first-language learning in children and that these differences require radically different processes. Then I turn to the arguments of those who regard the differences as essentially quantitative and who see no reason for believing that an adult learns a second language in a manner radically different from that in which a child learns a first language.

The argument for a difference in kind. Those authors who accept the critical period notion usually favor the view that second-language learning in adults is qualitatively different from first-language learning. They hold that the individual is biologically programmed to acquire language before puberty and that optimal grammatical coding is available only to children, not to adults (Halle, 1962; King, 1969; Saporta, 1966; Wilkins, 1972, 1974). The child is thought to process language in a manner different from and superior to the way that an adult processes language (Andersson, 1969; Echeverría, 1974).

According to this view, the language acquisition device of the child is radically different from (and superior to) that of the adult. The child processes language in terms of a preprogrammed linguistic coding ability; the adult processes language in terms of a general coding ability. Thus there are two models (see Figure 3.2) for language acquisition (Echeverría, 1974).

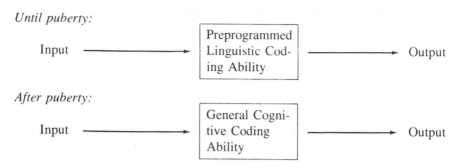

FIG. 3.2   Models of language acquisition before and after puberty (Echeverría, 1974).

This seems to be the view of Noam Chomsky (1968), who at one point suggested that the mind is divided into faculties: whereas first-language acquisition takes place through the faculty of language learning, which atrophies at a certain age, he postulated that languages can still be learned after that age by using such other faculties of the mind as the logical or the mathematical.

One reason given for the qualitative difference between second-language learning in adults and first-language learning is that structural changes result from first-language acquisition. If a new language is learned in adulthood, it must be filtered through the learning acquisition system of the individual, modified by the first language (Stern, 1970). The older the individual is, the more the rules and habits of the first language *interfere* with learning a second language; once people are in their teens, they can no longer learn a language as they acquired their first language (Politzer, 1965).

The interference argument rests largely on errors made by individuals learning a second language. These errors do not appear in first-language acquisition data; hence the second-learning experience is seen to be qualitatively different. For example, when an English-speaking adult says *Ich warte für ihn* in German, the English prepositional construction in the English equivalent, *I wait for him,* has interfered with and displaced the correct German form, *Ich warte auf ihn.* Children acquiring German as a first language do not make such mistakes; hence the two experiences involve basically different processes.

Another argument is that it is said to be more difficult for speakers of English to learn certain languages—e.g., Chinese—than to learn others—e.g., French, whereas the opposite is true for native Japanese speakers (James, 1971). That is, it is argued that comparison of the second-language learning experiences of speakers of different first languages reveals different degrees of interference due to the different first languages (Eckman, 1977; James, 1980). This again suggests that the learner of a second language must "filter" that language through a language acquisition device that has been modified and restructured by the first language.

Roger Brown (1973b) thought that second-language learning may be responsive to familiar sorts of learning variables whereas first-language learning may not. He cited evidence that grammatical morphemes are always learned by the child, although it seems that listeners do not really need them. He noted that adult Japanese learning English as a second language do not seem to learn how to use articles correctly, whereas the child acquiring English as a first language does. Similarly, children acquire tag questions in English without difficulty, whereas adults learning English as a second language often do not learn them at all. Brown was inclined to see first-language learning as a unique experience and thought that it may be "profoundly and ineradicably different [p. 104]" from second-language learning in adults.

The argument against a difference in kind.   On the opposite side of the fence are a number of authors who maintain that language learning in childhood and second-language learning in adulthood involve esentially the same processes (Cooper, 1970; Corder, 1967; Macnamara, 1973; Newmark & Reibel, 1968; Roberts, 1973). These authors admit that there are differences between the way an adult learns a second language and the way a child learns a first language, but they argue that these are mostly quantitative differences and do not constitute differences in kind.

The argument from interference is rejected, because it rests on a false assumption about the process of language learning and because it lacks empirical support. The interference notion derives from a learning-theory approach, according to which language learning involves a process of habit formation. Interference results from the fact that old habits have not yet been extinguished. Such an approach leads logically to the untenable position that old habits (the first language) must be unlearned or extinguished before new habits (the second language) can be mastered (Dulay & Burt, 1972). Even learning theorists have expressed dissatisfaction with theoretical formulations relating to interference phenomena (Tulving & Madigan, 1970). The essential issue is an empirical one: is there evidence that in learning a second language a person inevitably uses first-language structures and that errors result from the interference of the first language?

The argument that differential interference results from two different first languages when learning a particular second language does not necessarily prove the qualitative difference position. The fact that an American learns French or German easier than Chinese and that for a Japanese the reverse is true may simply be due to the way in which the material is taught (Littlewood, 1973). With appropriate teaching methods these differences may cancel out. Here again, the question is an empirical one and must be settled by empirical methods.

Of course it is difficult not to be impressed by the differences in first- and second-language learning. These differences have been commented on repeatedly. Children generalize more between words that sound alike and confuse the meaning of similar-sounding words (Ervin–Tripp, 1967). Children seem to attend to sounds—to the surface of language—whereas adults penetrate the surface of the utterance to its meaning (Ervin–Tripp, 1970b). Children are also limited, as we have seen in the preceding chapter, by the inefficiency of their information processing and mnemonic devices. Their language development is constrained and determined by their cognitive development.

In addition, the way in which children are exposed to their first language differs markedly from the way in which adults are usually exposed to a second language. Children learn their first language without focusing on linguistic form, through direct experience with events at hand in a natural communication setting. Adult language learning, in contrast, typically involves formal instruction and an artificial linguistic environment. The adult is taught to apply rules consciously, whereas the child receives no such instruction.

The question is whether such differences in how children and adults are exposed to language mean that different processes are employed in the two cases. Those who view language learning in processing terms, as a series of strategies employed by a changing language acquisition system, tend to see no need to posit a qualitative difference between first-language acquisition and second-language learning in adults. The basic features of the language acquisition system remain the same, although input conditions may be different for adults and children (Ervin–Tripp, 1973a, 1981). Memory heuristics improve with age, making it possible to retain longer input and discover meaning; yet there is a basic similarity of process. Although the use of written materials and formal instructions increases efficiency and speed of learning in adults (Braine, 1971b), an adult learning a second language faces the same task and uses essentially the same strategies as the child learning a first language.

Thus Taylor (1974) maintained that children in the acquisition of their first language do not operate under an imitation and repetition strategy, but rather under a strategy that encourages them to simplify and regularize the syntactic structure of the language they are acquiring. Taylor argued that this strategy of simplifying the target language applies to second-language learning as well. Both adults and children overgeneralize target language rules, reduce grammatical redundancies, and omit those rules that they have not learned, presumably because of their apparent arbitrariness.

Because of their cognitive maturity, second-language learners do not produce the one- and two-word utterances found in the speech of children acquiring the first language. But this does not mean that there is a qualitative difference between first-language learning and second-language learning (Ervin–Tripp, 1974):

> Now it is certainly the case that the second language learner makes use of prior knowledge, skills, tactics, but it is also true that the first language learner does this. That is, any learning builds on what has happened before, and it remains a major question just how this occurs. A child learning a language at four, whether a first or second language, has knowledge of the world, knowledge of spatial and object relations, knowledge of causality, which a child of one does not have. A child hearing a sentence he has never heard before, at the age of four, can bring to it knowledge of sound groupings, configurations, which a child of one does not have—whether or not he is listening to a new sentence in his mother tongue or a second language. The fact that the second language builds on prior knowledge is not what differentiates it from first language learning [p. 112].

What differences exist are thought to be quantitative in nature, resulting from the greater cognitive maturity of the second-language learner and from social and affective factors. In processing terms, first-language acquisition and second-language learning are seen to be identical, as evidenced by the kinds of errors observed (Taylor, 1974).

Some Empirical Findings

There are obvious problems comparing children learning a first language with adults learning a second. For one thing the two groups operate at different levels of mental functioning, yet methods of testing must be the same for both groups. Nonetheless, there are some data on the important question of whether adults learning a second language go through the same stages of development as children do acquiring that language as their first language. In addition, there have been empirical studies of interference that bear on the question at hand.

Developmental evidence.   Vivian Cook (1973) studied 20 foreign adults learning English and 24 English-speaking children, who ranged in age from 2 years, 11 months to 4 years and 9 months. The adult subjects came from a number of different countries and had been studying English in England for less than a year, though they had exposure to varying amounts of English in their own countries. All subjects were shown a picture and were read a sentence that the picture illustrated. They had to repeat the sentence and in some cases answer a comprehension question. In essence, this was the method of elicited imitation (Slobin & Welsh, 1973), often used to determine linguistic competence.

Both groups performed rather poorly on a series of sentences designed to test various syntactic features of the relative clause in English: *This is the man that drives the bus, The lady the boy is drawing is funny, The hammer that is breaking the cup is big,* and so forth. The children's imitations were correct only 8% of the time and the adults' 26% of the time. Both groups seemed to have approached the task in much the same way, as reflected in the errors they made. Both groups often omitted *that,* even when it was required grammatically; both groups replaced *that* with grammatical alternatives; both groups found the relative clauses following the subject of the sentence easier to imitate than those following the object of the sentence; and both groups recoded syntactic structure to preserve the sentences' meaning. In contrast to the adults, children used more substitutions for the relative (especially *what* for *that*), sometimes shifted the subject of the relative clause to the main clause, and occasionally repeated the last few words of the sentence in giving their answers (. . . *drives the bus,* . . .*is funny,* and so forth).

In general, the trend indicated that adult second-language learners and children made the same kinds of mistakes. Children even made some mistakes that are regarded as typical of foreigners, such as omitting the subject of the relative clause or omitting the "s" from the third-person singular form of the verb. Both groups did equally poorly on comprehension tests. The differences between the two groups probably reflected differences in the conditions under which they acquired the language; children were allowed to make more grammatically unacceptable substitutions and mistakes than the adults, who were closely monitored in an audio-lingual setting. The occasional echoing responses, in which children gave only the last few words of the sentence, probably reflected a strategy of seizing what remains in short-term memory; whereas adults use a more complex strategy because their operative memory is more effective.

In a second experiment, Cook tested 66 adults who had averaged 8 months of English instruction in England and 3 years and 8 months of instruction prior to coming to England. They were tested on sentences such as *The wolf is happy to bite* and *The duck is hard to bite.* The subject's task was to tell who was doing the biting in each sentence—the duck or the wolf. Cook found that he could sort his subjects into three types:

- *Primitive rule users,* who consistently regarded the subject of the sentence as the agent of the action.
- *Intermediates,* who gave mixed answers—sometimes following the primitive rule and sometimes giving the correct interpretation.
- *Passers,* who gave completely correct responses to all sentences.

These categories reflected the amount of exposure subjects had to English (Table 3.2) and appeared to represent developmental stages. Apparently, the first strategy used developmentally is to regard the subject of the sentence as the agent of the action, then there is a period of uncertainty, and finally the learner is able to interpret the sentence in terms of its deep structure rather than by relying exclusively on surface structure. There is evidence (Cromer, 1970) that children go through a similar process.

Cook pointed out that his results raise some problems for the critical period hypothesis. If adults lose the ability to acquire a language as children do, one would suppose that adults would utilize what knowledge they have to learn a new language. Adults have learned, for example, that sentences can contain sentences embedded in them. One would expect them to use this information and consequently to have less difficulty comprehending embedded relative clauses than a child does. But this did not happen in Cook's first experiment. When presented with sentences such as *The lady the boy's drawing is funny,* adult second-language learners fell into the same trap as children did. The adult's learning seems not to have been facilitated by the first language; as Cook's second experiment suggests, the second-language learner appears to go through essentially the same stages as the child.

Cook also noted that other studies tend to support the notion that children and adults approach language in basically the same way. For example, Palermo and Howe (1970) found that adults, in an analogous experimental learning situation, employed the same strategies as children do when learning regular and irregular past-tense inflections in English. Similarly, Stolz and Tiffany (1972) showed that the characteristic differences between word associations of children and adults could be canceled out by giving adults unfamiliar words.

In a study designed to investigate the acquisition of a set of complex English structures in adult learners of English as a second language,

TABLE 3.2
Average Amount of Exposure to English for Groups
Giving Different Types of Responses[a]

Type of response	Amount of instruction in England	Amount of prior instruction
Primitive rule users (7 subjects)	2 months	2 years, 2 months
Intermediates (45 subjects)	7 months	3 years, 5 months
Passers (14 subjects)	12 months	4 years, 8 months

[a]From Cook, 1973.

d'Anglejan and Tucker (1975) found results quite similar to Cook's. In their study, d'Anglejan and Tucker tested adult second-language learners of two levels of proficiency—beginners and advanced. The grammatical structures investigated were those complex English structures used by Carol Chomsky (1969) in her study of the acquisition of syntax in children between the ages of 5 and 10. Adult second-language learners were found to process the linguistic data of the target language without relying on the syntax of their first language. The developmental pattern observed for the acquisition of the complex structures paralleled those observed in Chomsky's children. In no case was there evidence of the use of strategies that differed from those used by children learning English as a first language.

Thus there seems to be little evidence from studies comparing language learning in children and second-language learning in adults that the two groups go through radically different processes. What evidence there is points to the conclusion that the processes involved are basically the same. Older learners have the advantage of greater knowledge of semantic systems and strategies of conversation, but there is no evidence that the language-acquisition system that is effective in first-language development suddenly atrophies (Ervin–Tripp, 1981). Of course, this need not be the last word on the topic, and more research is needed directly comparing the adult second-language learner and the child acquiring a first language before any definitive statements are possible.

The evidence from interference. As we have seen, those who view second-language learning in adulthood as qualitatively different from first-language acquisition in childhood base their argument in part on the evidence for interference in second-language learning. Because one finds adult learners making mistakes that reflect their first language and children making no such mistakes in acquiring their first language, the argument runs, the two experiences must be different in kind. Second-language learning is dependent on habits acquired during the process of first-language acquisition.

This view derives ultimately from traditional interference theory in verbal learning and memory research. We have seen that there is a logical problem with such a theory: old habits must be unlearned or extinguished before new habits can be learned; otherwise they interfere with the new habits. It follows that the learner would have to extinguish (forget) the first language to learn a second language without interference. This is obviously contrary to what actually happens when most people learn a second language.

How then should one think of interference? I shall define *interference* as those errors that occur in the learning of a second language (B) that reflect the acquisition of a previous language (A) and that are not found in the normal development of those who acquire that language (B) as a first language.

Such errors must be distinguished from at least three other types of errors (Dulay & Burt, 1972):

- Developmental errors: those errors that do not reflect the learner's first language (A), but are found among those who acquire the second language (B) during childhood as a first language.
- Ambiguous errors: those errors that can be categorized as due either to interference or as developmental errors.
- Unique errors: those errors that cannot be categorized as due either to interference or as developmental errors.

If acquiring a first language brings about structural changes that require subsequent second-language learning to be filtered through a language acquisition system modified by the first language, then one would expect the majority of second-language errors to reflect the interference of first-language structures. Yet the common finding is that the majority of errors are not traceable to first-language structure (Brudhiprabha, 1972; Dulay & Burt, 1972; Ervin–Tripp, 1970b; George, 1972; Lance, 1969; Peddie, 1982; Richards, 1971). In most of these studies only about a third of the errors was attributable to first-language structures. Many errors reflect the learner's attempt to generalize and apply the rules of the second language before they are mastered. Others are morphological and syntactic simplifications of first-language learners (Ervin–Tripp, 1969). Others seem to be unique in that they do not reflect first-language structure and are not found in the developmental acquisition data of native speakers of the second language.

This is not, however, to deny that interference errors occur. The argument is to what extent the adult learner of a second language is inhibited by first-language structures. Those who hold that the two types of language learning are qualitatively different are committed to the view that interference from first language is the main source of mistakes in second-language acquisition, because the structures of the first language determine those imposed on the second. The evidence does not seem to warrant such a conclusion. There is some evidence that interference errors predominate in the early stages of second-language learning in adults (Taylor, 1975), but such errors are much less frequent at later stages and by no means constitute the majority of errors.

Indeed, even the minority of errors that are due to interference may not all reflect negative transfer or inhibition. The adult second-language learner may be trying out strategies based on those successfully used in the first language. This intentional use of patterns from the first language to crack the code of the second does not seem to involve interference in the usual sense of the word. Nor does this mean that the second-language learner is necessarily using different processes in learning the language. The child also uses the patterns of the known language to comprehend those that are not known.

SECOND-LANGUAGE LEARNING IN CHILDREN AND ADULTS

Until now, the discussion has focused on the comparison of second-language learning in adults with first-language learning in children. Now I will turn briefly to the topic of second-language learning in children and adults. Both children and adults can learn a second language naturalistically, without formal instruction. And both children (at least older children) and adults can learn a second language in the classroom through deliberate instruction, rule isolation, and error correction. What evidence is there that adults and children learn a second language differently?

It is often argued that the child has a superior biological predisposition for language acquisition (this applies to second or third languages as well as to first languages). Hence the young child is thought to acquire a second language easily and quickly. The evidence, however, does not support this viewpoint. The few studies that have been conducted suggest that older children and adolescents do better than younger children in acquiring a second language in a natural environment (Ervin–Tripp, 1974; Kessler & Idar, 1979; Snow & Hoefnagel–Höhle, 1978).

Direct comparison between young children and adolescents or adults acquiring a second language is difficult because of several factors. First, the criterion for success is vastly different for the child as compared to the adult. Children are considered fluent when they can communicate at a level appropriate for their age. An adult must communicate with other adults about much more complicated issues, where deficiencies in vocabulary and syntax show up more readily. It is also difficult to hold constant such factors as motivation to learn and exposure to the second language across different age groups. Another factor that is difficult to control concerns differences in test-taking abilities between younger and older subjects (Hakuta, 1983).

Nonetheless, there are some interesting studies comparing younger with older learners. Asher and his associates (Asher, 1965, 1969; Asher, Kusudo, & de le Torre, 1974; Asher & Price, 1967) attempted to mimic the way in which children acquire languages in the natural setting. Asher argued that one possible reason why children acquire second languages faster than adults (assuming they do) is that their language acquisition is often synchronized to physical responses. The child has to make action responses in play and in response to commands. In contrast, an adult attempts to learn the language quite independently of physical behavior. What would happen, Asher asked, if adults were required to acquire language as children do, by synchronizing their second language with physical responses?

In one of his studies (Asher & Price, 1967) four age groups were compared in their acquisition of Russian: children from second, fourth, and eighth grade classes and a group of college undergraduates. All subjects were English speakers with no knowledge of Russian. They were divided into two groups at each age level. In the first group—called the Act–Act group—subjects were to imitate an adult model who physically responded to Russian commands to stand, sit, walk, stop, turn, squat, and run. Each utterance was presented 10 times in a random sequence. There were retention tests immediately after the training phase, 24 hours later, and 48 hours later. After each retention test new training was conducted with increasingly complex constructions. By the last training session, the subjects heard such commands as *Pick up the pencil and paper and put them on the chair* and *Walk to the door, pick up the pencil, put it on the table, and sit on the chair.*

Training and retention tests were the same for the second group—called the Observe–Act group—except that this group merely saw the model perform the Russian commands; only during the retention tests were subjects to act out commands. This, however, did not significantly affect their performance relative to the Act–Act group (Figure 3.3). Both groups performed approximately as well at each age level. All groups of children were significantly poorer than adults on measures of retention. Thus, in spite of the fact that the task appears to approximate closely the way in which languages are acquired in the "natural setting," children displayed no superior language acquisition capabilities.

The superiority of the adults in such tasks no doubt reflects cognitive maturation. *In situ,* this may be offset by other factors that favor children. Anecdotal and impressionistic evidence that children are superior in second-language acquisition most likely stems from nonlinguistic and nonbiological factors such as amount of exposure, motivation, lack of inhibition, and other personality variables. When the child is placed in an experimental situation where these factors are controlled or do not operate, performance is inferior to that of an adult.

If we turn to the more formal learning situation, we find generally the same pattern of results. There is, for example, some experimental research in which adults and children learned a miniature artificial language under controlled conditions. In this research (Braine, 1971a), the learning of adults was superior to that of children. In addition, there is the evidence, cited earlier, that older children perform better than younger children in the classroom, second-language learning situation (Bühler, 1972; Politzer & Weiss, 1969). In a study of third and fourth grade children learning Japanese as a second language, Grider, Otomo, and Toyota (1961) also

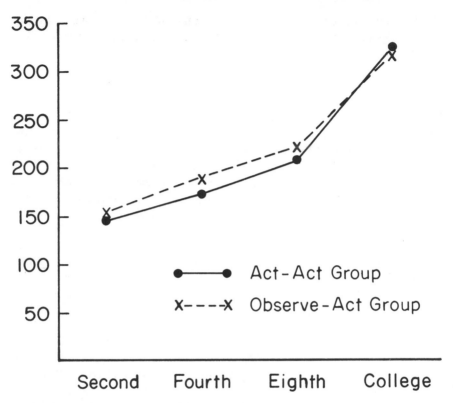

FIG. 3.3   Retention of commands as measured by mean total recall scores on all retention tests (based on Asher & Price, 1967).

found that older children performed better on tests of language skills. All of
these findings run against the argument that younger children have superior
ability in learning a second language.

Indeed, research suggests that adult and child second-language learners
pass through essentially the same developmental stages in their acquisition
of selected linguistic forms. For example, studies of the accuracy with which
learners of English as a second language correctly supply the required morpheme in obligatory contexts indicates that the same accuracy hierarchy
results regardless of age, language background, or the nature of the
learner's exposure to English (Bailey, Madden, & Krashen, 1974; Fathman,
1975; Krashen, Sferlazza, Feldman, & Fathman, 1976; Larsen–Freeman,
1976a). There may, however, be differences in performance due to the
cognitive superiority of older learners. Heilenman (1981) found that
although the performance of college students was quite similar to that of
children learning French as a second language (Tremaine, 1975), there were
differences on items involving semantic-syntactic relationships. College

students performed better than children on tasks that involved complex relationships within and across sentences. It may be that such relationships involve a certain level of cognitive maturation that young children do not yet possess.

Krashen (1975, 1982) suggested that changes in cognitive development that occur around puberty—such as the onset of "formal operations" in Piaget's sense—relate to adult–child differences in second-language development. Though ruling out an explanation based on the development of cerebral dominance, Krashen (1975) thought that it was possible that there are neurological events related to the cognitive maturation of the individual that in turn affect the development of a second language. Krashen (1982) also stressed the role of affective factors in accounting for adult–child differences, as have a number of other authors (Curran, 1961; Lambert, 1967; Schumann, 1975; Titone, 1973), most of whom played down the role of neurological factors. This view was summarized by Taylor (1974), who argued that the psychological learning strategies involved in second-language development are basically the same for children and adults, differing essentially in the degree of cognitive maturity of the learner. Affective variables set limits to what is learned but do not affect the basic process.

In any event, there is considerably more to be known about the biological substratum of language. Certainly biological development affects first-language development, but not enough is known about how and to what extent. There does not seem to be evidence of biological limits to second-language learning. An unqualified "frozen brain" theory does not seem supported by available evidence. Nor is there evidence that children possess special, biologically based language abilities that given them an advantage over adults in language learning. Clearly, however, there is room for more research in this area, especially research in which adults and children are compared in various learning contexts.

4 Simultaneous Acquisition of Two Languages in Childhood

This chapter is concerned with the study of children who acquire two languages simultaneously. In such cases, it is inappropriate to speak of first and second languages. Both languages are first languages, although one usually dominates in certain situations or with certain persons. If children hear one language from their parents and another from their playmates, for example, they will tend to speak the parents' language when in contact with them and will restrict the other language to the play situation. If contact with parents is much more extensive than contact with playmates, the language the child speaks with parents is likely to predominate. Perfect linguistic balance across situations seems difficult, if not impossible, to achieve, since amount of exposure across situations is never constant.

Bilingualism admits of degrees, however. This is consistent with the definition adopted in the first chapter: the ability to produce complete and meaningful utterances in two languages. Although bilingual children may be more fluent in one language in certain spheres than in the other language, they can produce complete and meaningful utterances in both. For the most part, the children studied in the research considered in this chapter were able to communicate with ease at a level appropriate for their age in either language. In some cases there were shifts in dominance from time to time as the child moved from a bilingual to a monolingual environment, but usually the child adjusted to the bilingual environment when placed in it again.

One problem in speaking of the simultaneous acquisition of two languages is defining a cutoff point at which one language can be said to have been established. If a 2½-year-old, English-speaking child moves to France and starts to acquire French, is the child simultaneously acquiring two languages; or has English been established already, with French being acquired as a second language? As mentioned in Chapter 1, I have arbitrarily set the cutoff point at 3 years of age. The child who is introduced to a second language before 3 years will be regarded as acquiring the two languages simultaneously; the child introduced to a second language after 3 will be considered to have had one language established and to acquire the second successively, as a second language. I do not mean by this that the first language is fully acquired at the age of 3 years; I do not believe that it can be said to be fully acquired at 6 years. But by the age of 3, it would seem that the child has had a considerable head start in one language; it is no longer a question of acquiring the two simultaneously.

Of course both groups—children who acquire two languages simultaneously and children who acquire them successively—can achieve bilingual competence. The child's ultimate bilingualism is not a function of how early a second language is introduced. Simultaneous acquisition of two languages is not necessarily superior to successive acquisition in assuring retention of both languages. A child brought up in a bilingual environment from birth may lose that bilingualism when contact with one of the original languages is lost. Ultimate retention of two languages depends on a large number of factors, such as the prestige of the languages, cultural pressures, motivation, opportunities of use—but not on age of acquisition.

STUDIES OF BILINGUAL CHILDREN

Most of the studies I discuss here are case studies based on diaries or other records kept by parents whose children were introduced simultaneously to two languages. Usually the parent keeping the record was a professional linguist, although this is not always the case. In some studies linguists or psycholinguists used records made available to them by parents. In other studies linguists reported on their observations of other people's children.

There is considerable variation in the quality of these studies. Some, which I do not consider at any length here, are anecdotal and impressionistic. Those that I do discuss are more objective, although in all studies the issue of reliability looms large. There is ample room for error in observational research (especially if one is observing one's own child). The child may be seen to have abilities he or she does not possess; ill-formed utterances may be transformed into well-formed sentences; mistakes may be overlooked or suppressed (or seen to occur when they do not). The tendency is to see what supports one's hypotheses and to ignore the rest.

Another problem with the case report is that the information provided is not always what could be hoped for. The observer may have been quite meticulous and scrupulous in taking notes on the child's speech but may have overlooked much that is of interest from the perspective of present-day linguistics and psycholinguists. Observation must be a selective process. The speech of even very young children provides too much data for everything to be recorded. Only in recent years are there studies that deal systematically with particular theoretical issues in bilingual language acquisition. Most of these studies involve children who acquired a second language subsequent to the first language, a topic that concerns us in the following chapter.

Nonetheless, a great deal can be learned from the diary literature pertaining to children who were simultaneously exposed to bilingual language presentation. Most of the studies discussed here are linguistically sophisticated and carefully conducted. In some cases they reflect a Herculean labor of recording and analyzing the child's speech. The landmark study in this respect is Leopold's classic report (1939, 1947, 1949a, 1949b) on the language development of his daughter, Hildegard. This still stands as the single most valuable source of information about bilingualism in the young child. I group the studies around Leopold's, looking first at earlier studies and then, after a discussion of Leopold's findings, examining more recent studies of bilingual language acquisition.

Early Studies

The earliest detailed study of childhood bilingualism is that of the French linguist Jules Ronjat (1913). In the summer of the year 1908, Ronjat, whose wife was German and at that time pregnant with their son, received the following advice concerning bilingual language training from his colleague, Maurice Grammont:

> There is nothing for the child to be taught. It is sufficient simply to speak to him when the occasion to do so arises in one of the languages he is to learn. But here is the crux: *each language must be embodied in a different person.* You, for instance, should always talk French to him and his mother German. *Never switch roles.* In this manner he will begin to speak two languages without noticing it and without having to put forth any special effort in learning them [Ronjat, 1913, p. 3].

This method was strictly enforced by Ronjat and his wife, with considerable success. The child appeared to distinguish the two languages quite early. Before his second birthday he had developed a system of testing new words by using the word with German and with French pronunciation until he was prepared to assign it to "mama's box or papa's box" ("*le casier mama ou le casier papa*"). This testing period (*temps d'essai*) never lasted longer than a week, and after the word was assigned there was never any doubt as to where it belonged.

Ronjat reported that by 3 years and 5 months his son Louis could correctly utter the phonemes of both languages. This represented a slight retardation when compared to the norms available for monolingual-speaking French and German children. The retardation was in the normal range, however, and Ronjat did not regard this as a negative consequence of bilingual presentation.

In his vocabulary development, Louis Ronjat initially tended to favor his "mother" tongue. This imbalance was temporary, however; and before long the child deliberately tried to learn words in both languages simultaneously. If he knew the name for something in one language only, he would ask for its name in the other. There seemed to be no evidence of confusion between languages.

This is clearly the most important aspect of Ronjat's study. The child spoke both languages as a native-speaking child would. Even when he used loan words from one language in the other language, he gave the word its appropriate pronunciation; French loan words in German were given German pronunciation and vice versa. Each language was person-specific—a nurse or servant was identified (after some initial confusion) as French- or German-speaking and thereafter was spoken to only in that language. If his father spoke to him in French with a message for a German-speaking servant, the boy gave the message in German without any apparent effort. It was not as if the boy were translating but, as we would say today, simply shifting registers or language codes.

Although Ronjat spoke only French to the child and his wife only German, there were occasional slips. These did not faze the child; he simply responded in the correct language. At table his parents spoke German to each other; but if the child broke in with something to say to his father, he always did so in French. On one occasion the father used the word *approbation* at dinner in German and with a German pronunciation. The boy did not know the word and asked his father, *Qu'est-ce que c'est, approbation?* with the correct French pronunciation.

The child showed remarkably few signs of interference between languages. Those rare mistakes that his father observed were mainly grammatical and syntactic. There were almost no mistakes due to clang associations—confusion of meaning between similar sounding words. Nor were word order mistakes common. The child, for example, would never say *Wein rot* for *Rotwein* on analogy with *vin rouge*. Thus, although interference errors did occur, they were not very frequent. The predominant impression was that the child kept the two languages independent of each other.

Ronjat reported that his son learned both French and German equally well and that his bilingualism had no deleterious effect on his intellectual development. Ronjat attributed the child's success in not confusing the two languages to the strict observation of the principle *une personne, une langue.* In contrast, Ronjat noted that another bilingual child, whose parents were not as consistent in their behavior, had considerably more difficulty learning the two languages. Ronjat concluded that imbedding each language separately in a specific and constant person greatly facilitates learning.

The importance of making the two languages person-specific was also emphasized by the Serbian linguist, Pavlovitch (1920), whose son grew up in France. The family spoke Serbian, but when the child was 1 year and 1 month, a French friend of the family began to spend a great deal of time with him. Both languages appeared simultaneously, and there was no obvious confusion between them. Corresponding phonemic systems of both languages were mastered at approximately the same time and without confusion. Initially, French vocabulary developed slower than Serbian, and the child seemed to use words with the same reference as synonyms. This continued from the age of 1 year and 9 months to 2 years. At that point, the child seemed to become aware that he was exposed to bilingual presentation, and thereafter confusion between the languages ceased. Both languages were kept consistently independent of each other.

Pavlovitch attributed the child's ability to distinguish the languages to the fact that the use of one or the other language was associated with a particular person. As with Ronjat's child, this sharp differentiation of the two languages appeared to help acquisition and to prevent confusion. Although the child realized that his parents could speak and understand French, he consistently spoke Serbian to them in the family environment. Unfortunately, Pavlovitch's study ends when his child was 2 years of age and leaves important questions unanswered, such as the development of inflections, which is quite different in the two languages.

In another early study of a child exposed to bilingual presentation, Hoyer and Hoyer (1924) carefully observed the babbling of their infant, who heard Russian from his mother and German from his father. The child began to utter comprehensible words at 11 months but reduced his utterances in such a way that whole syllables were dropped (especially unstressed syllables). He seemed to employ only those sound elements that were present at this time in his babbling monologues. Whether these particular sounds resulted from his exposure to the languages in his environment or whether they are universally found in children at this period could not be answered with any assurance; some of the sound elements in the child's babbling did appear to reflect sound combinations to which he had considerable exposure.

Recent research on babbling suggests that the sound features the child produces are universal (McNeill, 1970) and that there are many sounds in the environment that children do not produce when babbling (Clark & Clark, 1977). This was the conclusion of some early investigators as well

(Bühler, 1930; Grégoire, 1937). Ronjat (1913) observed that sounds the infant had never heard appeared in his son's early babbling. Thus the notion that bilingual presentation has an effect on a child's babbling seems unsupported by available evidence.

One of the few if not the only early study of bilingual children by an American was Madorah Smith's (1935) report on the language development of eight children from an English- and Chinese-speaking bilingual family. The children were born in China of missionary parents and lived there, except for 1 year in America, until the youngest child was 20 months old. They heard Chinese from their native nurses, other servants, and practically all Chinese children and adults. All of their non-Chinese acquaintances spoke English. Their parents used both English and Chinese in speaking to the children.

Smith's study was based on data from the mother's diary, kept from the time the oldest child was born until the family returned to America. These data were not ideal, because they were unsystematically gathered; nonetheless, they allowed some comparison across children. They were analyzed for sentence length, number of errors per 10 words, number of inflected forms of English words in proportion to the total number of English words, percentage of Chinese words used. The most interesting information for our purposes was the percent of mixed sentences, since this provides some index of the amount of confusion between the two languages.

Much more mixing was reported by Smith than by Ronjat or Pavlovitch. The two languages were confused until the third birthday of most of the children. The average age of the children at the time of the last recorded mixed sentence was 39 months. This was most likely due to the parents' use of both languages. Even among themselves, the children—though preferring English—also occasionally used Chinese. Apparently, this lack of consistency in presentation caused younger children to confuse the two languages. There was no clear demarcation between Chinese and English. Smith concluded that it is best for young children to receive two languages from different sources, with each adult in the home using one language consistently.

There is some evidence that children are capable of acquiring more than two languages simultaneously. Geissler (1938), a German teacher in Belgrade, reported that some young children he observed were able to master as many as four languages without mixing them. They did this quite naturally without the kind of disciplined presentation characteristic of the training of children such as the sons of Ronjat and Pavlovitch. Geissler's report is highly impressionistic, however; and his comments on language development are vague and based on scanty evidence.

Nonetheless, his study is a paragon of objectivity for German research on bilingualism during the 1930s. At this time, German authors such as

Schmidt–Rohr (1933) were inveighing against the dangers of bilingualism: the mother tongue—*die Muttersprache*—must be preserved in its purity, or else the child would be in danger of losing his German nationality and would become an atheist. Bilingualism was harmful to the individual: after all, people were not required to live with two religions . . . (Weisgerber, 1935).

Lenna Emrich (1938) reflected this mentality in her study of a German child (her own?) raised from her 6th week in Bulgaria. The child's parents spoke to her in German, but her nurse spoke only Bulgarian. The child showed the typical bilingual development: she understood both languages with ease, learned the sound systems of both languages, and began to build up her vocabulary in both languages. When she was 1 year and 9 months, however, the family returned to Germany for 3 months. The child was reported to have had serious problems adjusting to this change, but was seen to be making steady progress in German. Shortly after the girl's second birthday, the family moved to an area where another (unspecified Slavic language was spoken. The new nurse was bilingual, but the child refused to speak the Slavic language with her. Emrich saw this as an indication that German was now internalized as the child's language—a happy ending since bilingualism had, supposedly, created only problems for her.

We should remember, however, that at this time the attitude of most Americans toward bilingualism was similar to that of their German contemporaries. In the 1920s and 1930s a prime goal of the American school system was to eradicate bilingualism, which was thought to be a social evil. Perhaps this is one reason why there was so little interest in bilingualism among American researchers at this time. In 1939, however, this situation changed with the publication of the first volume of Leopold's monumental *Speech development of a bilingual child* (1939, 1947, 1949a, 1949b).

Leopold's Study

Werner Leopold's four-volume work is a detailed analysis of the language development of his daughter Hildegard, who was spoken to in German by her father and in English by her mother. Except for a short visit to Germany at the end of her 1st year and a longer visit (7 months) when she was 5 years of age, the child was always in an English-speaking social environment. Thus the German language was essentially a private language whereby she communicated with her father. Hildegard obviously did not achieve the amount of balance in her bilingualism that the sons of Ronjat and Pavlovitch achieved. After her second birthday, this imbalance became increasingly noticeable as her father's influence became lessened, relative to the widening circle of English-speaking individuals in the child's environment. German tended to become more and more passive, and English words were increasingly chosen for active employment.

In the first volume of his work (1939), Leopold carefully analyzed his daughter's vocabulary to the age of 2 years. His analysis included a chronological survey of word acquisition, mortality statistics, phonetic accuracy, semantic classification, and bilingual synonyms. Of particular interest is his discussion of how certain words appeared in the child's early speech, only to drop out of active use later. There were 241 words that were actively employed at the age of 1 year and 11 months, out of a total of 377 words that had been used by the child to this point (Table 4.1). Of these active words, 46 (19%) had both English and German prototypes. Note that mortality was large for German words, suggesting that English was beginning to become more dominant, although the loss of English words accounted for about ⅓ of the total loss. Furthermore, many English words were more recent than the German words and therefore had a smaller mortality. Seventy of the 195 English words had been acquired during the last month in this period.

Leopold suggested the following possible reasons for the mortality of words in the child's vocabulary:

- Phonetic form: certain words dropped out because of phonetic difficulty. *Radio* appeared early but apparently proved too difficult for Hildegard to cope with.
- Homonymy: other words may have lost certain meanings in the child's early speech. Hildegard used *mama* to mean food and mother; but its use with the first meaning was discontinued, perhaps because it interfered with its use with the second meaning.
- Acquisition of more specific terms: overextended words (*pretty* to refer to all admired objects) are abandoned in favor of specific names of objects.

TABLE 4.1
Mortality Statistics Based on Hildegard's Early Speech[a]

	German	German-English	English
Total words (377)	104 (28%)	78 (21%)	195 (52%)
Active words at 1;11 (241)	43 (18%)	46 (19%)	152 (63%)
Inactive words at 1;11 (136)	61 (45%)	32 (24%)	43 (32%)

[a] Data from Leopold (1939).

- Change of interest: the word *Schnee* (*snow*) disappeared from the child's vocabulary when winter passed; the word *measles* was used only during the family epidemic; and so forth.
- Rejection of nonstandard terms: emotional and self-expressive words such as [bu::] for thunder and [k$_x$] for disgust with the taste of food appear sporadically but are not established.
- Struggle with synonyms: some words are abandoned as synonyms took their place. This happened within both languages as overextensions were abandoned for terms with more precise meanings. In addition, there were shifts from a word in one language to its equivalent in the other. This usually involved shifts from the German word to its English equivalent (e.g., *Augenblick* replaced by *wait*), but there were cases where the English gave way to the German (e.g., *mitten* to *Handschuh*).
- Lack of stability: no specific reasons for instability can be found. The use of the word appeared simply to be a passing vogue.

Of particular interest in the present context are shifts in usage from a word in one language to its equivalent in the other. Although some bilingual synonyms were acquired simultaneously in both languages, in other cases a word occurred first in one language and only subsequently did its synonym in the other language appear. For a while, the two words seemed to be in competition with each other and one tended to be preferred. The child seemed to have adopted the strategy of giving things one name only. However, once she realized that there were two languages in her environment, this competition ceased and she managed to use the appropriate words in both languages (although the increasing predominance of English complicated this task).

In Leopold's (1947) second volume he discussed the child's sound system during the first 2 years. His analysis is typically thorough and includes tabulations of Hildegard's representation of standard sounds, an analysis of sound substitutions, and an analysis of her phonetic system. He applied Jakobson's (1941) theory of contrasts to his data and found it to match relatively well, although not in all details. Like Jakobson, Leopold maintained that the sound system develops phonemically rather than phonetically and that sound substitutions reveal method and system rather than randomness.

Like Ronjat (1913) and Pavlovitch (1920), Leopold found little evidence of interference between the two languages on the phonetic level. Even though Hildegard heard two different *l* sounds in the two languages, for example, the effect of bilingual presentation on her speech production was brief. There was no instance where Leopold found unequivocal evidence of a phonetic effect of bilingualism. The simplifications and phonetic substitutions that occurred have also been found in the speech of monolingual children.

In the third volume, Leopold (1949a) discussed questions of syntax and morphology with reference to his daughter's speech during the first 2 years. From 8 months to 1 year and 8 months, one-word utterances prevailed. These Leopold viewed as generally taking the place of what we would call sentences in standard speech. As the speech of the child developed, it changed from a noninflected language to a language with endings comprehended as structural elements. This transformation was not the product of steady growth over time but rather seemed to occur "by leaps and bounds."

Leopold's account of the development of syntax corresponds in many respects to observations made by later investigators of children's language development as described in Chapter 2. He noted the importance of word order, the initial preference for *what* and *where* over *why* questions, the slow development of auxiliary and modal verb constructions, and the relatively late appearance of conjunctions and compound sentences. Hildegard did not achieve subordination of one clause to another in the time studied, and in general her syntactic development was still in a primitive stage at the end of the first 2 years.

Morphological development was also relatively primitive during this time, lagging behind more conspicuous syntactic structures. Hildegard did learn some English plural forms, including the irregular plural *feet*; but German plurals were rare, although the German plural *Füsse* also appeared. German noun inflections did not appear, except for the possessive, which also appeared in English. There were a few instances of adjectival inflections in Hildegard's German, but they seemed to be immediate echoes of her father's speech. Her verbs usually lacked endings in German, probably because she preferred to use the uninflected form. There was no conclusive evidence that the third-person endings were applied to English or German verbs. In general, Hildegard at this time had taken only the first steps toward learning the morphology of the language.

Leopold (1949a) found no evidence for an effect due to bilingual presentation on the child's syntactic or morphological development. One problematic factor was his daughter's failure to use the -*en* ending in her German infinitives. This could possibly be attributed to English influence, but Leopold was not willing to ascribe this to bilingualism. It was also possible that Hildegard—as a German monolingual—would have favored the pure stem, which is often heard in German imperatives and is also early in monolingual German speech (Preyer, 1882).

Although Leopold found no conclusive evidence for interference between languages in the first 2 years, it should be pointed out that this situation changed later when English became more dominant and German was pushed back to a subsidiary position. German pronunciation was then affected by English habits of articulation; there was a common mixture of English words in German sentences, and hybrid forms appeared. English words generally were given German endings and prefixes (*pouren, practicen, geyawnt,* and *monthe*).

A somewhat similar process was observed in the area of syntactic development. Initially, during the first 2 years, there was a free mixing of English and German within a single utterance. The constructions were primitive and incomplete, and the two languages were not used as separate instruments. Hence it was impossible to find an influence of the constructions of one language on those of the other. Even those cases of puzzling word order that were observed could not be regarded as due to the interference of competing syntactic models. Leopold argued it was more likely that since Hildegard had absorbed neither English nor German syntactic patterns with sufficient assurance at this time, variations in word order were due to psychological factors—e.g., the desire to give the psychological subject (an item of dominating interest) an emphatic position. Later, when English began to predominate, the influence of English on the structure of sentences and on the composition of idiomatic phrases became very noticeable.

Leopold (1949a) also analyzed semantic development during the first 2 years, especially the question of how standard meanings are acquired by the child and how and why certain words are overextended. In Hildegard's speech, for example, *wauwau* was used to refer to all sorts of animals including bedroom slippers with a simulated dog's face on them. Other words also were given similar extension: one ingenuous example was her combination of the word *auto* with her word for bird, *peep-peep*, to signify *airplane.*

The last volume (1949b) is Leopold's diary of Hildegard's speech development from her 2nd to her 12th birthday. In addition, Leopold included a brief section on the development of the speech of his younger daughter, Karla, from her 2nd year to her 10th. Leopold felt that in both of his daughters consciousness of dealing with two languages began early in the 3rd year. Only at the end of the 3rd year did the active separation of the two languages begin. From that point on the two languages developed as separate systems.

Studies of Bilingual Children After Leopold

The tradition of the linguist–parent was continued after Leopold by the social anthropologist, Robbins Burling (1959), whose son Stephen acquired Garo, a language belonging to the Bodo group of Tibeto–Burman. The child heard English exclusively until his arrival in India at the age of 1 year and 4 months. Subsequently, he had more contact with Garo speakers than with English speakers (especially since his mother was hospitalized for part of this time), and the Garo language became predominant.

Burling noted that certain elements in his son's English phonemic system developed later than the corresponding elements in Garo, the Garo phonemes being used initially in place of the English ones. In fact, although at 2 years and 9 months or so, a systematic separation of Garo and English vowel systems seemed to occur, the consonant system never became differentiated; the Garo sounds were simply used as replacements for the English ones.

Morphological development in English remained very primitive during the time studied (to 2 years and 10 months). The child used some plural endings but not with consistency. In contrast, morphological development in Garo was extensive. This language consists of several stretches of syllables set off by characteristic junctures that can be called words (*ba-bi on-a-ha* for *Babi gave it to me*). Before his second birthday, Stephen had learned various verb suffixes to create past, future, imperative, and other constructions. Shortly thereafter, he acquired adverbial affixes, interrogative suffixes, noun endings, and numerals. In spite of the complexity of the system, the child never used an incorrect morpheme order. Nor did he have trouble with word order in English (in contrast to Burling's daughter, a monolingual, English-speaking child).

Burling's son assimilated his English vocabulary into Garo and appended Garo endings on English words without hesitation. His sentences were Garo in morphology and syntax, although some lexical items were English. Later, when English sentences appeared, the same process occurred in reverse, with Garo words given English morphology and syntax. Nonetheless, the child's usage was consistent; there was never any question of which language he was using, since morphology and syntax were either all Garo or all English.

Burling's study was unusual in that it is one of the few case studies of bilingualism involving a child learning a non-European language. The report of the French psychologist, Tabouret-Keller (1962), is also unusual in that it is one of the few studies of a child whose parents were from a working-class background. The child's father was a mine worker and her mother came from a poor rural background. The father was bilingual from childhood in French and a German dialect; the mother was raised speaking the German dialect but had learned French in school. Tabouret-Keller observed that both parents mixed both languages in speaking with the child, who heard French roughly ⅔ of the time and the German dialect ⅓ of the time.

By 2 years of age, the child had a larger French than German vocabulary; ¾ of her words were French and ¼ German. Tabouret-Keller was not able to ascertain why certain words were chosen from one language and other words from the other, although she speculated that certain dialect words were preferred because they were more easily inflected than the French equivalents. About 60% of the child's early sentences were mixed in that both French and German words appeared in them. The child's usage could not be predicted from a probabilistic model based on parental input, since such a model predicts—as Tabouret-Keller demonstrated—a far greater proportion of homogeneous French sentences than was actually obtained (20%) and far fewer homogeneous dialect sentences than the child used (also 20%). Tabouret-Keller attributed this lack of correspondence to the influence of the child's playmates on her speech. These children all spoke the German dialect, and this had the effect of increasing her usage of dialect words over what would be predicted by a probabilistic model.

Both Burling and Tabouret-Keller observed considerable mixing in the children they studied. This was also true of Murrell's (1966) study of his daughter, who acquired language in a trilingual environment. For the first 2 years of her life, the child heard Swedish at home and Finnish from a nurse and in kindergarten, with the exception of 2 months (from 1 year and 2 months to 1 year and 4 months) when the family was in England. When the child was 2 years and 1 month old, the family moved to England; and English began to predominate, although the child's mother and occasionally her father continued to speak to her in Swedish.

The child's speech development seemed to be impaired by this experience. She was slow in her morphological development; and there were no word-order regularities in her speech by 2 years and 8 months, although the subject usually appeared before the predicate. There was extreme interference between the languages, and hybrid phrases such as *on bordet* for *on the table* were frequent. There was also sound fusion: for example, the Swedish *bussen* and the English *bus* were combined to form *bas(s)en*. Murrell did not attribute this to morphological fusion (the English *bus* with the Swedish *-en*), since at this point in the child's development the meaning of the affix morphemes was unknown.

Rūķe-Draviņa (1965, 1967) also found sound confusions in the speech of two Swedish–Latvian bilingual children who were learning to speak a language with a rolled apical /r/ (Latvian) together with one possessing the uvular /R/ (Swedish). She found that the uvular /R/ was acquired earlier and tended to intrude and replace the apical /r/ in the other language. Sound borrowing occurred most often in words with the same form in both languages. This same phenomenon was observed by Zaręba (1953) in the speech of his Swedish–Polish bilingual daughter. Both Rūķe-Draviņa and Zaręba found that Swedish word intonations and phraseology intruded in the less dominant Latvian and Polish speech of their children. Rūķe-Draviņa (1967) argued that interference is always present in bilingualism and is more marked, the closer the languages are in their phonological and morphological characteristics.

In contrast, Engel (1965) noted in her case study of her son that confusion of speech sounds rarely occurred. The boy was exposed from birth to English and Italian with Italian predominating. He heard English only from his father, although his parents spoke English to each other. It seemed that the child's ability to keep the sound units distinct, especially sound sequences and intonation, was the means by which he differentiated the two languages.

Engel pointed out that her son's English, though much the weaker of his two languages, developed contemporaneously with his Italian. There were some semantic confusions and hybrid words- Italian endings were often attached to English words without the child being aware of mixing English and Italian morphologically. Yet though there was confusion on this level, there was none with respect to sounds. Engel saw this as an indication that language is not monolithically structured but has two levels: phonetic and morphological–semantic. This distinction seems consistent with my comments in Chapter 3 on the critical period hypothesis. Perhaps the critical period notion as elaborated by Lenneberg applies to the phonetic level of language but not to what Engel called the morphological–semantic level.

Totten (1960), whose children were raised bilingually in Swedish and English, reported that they initially tended to mix both languages. It was only after they distinguished the languages that the problem of interference between the two disappeared. There was no problem learning different sound systems, however, in that the children acquired the accent of the more fluent parent in both languages. The child's plasticity in this regard was also noted by Metraux (1965), who observed that the influence of friends and playmates was extremely effective in counteracting a child's accent. In her comments on French–English bilingual children, Metraux noted that the children would often pretend not to understand another language if it was not the language with which they were accustomed to speaking with a particular person. When parents spoke to children in another language or tested their knowledge in a language they had habitually used with someone else, the children would refuse to answer.

This specificity in the use of linguistic systems was also observed by Oksaar (1970) in a case study of her 3-year-old, Swedish–Estonian-speaking child. This child spoke Swedish with his playmates and Estonian to his parents. The two domains were usually kept apart, but there were cases where both playmates and parents were present. In such cases, the child spoke Swedish, even if he was in the Estonian home environment.

Oksaar recorded her son's utterances on a tape recorder from the 2nd month of his life. Emphasis was placed on collecting data about the child's speech in different contexts—alone, with other children, and with his parents. In addition, recordings were made at certain times twice a month on 3 successive days. It was observed that the child's use of the sound system of Estonian was not influenced by the speech of a Swedish playmate with whom he was in constant contact, although one might expect confusion because of the similarity of the two systems. The finding that the bilingual child is able to keep sound systems distinct corresponds to the observations of Engel (1965) and Totten (1960).

In contrast, Oksaar found obvious interference and mixing in morphology and syntax. The child attached the endings of one language to stems of the other. He also attached Estonian endings to Swedish verb forms in Estonian sentences. His choice of a particular form seemed to follow a simplicity principle: the more simple the form, the more likely it was to be chosen.

Imedadze (1960, 1967) reported the case of a child whose mother and father spoke to her in Georgian and whose grandmother-nurse spoke to her in Russian. Imedadze felt that the child went through an initial stage of confusion where elements of both languages appeared and—at about 20 months—through a period of differentiation where the elements were separated from each other. There also seemed to be an interaction of corresponding grammatical structures. For example, the genitive and instrumental of both languages emerged at the same time. This Imedadze attributed to the fact that these forms express the same semantic relationships in analogous fashion in the two languages. In contrast, the subject–to–object relation in Georgian was expressed first by analogy with the Russian form, which adds an accusative ending: *Dali unda kabas (Dali wants a dress)*. Only later did the more complicated Georgian form appear, which demands a dative case ending for the psychological subject and the nominative case for the psychological object: *Dalis unda kaba.*

In such instances it is important to have information about the course of monolingual syntactic acquisition. Bubenik (1978) noted that her child expressed the future tense in Czech in a way that could have shown the influence of English (the child's other language) or the influence of simplification strategies common in monolingual learners of Slavic languages. Without data concerning the acquisition of syntactic structures in monolingual Czech (and Serbo-Croatian) children it is impossible to determine whether the observed pattern is due to bilingual presentation.

There are some instances where the effect of bilingual presentation is clear. For example, Vihman (1982) reported a case of direct borrowing of morphological forms from one language into another. Her child, Raivo, avoided Estonian morphological markers and, for a time, made use of the English *has* followed by an uninflected Estonian noun to express possession in Estonian. Vihman saw this as a simplification strategy that enabled the child to avoid the complexities of the Estonian construction.

Other children have been observed to use the syntax of the stronger language in both languages. Swain and Wesche (1975) studied a French-English bilingual child whose English at the beginning of the study was relatively poor compared to his French. For the most part, the child used French syntax, with both French and English lexical items. At times, however, he employed English syntax, even with French lexical items. This suggests that the two grammatical systems were internalized, but that their linguistic allocation was not yet under control.

Occasionally, the same semantic relation may emerge at different times in the languages of a single bilingual child. Such a case was reported by Mikeš (1967; Mikeš & Vlahović, 1966) in the study of two Serbo–Croatian–Hungarian bilingual girls. Before the age of 2, these children expressed locative relations in Hungarian but not in Serbo–Croatian. Since the Hungarian language requires only case inflections to express locative relations, and the Serbo–Croatian language requires case inflections and a locative preposition, it seems reasonable to suppose that the difference in complexity of the formal devices needed to express the relationship caused the delay in production.

Volterra and Taeschner (1978) reported that the two children they studied, who acquired Italian and German simultaneously, initially developed a single synctactic system that was applied to the lexicon of both languages. This syntactic system appeared to be different from that of either language. They suggested that children initially fashion a unique system; then the system of the language with the more simple syntactic structures becomes dominant; and finally, the two syntactic systems become differentiated.

Itoh and Hatch (1978) studied the language development of a Japanese boy who learned English at the age of 2½. Some structures in the child's first language had already been acquired by this time, although other constructions developed simultaneously. The imbalance led to initial confusion, especially in the sound system. Of particular interest in this study was the acquisition by the child of formulaic expressions that were acquired wholistically and subsequently broken down. For example, *I wanna* first appeared in such utterances as *I wanna orange juice . . . more* and *I wanna driver*. Later forms such as *I wanna down* and *I wanna cake* appeared. Finally, there were utterances like *I wanna play* and *I wanna open it*. The child appeared to be analyzing such formulaic expressions and working out their appropriate usage. As we shall see in Chapter 6, the same process has been noted by other authors studying successive acquisition of a second language.

LANGUAGE ACQUISITION PROCESSES IN BILINGUAL CHILDREN

Because childhood bilingualism is a topic that has received a great deal of attention in the past decade, it is impossible to review all studies here (see Redlinger, 1979; Vihman & McLaughlin, 1982). Table 4.2 summarizes some

TABLE 4.2
Case Studies of Simultaneous Bilingual Acquisition[a]

Author	Languages	Age of child at time of study	Concerns of study
Ronjat (1913)	French–German	First 5 years	Sp S, Sem, Interf
Pavlovitch (1920)	French–Serbian	First 2 years	Sp S, Sem, Ext, Interf
Hoyer & Hoyer (1924)	Russian–German	First year	Bab
Smith (1935)	English–Chinese	Eight children, first 4 years	Sem, Interf
Emrich (1938)	German–Bulgarian	First 3 years	Interf
Leopold (1939, 1947, 1949a, 1949b)	German–English	First 2 years (and from 2 to 12)	Bab, Sp S, Sem, Ext, Sy, Mor, W O, Dvlp Seq, Interf
Burling (1959)	Garo–English	1 year, 4 months, to 2 years, 10 months	Sp S, Sem, Sy, Mor, Interf
Imedadze (1960)	Russian–Georgian	11 months to 3 years	Sem, Ext, Sy, Mor, Dvlp Seq, Interf
Tabouret-Keller (1962)	French–German	1 year, 8 months to 2 years, 11 months	Sem, Interf
Engel (1965)	English–Italian	First 4½ years	Sp S, Sem, Mor, Interf
Murrell (1966)	Swedish–Finnish–English	2 years to 2 years, 8 months	Sp S, Sem, Sy, Mor, W O, Interf
Rūķe-Draviņa (1967)	Swedish–Latvian	Two children, first 6 years	Sp S, Sem, Dvlp Seq, Interf
Mikĕš (1967)	Hungarian–Serbo-Croatian	Three children, first 4 years	Sy, Mor, Dvlp Seq, Interf
Oksaar (1970)	Swedish–Estonian	2 months to 3 years	Sp S, Sem, Ext, Sy, Mor, Interf
Swain (1972)	French–English	2 years, 4 months to 4 years	Sy, Mor, Dvlp Seq, Interf
Volterra & Taeschner (1978)	Italian–German	Two children, 1 to 3 years	Sem, Ext, Sy, Mor, Interf
Itoh & Hatch (1978)	Japanese–English	2½ to 3 years, 1 month	Sp S, Sem, Sy, Mor, Interf
Celce-Murcia (1978)	French–English	2 years, 4 months	Sp S, Sem, Sy, Mor, Interf
Vihman (1982)	Estonian–English	1 year, one month to 2 years, 10 months	Sp S, Sem, Sy, Mor, Interf

[a]Abbreviations: Sp S = Speech Sounds; Bab = Babbling; Sem = Semantics; Ext = Extensions of Word Meanings; Sy = Syntax; Mor = Morphology; W O = Word Order; Dvlp Seq = Developmental Sequences; Interf = Interference Phenomena.

of the case studies of children who were raised under conditions of bilingual presentation during the first 3 years of life. The studies vary considerably in the topics they deal with and appear in several instances to be contradictory. There are, however, general points of agreement that I will attempt to elucidate by looking at what these and other studies say about the developmental sequence of acquisition in the bilingual child's two languages, about interference between languages, and about code switching in bilingual children.

Developmental Features

In the discussion of processing models of language acquisition in Chapter 2 I noted that an adequate language acquisition system includes sound system processing, lexical processing, and grammatical processing. Looking at *sound system processing* first, it appears that the bilingual child's development is not very different from that of the monolingual child. The child must recognize and distinguish stress-pitch features of prosodic contours, as well as the quality of stressed vowels, timing and length of stressed syllables, and the location of marked features such as friction and nasal consonants. This requires some kind of analytic ability that permits matching of a particular string in short-term memory with the acoustical features of lexical items as they are stored in long-term memory (Ervin–Tripp, 1970b).

The bilingual child's task is complicated by the fact that two sound systems must be distinguished from each other. A number of observers have noted that there is an initial period of confusion (Leopold, 1947; Rūķe-Dravina, 1967), especially when the corresponding phonemes in the two languages are differentially difficult to acquire. In such a case, it seems likely that the easier phoneme will be applied in both languages (Murrell, 1966; Rūķe-Dravina, 1965). If the two languages are in balance the period of confusion is relatively short (Pavlovitch, 1920). In fact, some authors reported no evidence of confusion of sound systems (Engel, 1965; Oksaar, 1970). When one language predominates, however, as with Burling's (1959) son, the sound features of the dominant language may be substituted for those of the subordinate language. Similarly, words that are difficult to pronounce in one language may be systematically avoided (Celce–Murcia, 1978).

Leopold's daughter Hildegard developed by 2 years of age a vowel system consisting of 12 phonemes. She appeared to be experimenting beyond the model provided by English. For example, although English makes no use of the vowel length, Hildegard did: she distinguished [wɔk] *walk* and [wɔːk] *fork*. Furthermore, she used a number of diphthongs that did not occur in the speech of the adult model: [ɛa], [oi], [oɪ]. She seemed to be using her ability to combine two vowel qualities into a diphthong as a productive process to construct new words with complex vowel nuclei not present in standard English (Moskowitz, 1970). Perhaps such experimentation with sounds from the bilingual repertory is common with bilingual children, but it has rarely been commented upon in the literature.

Another interesting aspect of bilingual phonological development is the use of blends. Bilingual children will occasionally settle on a single phonological shape to express the same concept in either language, usually when the words are somewhat similar in the two languages. Thus, Leopold (1939) reported that his daughter used [das] for *scratch* and for *kratzen* in German. Vihman's son used [nu:et] for *new* and for *uued, "new"* plural in Estonian (Vihman & McLaughlin, 1982). Such blends drop out as the two language systems become differentiated.

In the discussion of *semantic processing* in Chapter 2, I noted that one of the tasks involved in semantic development is to attach words to their referents and to abstract concepts. There is a period between the ages of 1 year and 1 month and 2 years and 6 months when overextensions are common (E. Clark, 1973). Detailed studies reveal that overextensions relate to vocabulary growth and rarely last more than 8 months. Only certain words are overextended; others appear to be used in a manner consistent with adult criteria from the moment of their introduction into the child's speech (Leopold, 1949a; Pavlovitch, 1920). When overextensions do occur, their features appear to be derived predominantly from perceptual input—from visual, tactile, and auditory sources (E. Clark, 1973). Both Pavlovitch (1920) and Leopold (1949a) reported that the meaning of over-extended terms is narrowed down by the addition of new words that take over subparts of the semantic domain of the overextended word. In Hildegard's speech, for example, *sch* was initially used for all moving objects, but when the words *auto* and *choo-choo* were introduced to her vocabulary, they took over the domain of *sch*. Subsequently *choo-choo* was abandoned (except for *choo-choo train*) when *train, wheelbarrow,* and *airplane* were acquired.

Pavlovitch (1920) provided a number of examples of overextensions in his son's speech. One of the most interesting examples was the word *bébé,* which was initially used to refer to all reflections of the self in mirrors, photos of self and photos in general, pictures, all books with pictures, and books in general. In time, the word was narrowed down and distinguished from other words. This process is schematized in Table 4.3.

It sometimes happens that the bilingual child gives different extensions to words that have a single meaning for an adult. Volterra and Taeschner (1978) found, for example, that the German *da (there)* and the Italian *la (there)* had different meanings for one of their children. *La* was used for things that were not present and not visible; *da* was used for things that were

TABLE 4.3
The Restructuring of Overextensions[a]

	Word(s)	Semantic domain
Stage I	bébé	Reflections of self in mirror; photos of self; all photos; all pictures; books with pictures; all books.
Stage II	bébé	Reflections of self in mirror; photos of self; all pictures; books with pictures; all books.
	deda (grandfather)	All photos.
Stage III	bébé	Reflections of self in mirror; photos of self; books with pictures; all books.
	deda	All photos.
	káta (karta = card)	All pictures of landscapes, views.
Stage IV	bébé	Reflections of self in mirror; photos of self.
	deda	All photos.
	káta	All pictures not of people.
	kigh (book)	All books.
Stage V	bébé	Self; small children in pictures
	deda	Photos.
	káta	Pictures.
	kigh	Books.
	slika (reflection)	Reflections in mirror.
	duda (Douchan, own name)	Photo of self.

[a] Data based on Pavlovitch, 1920 (table from E. Clark, 1973).

present and visible. They argued that initially all words of the child's speech form a single lexical system; only gradually does the child differentiate the lexical items of the separate languages as these languages are experienced in different linguistic and nonlinguistic contexts.

Turning now to *syntactic processing,* we observe once again the importance of word-order regularities (Braine, 1971a; Ervin-Tripp, 1973a). Children probably store features of invariant order and probabilities of order for various semantic relations (Ervin-Tripp, 1973a). In inflected languages there may be morphological realization of semantic relations. As Slobin (1971) noted, linguistic realization of semantic relations can occur at different times within the two languages of a bilingual child, reflecting the perceptual salience of the features needed to mark the relationship in the two languages. Thus Serbo Croatian–Hungarian bilingual children (Mikeš, 1967; Mikeš & Vlahović, 1966) demonstrated locative relations in Hungarian (where the locative marker is expressed by noun inflection) earlier than in Serbo-Croatian (where noun inflection and preposition are needed to express the locative). This seems to reflect a processing strategy according to which word endings are scanned for their linguistic input earlier than prepositions.

Mikes̆ (1967) pointed out, however, that the order in which various syntactic structures are acquired by bilingual children is the same as for monolingual children. The Serbo-Croatian locative construction is also acquired relatively late by monolingual speakers of that language. Furthermore, the syntactic development in languages of different structural types follows basically the same sequence. Mikes̆ concluded that bilingual presentation has little effect on syntactic development.

The same conclusion was reached by Imedadze (1960) on the basis of her study of a Russian-Georgian bilingual child. The sequence with which grammatical categories appeared depended on their difficulty—as is true of the monolingual child. Syntactic structures followed the same developmental order in both of the child's languages as they did for monolingual children. If both languages express a semantic relationship similarly, it tends to be acquired simultaneously in both languages; if it is more difficult in one language, it is acquired later in that language—as is true in the development of the monolingual speaker of that language.

One exception to this general rule was reported by Rūķe-Draviņa (1967) who found that her children used the Latvian double negative before the simple negative of Swedish. This was probably because Latvian was acquired earlier, in the home, whereas Swedish was acquired later through contact with playmates. Presumably, the child was exposed to the Latvian construction earlier and hence acquired it before the easier Swedish form.

Morphology usually follows syntax except in some languages that are so structured that morphological and syntactic features must be acquired simultaneously (Burling, 1959). Murrell (1966) found no affix morphemes in his daughter's speech at 2 years and 8 months, and Leopold (1953) also noted that almost no morphological devices indicating declensions and conjugations were acquired by his daughter in the first 2 years. Syntactic relations were made clear by word order, although there were occasional mistakes, especially when a focal word was put first in the sentence (*Meow bites wauwau* at 1 year and 11 months). In the course of time, communication difficulties became a strong source of motivation for Hildegard to learn standard morphological features.

In a study of 3- to 10-year-old, bilingual, Mexican-American children, Carrow (1971) found that there were specific areas where the children studied were, as a group, significantly delayed when compared to a control group of English-speaking children. The comprehension of pronouns, negatives, and some tense markers caused difficulty for children in the bilingual group. Nonetheless, the sequence of development of the various form classes and grammatical structures was the same for both groups and within the Mexican-American group in both English and Spanish. Carrow concluded from this that language development follows systematic growth patterns regardless of language.

Kessler (1971, 1972) also found in her research on 6- to 8-year-old bilingual children who spoke Italian and English that structures shared by both languages were acquired at approximately the same rate and in the same sequence. If the structure is not shared by both languages, it is acquired later—linguistically more simple structural variants being acquired before those that are linguistically more complex. For example, the subject and indirect object relation (e.g., *The boy is handing the book to the mother*) gave the bilingual children very little difficulty in either language, whereas sentences with the prepositions *for* and *to* presented the greatest difficulty in both languages (e.g., *The baby gives the ball for the cat to the dog*). Other constructions such as the object pronoun (*He is giving her the book*) or the possessive adjective (*his ball*) seemed to have been acquired by the children in English but not in Italian. Similarly, the reflexive reciprocal construction (*The girls see themselves*) was not established in English, although it presented no problem in Italian.

Although both the Carrow and Kessler studies compared children at different ages and did not involve the longitudinal study of individual children, their findings are consistent with reports from case studies of bilingual children (e.g., Engel, 1965; Imedadze, 1960; Leopold, 1949a; Mikès, 1967). The consensus is that language acquisition follows the same basic developmental pattern in the bilingual child as in the monolingual child. In the bilingual child, certain syntactic structures in one language will lag behind those of the other language because they are more complex. The pattern for each language, however, is the same as it is in the monolingual child (although it may be somewhat retarded in some bilingual children).

In short, it seems that the language acquisition process is the same in its basic features and in its developmental sequence for the bilingual child and the monolingual child. The bilingual child has the additional task of distinguishing the two language systems, but there is no evidence that this requires special language processing devices. In fact, the child most likely employs a single set of rules and heuristics with those sounds, lexical items, and formal structures that require differentiation tagged as specific to a particular system. This is a point to which I shall return shortly.

Interference Between Languages

Investigators of childhood bilingualism differ greatly in the amount of interference between languages they report. Both Ronjat (1913) and Pavlovitch (1920) reported that their children showed very few signs of interference and kept both languages separate on all levels. Other investigators, however, found considerable confusion (Burling, 1959; Murrell, 1966; Rūķe–Draviņa, 1967; Tabouret–Keller, 1962).

As we have seen, Rūķe–Draviņa (1965) and Zaręba (1953) both reported substitution of the easier uvular /R/ sound for the more difficult apical /r/, Leopold (1947) also found an early preference for /R/ in his daughter's speech. In addition, all three authors observed a period during which /l/ sounds in the different languages were confused, but all noted that this confusion was of short duration. Leopold (1949a) argued that on close examination those phonetic mistakes that his daughter made could have occurred if his daughter had been exposed to one language only. They were not, he maintained, evidence of interference between languages but could be attributed to processes that operate in the phonological development of monolingual children as well. He pointed out, however, that when the balance between the two languages was shifted in favor of one or the other, his daughter's speech showed signs of interference. The same was true of other bilingual children when one language predominated (Burling, 1959; Zaręba, 1953).

For the most part, children seem to be able readily to acquire and discriminate the sounds they hear in the bilingual environment. Engel (1965) noted that this was the most stable aspect of her son's speech, which otherwise was marked by considerable confusion between English and Italian. She mentioned at one point in her article the case of a French–American family in which children spoke French without an accent to their French mother but French with an American accent to their American father. Apparently such discriminations are readily made by children whose facility in programming the sounds of a language may, as was suggested in Chapter 3, have a physiological basis.

A number of observers have noted a tendency on the part of the bilingual child to mix words from different languages in the same sentence (Burling, 1959; Leopold, 1949a; Rūķe–Draviņa, 1967; Tabouret–Keller, 1962; Totten, 1960). Mixing was especially noticeable in the child observed by Tabouret–Keller, (1962) where 60% of the child's three-word sentences contained words from both languages. In this case the fact that the parents constantly mixed both languages probably played a considerable role in the child's confusion.

Even where this does not happen, however, some mixing occurs. Ronjat (1913) remarked that his son initially tried out words in both languages before settling on the appropriate one. Leopold (1939) found that a small number of bilingual synonyms were used interchangeably in his child's speech. *Hot* and *heiss,* for example, were used synonymously until the 3rd year. Other examples include the words *Schnee* and *snow, ja* and *yes, bitte* and *please, kaputt* and *broke, alle* and *all gone.* In these cases the words were used in both languages concurrently.

In other cases, there seemed to be a struggle going on between two words for predominance. *Nein* and *no* coexisted briefly, but eventually the German word dropped out. *Mehr* was so well established that *more* never appeared in the first 2 years. *Auge* and *eye* appeared at the same time, but only *eye* became active. *Weg* rose ineffectually against *away,* as did *hair* against *Haar. Doggie* entered late as a feeble competitor to the well-established *Wau-wau.* Leopold concluded that such cases indicate that the child is striving to make one unit out of the split presentation. Only when Hildegard became aware that she was being presented two different languages did she begin to use the appropriate word in both languages. Once this realization is achieved, the child may begin simultaneously to learn the words from both languages that refer to objects and abstract concepts (Burling, 1959).

Leopold (1947) also noted that the child may use knowledge of the vocabulary of one language to generate words in the other language. For example, his daughter at 3 years and 6 months did not know the German word for *candle,* so she generated the word *Kandl* with a German *a* sound. Similar examples have been reported by other authors (Engel, 1965; Murrell, 1966; Rūke–Draviņa, 1967).

Oksaar (1970) observed considerable interference from the predominance of Swedish in the speech of her Swedish–Estonian bilingual child. Swedish morphemes occurred with Estonian endings in the home, where Estonian was spoken; but with playmates the Swedish forms predominated. Engel (1965) also found a great deal of morphological confusion in her son's weaker language, English. Burling (1959) noted morphological and syntactic mixing, although his son seemed aware that he was mixing the two languages. Difficulties with prepositional constructions were noted by Carrow (1971), and Murrell (1966) found no word order regularities in the speech of his English–Swedish-speaking daughter at 2 years and 8 months. Word order and prepositional constructions seem to be the most incorrigible tasks in bilingual language development and may not be entirely mastered in adulthood (Elwert, 1960).

Leopold (1949a) felt that because of the mixture of two languages in his daughter's speech it was impossible to find evidence of syntactic interference. Hildegard's constructions in both languages were so primitive up to the 3rd year and so incomplete that no language differences could be established. It was only when English began to predominate that its influence on German syntactic constructions could be clearly established.

The findings concerning interference seem contradictory until one considers how the two languages were presented to the child. It seems that interference between languages can be held to a minimum if the domains of use are clearly defined and if the two languages are maintained somewhat in balance. This seems to have been true of the children of Ronjat (1913) and Pavlovitch (1920) and initially of Leopold's daughter. These studies suggest that the optimal conditions for reducing interference require that both languages be spoken in the home consistently by different persons. A *caveat emptor* is in order here, however, since in all three cases the children were raised in upper-class or at least upper-middle-class families. No information is available on how this method works in a middle-class or lower-class family environment. Furthermore, Ronjat and Pavlovitch were fairly authoritarian in their upbringing of their children (Tabouret–Keller, 1962), and the rigorous application of the one-person, one-language rule requires considerable discipline on the part of both parents and child.

In looking at other situations of bilingual presentation, one finds that optimal results are rarely achieved. If one language is spoken in the home and the second is acquired through acquaintances and playmates, balance seems to be upset and interference is greater (Murrell, 1966; Oksaar, 1970; Rūķe–Draviņa, 1967; Zaręba, 1953). Kuo (1974) pointed out that, as children grow older, the peer group plays an increasingly important role in determining what language becomes dominant. Once one language begins to predominate and the other is reduced to subordinate status, interference between languages is clearly in evidence (Burling, 1959; Engel, 1965; Leopold, 1949a). This is not to imply that the child does not achieve bilingual fluency, but the balance is usually tipped in favor of one language or the other.

The greatest amount of interference between languages seems to be produced when adults in the child's environment mix the languages in their own speech (Burling, 1959; Tabouret–Keller, 1962). Another factor contributing to interference is similarity between the two languages (Geissler, 1938; Mikeš, 1967; Rūķe–Draviņa, 1967). However, there has been relatively little systematic reseach on the effects of various languages on each other's development, and it is not even known if the total amount of interference between two similar languages is less or more than between two dissimilar ones and if the mechanisms of interference differ (Vildomec, 1963). Nor has there been a careful analysis of the errors the bilingual child makes to determine whether the mistakes are indeed the result of interference or whether they reflect developmental errors common in the acquisition data of monolingual children or developmental strategies of various sorts. This type of analysis has been carried out mainly with children who acquired a second language after the first was established (see Bubenik, 1978 and Vihman, 1982 for exceptions).

Furthermore there is the possibility that much of what appears to be interference between languages is in fact language mixing of the sort that occurs commonly in adult speech in certain language communities (Lindholm & Padilla, 1977; Padilla & Liebman, 1975) and that is quite "grammatical" (Cornejo, 1973) in the sense that there is agreement between articles or adjectives in one language and nouns in the other (*una bike* for *una bicicleta* or *al shopping center* for *al centro*). This language mixing or *code mixing* refers to switches within sentences and should be distinguished from *code switching,* which refers to changing languages over phrases or sentences. Code mixing will be discussed in more detail in the next chapter; at this point I would like to turn to the question of code switching in bilingual children.

Code Switching

I pointed out in Chapter 2 that in addition to their other linguistic tasks, children learn styles, or codes, of talking to different people in different situations. The child, for example, learns to distinguish formal and informal codes, serious, intimate, slang, and colloquial codes. One way of viewing the simultaneous acquisition of two languages in children is to regard it as a task not significantly different from that faced by a monolingual child learning to differentiate various linguistic codes.

One argument against this position is that such an interpretation places too great a strain on the child's processing capacities. Yet in some languages, the amount of code switching within the language itself is much greater than what we are accustomed to in European languages. In Javanese, for example, there are a number of different codes among which any Javanese must switch from one situation to another. Many of the most common words vary depending on such variables as the age, sex, kinship, occupation, wealth, education, religion, and family background of the individuals communicating. It is as if a separate language had to be learned for each of these situations (Geertz, 1960).

Furthermore, the frequency of bidialectalism— whereby speakers switch between the standard language and a dialect—in societies throughout the world seems to rule out what Stewart (1971) has dubbed the "single space" theory, according to which an individual has room in the brain for only one language code. The achievement of primitive tribes who master a number of different languages of great complexity (Hill, 1970) would seem to bear eloquent witness to the human's capacity in this respect.

In the development of the child, it seems that initially an effort is made to make a single unit out of the bilingual presentation (Leopold, 1939). Language input remains undifferentiated, and the child does not appear to comprehend that input consists of split presentation. Even when comprehension processing shows that the child can understand the meaning of two words for the same referent or the use of two different forms, children seem to focus on one symbol or form in their spontaneous utterances.

Some evidence that the two languages of bilingual children are initially not encoded separately comes from a study by Swain (1972) of French–Canadian children, aged 2 years and 1 month to 4 years and 10 months, who had been exposed to French and English since birth. Swain argued that separate sets of rules for both codes would be inefficient in terms of memory storage. It is more efficient for the child to employ a common core of rules with those specific to a particular code tagged as such through a process of differentiation. The data indicated that the rules acquired first in the simultaneous acquisition of *yes/no* questions in two languages were those that were common to both languages. Rules that were language-specific or more complex were acquired later.

This seems to be generally true. Imedadze's (1960) finding that the Georgian subject–to–object relation was expressed first by analogy to the Russian in the speech of a bilingual child also suggests that the child initially tries to use a single code for both languages. Other authors also report the initial assimilation syntactically and morphologically of one language to the other (Engel, 1965; Mikěs, 1967; Rūķe–Draviņa, 1967).

At some point the child becomes conscious of speaking two different languages. Ronjat (1913) maintained that his child had this awareness at 1 year and 6 months, and Pavlovitch (1920) also put the date of awareness relatively early, at 2 years. Other authors (Elwert, 1960; Geissler, 1938; Imedadze, 1960; Rūķe–Draviņa, 1967) set the date somewhere in the 3rd or 4th year. Leopold (1949a) saw some signs of awareness on the part of his daughter at 2 years, but it was only at 3 years and 6 months or so that the child had a good feeling for the differences between the two languages.

One reason for the disagreement on this issue is that different authors use different criteria for awareness. Ronjat (1913) thought that the child was conscious of bilingualism when he used synonymous pairs of words from his two languages. Imedadze (1960) argued that this does not necessarily indicate an awareness of bilingualism; the child is simply trying to use the means at her disposal to communicate. For the child, the two words are part of a single linguistic code. Awareness of bilingualism begins when the child starts to use the two languages distinctly to communicate with different people in different languages. It is this practice of "translating" or using rough equivalents in interacting with different people that leads to an awareness of bilingualism, not the use of synonymous word pairs. Imedadze found this stage to begin near the end of the 2nd year in the child she studied and to be complete by 2 years and 4 months, when the child ceased to adopt words from one language to the other but asked for the corresponding word when it was unknown in one of her languages. Swain and Wesche (1975) also used spontaneous translation as evidence that the child is aware of the difference between languages. This approach, however, has its critics, as we shall see in Chapter 7 when the question of language differentiation is discussed in more detail.

Once the child becomes aware of and differentiates the two linguistic codes, language changing or code switching becomes a normal aspect of behavior with respect to certain known persons or situations. The bilingual child is able to switch languages with remarkable quickness (Gerullis, 1932; Mitchell, 1954) and even, apparently, in dreams (Braun, 1937; Elwert, 1960). Different codes are associated with different people and age groups (Elwert, 1960; Mitchell, 1954; Oksaar, 1970). Situational specificity was observed by Rūķe-Draviņa (1967), whose children spoke Latvian in the home and Swedish with playmates. When playing in the home, they used Swedish—the language associated with the play situation. Even different locations can be occasions for switching: Meertens (1959) reported that a small Dutch boy spoke Frisian when walking with his parents but switched to Dutch when going into a store and when going by his school and church.

This is not to imply that switching codes is always easy for the child. If parents or other adults try to speak to the child in a language other than the one in which they usually speak, the child is likely to become confused and may not understand what is said in spite of knowing the language (Metraux, 1965; Perren, 1972). Once a particular language code becomes temporarily predominant through use, it is difficult to switch back to the other language (Emrich, 1938; Leopold, 1949b). The child may go through a period of silence until some degree of balance is achieved (Engel, 1966; Leopold, 1949b).

There are also cases where language changes within phrases or sentences (code mixing) are quite common. For example, Spanish–English bilingual children in the southwestern and western sectors of the United States hear mixed utterances from their parents and others, and mixing occurs in their own speech. Since these children are capable by the age of 3 of distinguishing the two languages and apply different rules to each language (Padilla & Liebman, 1975), it is possible that mixing is for them still another code used for rhetorical, affective, or other purposes. This is a topic I discuss in more detail in the next chapter.

CONCLUSION

In conclusion, a few general comments are in order. Although most of the case studies we have discussed in this chapter were well conducted and have supplied us with valuable information, there is a danger in over-reliance on this method. The principal difficulty is assuring objectivity. How is the investigator (or the reader) to know that all of the data are being gathered, not just the data that fit the investigator's preconceptions as to how things should be? One improvement would be to use more objective methods of assessing the child's linguistic abilities. A large number of elicitation techniques are now available for testing young children. These include the Imitation-Comprehension-Production technique (Fraser, Bellugi, & Brown,

1963), Elicited-Imitation (Slobin & Welsh, 1973), Developmental Sentence Scoring (Lee & Canter, 1971), the "wug" test (Berko, 1958), and the Picture Verification technique (Slobin, 1966b). The use of such methods, in addition to traditional observational information, would greatly improve our knowledge of the processes involved in bilingual language acquisition.

Greater objectivity can also be achieved by technical means. For example, simply keeping notes on the child's speech as it occurs is not sufficient for accurate analysis (Oksaar, 1969). A regular procedure should be instigated for taking tape-recorded samples of the child's speech at different times and in different situations. The use of video tape is also a desideratum, as it frequently happens that the meaning of the child's utterance is clear only from context. Video tapes also could provide a great deal of information as to how the child learns the rules for code switching—presently a murky area.

Finally, investigators have to know what they are looking for. In the typical case study, the data are gathered more or less as they fall from the mouth of the child by an investigator who sits down afterwards and tries to put the pieces together. A better way to proceed is to know what one is looking for beforehand. There is still a lot to be learned. For instance:

- What developmental stages do children exposed to two languages go through in acquiring specific syntactic structures such as negative constructions, interrogative constructions, relative clauses, and so on?
- Are these developmental stages always identical with those followed by monolingual speakers?
- How do specific languages interact with each other phonetically, syntactically, and semantically?
- What regularities are to be found in semantic and morphological mixings?
- Do particular language combinations cause more retardation in individual language development than others?
- Is bilingual language acquisition more difficult for some children than for others? Why is this (if true)?
- What factors of language presentation affect bilingual development?
- What processes are involved in children's achieving an awareness that they are exposed to bilingual presentation?
- How are more subtle aspects of language acquisition—such as the acquisition of implied requests and more complicated grammatical constructions—affected by bilingual presentation?
- What can parents do to facilitate the child's learning of two languages?

The field awaits systematic research directed at answering such questions.

5 Successive Acquisition of Two Languages in Childhood

This chapter deals with research on the successive acquisition of two languages in childhood. The distinction between simultaneous and successive language acquisition is, as we have seen, a rather arbitrary one, the cutoff point being roughly 3 years. If the child is introduced to a second language before that age, I consider acquisition of the two languages to be simultaneous; if the second language is introduced after 3 years, acquisition is successive—one language having been relatively well established (though by no means fully established) by that age.

The questions of interest in this chapter are similar to those that concerned us in the previous chapter. What information can be gained from case studies of children acquiring a second language? What are the developmental consequences of acquiring two languages? Does the acquisition of a second language interfere with the acquisition of the first language, or vice versa? How does the child learn to switch codes—to move from one language code to the other?

The literature on the successive acquisition of two languages is reviewed chronologically, beginning with the early case studies. As was mentioned in the previous chapter, the literature on successive acquisition of two languages in childhood includes some recent studies dealing with particular theoretical issues in second-language acquisition. Some of these are case studies, and others are studies with groups of children that employ a combination of case study and elicitation techniques.

The discussion in this chapter deals with studies of children who acquire their second language without formal instructions in a natural milieu (i.e., by living in an environment in which they are constantly exposed to the language). The format for the present chapter is the same as in the previous one: first an overview of the research and then an examination of the language acquisition process when a second language is acquired following a first language.

STUDIES OF SUCCESSIVE LANGUAGE ACQUISITION

The studies are divided into two groups. The first group consists of case studies that deal for the most part with general phenomena of second-language acquisition. Most studies until recent years were of this sort—the description in broad terms of the linguistic development of children acquiring a second language. Rather than focusing on particular issues, parent–observers and linguists considered the whole process of second-language acquisition, describing some aspects in more detail than others, depending on their interests. Recently, there has been more concern with specific topics, especially particular aspects of syntactic development in children acquiring a second language in a natural setting.

Early Studies

The earliest study in the literature is the report of Volz (cited in Stern & Stern, 1907) of his child's acquisition of German as a second language. The child had lived for the first 3 years of his life in Sumatra, during which time he was exposed almost entirely to Malay. From 3 years and 1 month, the child heard only German. Volz observed a transition period from 3 years, 1 month, to 3 years, 3 months, when the child used both languages next to each other but did not mix them. If he did not know a particular German word or expression, he reverted to Malay but always added *malayu (in Malay)*. After 3 years and 3 months, Malay was used less frequently; and by 3 years and 8 months, the language seemed to be entirely forgotten. Nonetheless, Malay syntactic structures and word order persisted for some time. The child experienced a period of relative stagnation between 3 years and 6 months and 3 years and 9 months, attributed by his father to discouragement due to being often misunderstood and not understanding others and to frustration at not being able to express himself adequately. During this period he was often silent. At 3 years and 9 months, the boy began to speak more and tried with considerable effort to express his thoughts accurately. By 4 years of age, his ability in the German language began to approximate that of monolingual children his age. Volz made the interesting observation that when his son had completely forgotten all Malay, he displayed the sounds and intonations of Malay when speaking nonsensical gibberish or when imitating his parents reading. Apparently he had retained the motor patterns associated with the forgotten language.

Kenyeres (1938) observed her 6½-year-old daughter, Eva, acquiring French after the family had moved from Hungary to Geneva. Up to that point in her life the child had spoken only Hungarian and knew no French. She was strongly motivated to master the language so as to be able to communicate and play with other children. Within 10 months she was able, in her mother's judgment, to speak French as well as native children her age. Phonetic development was especially rapid. At first, only major differences (e.g., nasality) were attended to; after that, more subtle ones. By the end of the 3rd month she had mastered the French sound system.

During these first 3 months Eva tended actively to translate French into Hungarian. She analyzed the differences and began to practice with French forms. Initially she seemed to clutch at a known and dominant word in an otherwise incomprehensible sentence and deciphered the sentence by using that word as a focus and translating into Hungarian. Her French constructions were formed by analogy with the Hungarian. She consciously tried to find rules for gender and to determine to what extent French constructions corresponded to those she already knew. By the 6th month she used words for which she did not possess Hungarian equivalents, and French began to fulfill the function of her native language, although Hungarian continued to be used to supply certain forms not yet acquired in French.

Kenyeres concluded that her daughter had acquired her second language in a manner that was different from the way in which she acquired her first language. Her acquisition of the second language was based on what she knew of her first language. She operated by analogy, using her knowledge of the first language to derive the rules of the second. She consciously rehearsed, especially when playing alone with her dolls, apparently deliberately trying to learn words and phrases in her second language as an adult does via the audio-lingual method.

Malmberg (1945) provided an account of the acquisition of Swedish by a 4½-year-old, Finnish-speaking girl. The child tended to give certain Swedish words, especially those with Finnish cognates, the stress they would receive in Finnish. There was considerable difficulty with certain aspects of the Swedish sound system, especially with voiced stops. Nonetheless, it seemed that certain sounds—such as the uvular /R/—were acquired along with or instead of the sounds—such as the apical /r/—of her first language.

Finnish endings were initially applied to Swedish noun stems, and even after the Swedish suffix was learned, the Finnish postpositional continued to be used. Eventually the Finnish postpositional was replaced by a Swedish preposition, which still, however, followed the noun and its suffix. The final step in this process was the correct placement of the Swedish preposition. There were thus four steps in the child's development:

Stage 1:   Substitution of Finnish noun stem by Swedish noun stem with Finnish endings.

Stage 2:   Swedish noun stem receives Swedish endings but is followed by the Finnish postpositional as before.

Stage 3:   The Finnish postpositional is replaced by a Swedish preposition following the noun and its suffix.

Stage 4:   The preposition is correctly placed.

Tits (1948) reported on the language development of a 6-year-old Spanish refugee girl who acquired French and Flemish in Belgium. The child, like Kenyeres's daughter, used her first language as a starting point and demonstrated good progress in French. She declared on the 93rd day after her arrival in Belgium that she did not know Spanish anymore (although her foster parents tried to preserve this language and had her subsequently take Spanish in school). At the age of 8 and again at 10 years, she scored 2 years above the mean for her age on tests of French language skills. In general, Tits maintained that her development in her second language progressed through the same stages as one observes in a child acquiring this language as a first language, although at a much quicker pace and with less clear delineation between stages.

Valette (1964) reported on the acquisition of French by an American child whose parents moved to Paris when he was 3 years and 3 months old. The child was in a French kindergarten from 9 to 5 each day where the only language he heard was French; English was maintained in the home. He mastered a number of standard phrases in the first 6 weeks and by 3 months had acquired a few more functional phrases such as *C'est Rene qu'a fait ça, Comme ça, Ça y est.* During the period from the 3rd to the 6th month, he showed relatively rapid development, and after this period he could make himself understood to other children. If he did not know a particular French word, he would replace it by the English spoken with a French accent. By 9 months he had acquired an authentic French accent. During the period of his most rapid increase in vocabulary, from 8 to 9 months, Valette observed that he would make a number of mistakes that are typical of native French children, such as deducing from *un avion* or *un autre* that the basic form is *le navion* or *le nautre.* Verbs were learned first in the singular of the present tense; plural verb forms were acquired relatively late, as were other tenses. The infinitive was used in the future and in past constructions and in the subjunctive. Valette noted that acquiring the language was not easy for the child even with so much exposure, and after 1 year he was still a year behind his French peers in his command of the language.

Francescato (1969) found that his children, who learned Italian first and then Dutch, required about a year's time to reach the level of their peers in Dutch. In neither his study nor in Valette's were criteria given for language mastery, so comparison is difficult. In contrast to Kenyeres, Francescato did not feel that his children consciously compared the language system of their second language with their first language, but this is possibly because his children learned the second language at a younger age (3 and 4) than Kenyeres's child. He also argued that the young child of 3 or 4 can serve as a translator, not because the child actually translates from one language to another, but because the situation elicits certain verbal responses. If his children were simply given a sentence out of context to translate, they could not do so.

Recent Research

To this point the studies under review have been concerned with broad questions of language development and use and have rarely given extended and systematic treatment to phonological, semantic, or syntactic issues. The one exception is Malmberg's valuable analysis of the stages of acquisition of the Swedish prepositional construction by a Finnish-speaking child. Most recent studies are like Malmberg's in that they are centrally concerned with specific problems of theoretical interest, especially aspects of syntactic development and the question of interference between first and second languages.

For example, Ravem (1968) studied the development of English syntactic regularities in the speech of his 6½-year old, Norwegian-speaking son by attempting to steer the conversation in different directions to elicit from the boy different kinds of sentences referring to past, present, and future events. In addition, he gave his son a translation test at regular intervals involving 50 negative and 50 interrogative sentences that require an auxiliary in adult speech. The test consisted of a request in Norwegian to *Go and ask Mother if . . .* or *Tell Ranny that . . .* , with the indirect sentence containing the auxiliary verb. Comparison of this method with the child's spontaneous utterances showed it to be an accurate index of the child's syntactic development.

Ravem was principally interested in the acquisition of the modal *do* in his son's speech. He found that *do* was learned in a manner that followed the usual developmental sequence for English-speaking, monolingual children. That is, the modal was initially omitted in negative sentences, and the negative was marked by a negator between the subject and the predicate: *I not like that.* The modal was also dropped in yes–no questions, although here the Norwegian inversion pattern was retained: *Like you ice cream?* An English-speaking, monolingual child uses intonation without inversion at this stage: *You like ice cream?*

Ravem's son, however, did not usually invert the verb in *wh-* questions. On the basis of his formation of *yes–no* questions, where the Norwegian pattern persisted, one would expect *wh-* questions of the form: *What reading you?* or *What doing you now?* Instead, Ravem found constructions in which the child used the pattern of the declarative sentence in *wh-* question sentences, without inversion: *What you reading to-yesterday?* These constructions are similar to those observed in monolingual, English-speaking children. Ravem suggested that in the *yes–no* questions inversion is used as a question signal, but this does not explain why monolingual children do not use inversion in *yes–no* questions, whereas Ravem's son did. As we shall see, there are other possible explanations for this apparently anomalous finding.

Finally, Ravem's study contained information on the development of *do* as a tense marker. There appeared to be four stages:

Stage 1.   *Do* occurs in the context of isolated verbs, probably as a lexical variant of *not: I don't know, I don't talking to you.*

Stage 2.   *Do* occurs in the context of and as a variant of *you: What d'you like?*

Stage 3.   *Do* emerges as a tense carrier: *What you did in Rothbury? What d'you do to-yesterday?*

Stage 4.   *Do* emerges as a separate element with a present and past form. *Did* is used in sentences requiring the past tense, and *do* is almost invariably followed by the infinitive form of the main verb.

In a study using similar procedures, Ravem (1974) examined the development of *wh-* questions in the speech of his son and of his daughter, aged 3 years and 9 months. In general, the mistakes they made reflected English rather than Norwegian developmental features. For instance, the children failed to invert the auxiliary verb and the subject (*What she is doing?*), a mistake similar to that found by Brown (1968) in English-speaking children. They made this mistake although they already had learned the Norwegian rule that requires the subject–verb inversion. Similarly, *why* questions developed late, as they do in monolingual children, even though Ravem's children understood the notion of causality in their first language.

Taking into account the age and maturity of the children and the fact that they already knew one language, Ravem's findings suggest that the similarities in first- and second-language development are more striking than the differences. The children seemed to pass through essentially the same stages that first-language learners pass through. There were occasional exceptions to the rule—instances in which Norwegian forms appeared to influence the English ones—but these were rare.

Hernandez (cited by Ervin-Tripp, 1970b) analyzed the language development of a Chicano child of 3 learning English. He found that the influence of the new sound system was initially pre-eminent, suggesting that acquisition of the sound system is especially important for a child of this age learning a second language. Hernandez reported that a number of the Spanish-speaking children he observed attempted to speak English by using English phonological features with Spanish lexicon and grammar.

In a study of the acquisition of Spanish by seven English-speaking children from 4 to 6½ years of age, Dato (1970) reported that the children failed to invert the subject and verb in questions, although word–for–word translation from English to Spanish would lead to inversion. This finding is similar to that of Ravem (1974), suggesting once again that the developmental pattern in second-language learning follows the same sequence as is observed in monolingual speakers of the target language.

In general, Dato found evidence that second-language syntactic development was characterized by a learning sequence in which "base structures" are acquired first and then "transformed structures," a sequence typical of first-language acquisition as well. Although his tranformational analysis has been criticized (Dulay & Burt, 1972), his data suggest that second-language acquisition, like first-language acquisition, is characterized by a general trend of increasing complexity.

Dato (1971) extended his transformational analysis in a subsequent study concerned with the auxiliary verb. Again the evidence indicated that even in older children, simple forms are learned before more complex ones. The children in his study learned the imperative and copula first, closely followed by the present indicative. More complex forms developed later. The sequence in which the children learned person-number, tense, and other elements of the auxiliary was the same, although the children differed in age at the time of their introduction to Spanish.

Politzer and Ramirez (1973) conducted a study of Chicano children from 5 to 9 years of age, based on speech samples collected by having the children describe a silent movie they had watched. Their answers were recorded on tape, and deviations from standard English were counted and categorized. The results were interpreted as indicating that Spanish influence was the major cause of error as shown by such mistakes as nominalization by use of the infinitive rather than the gerund (*instead of kill birds*), uncertainty in the use of subject pronouns (omission of the pronoun in sentences such as [*He*] *pinch the man,* [I] *liked him, then* [*he*] *flew away*), the use of redundant pronouns (*The bird he save him, The man he came*), and confusion of word order (object–subject–verb constructions). Nonetheless, Politzer and Ramirez admitted that error classification of this sort is problematic. When the child says *He not catch the bird,* this appears to resemble the Spanish construction but may in fact represent a phase in the development of the negative construction that occurs in the monolingual, English-speaking child's language development as well. Whether a particular error can be attributed to the influence of the second language involves the difficult judgmental task of separating those errors that are found in the speech of monolingual speakers from those that are the result of interference between languages.

In a further discussion of this topic Politzer (1974) noted that there is ample evidence that many of the mistakes made by second-language learners are similar or identical to the mistakes made by children in the process of first-language acquisition. He also thought that there was some evidence that complex structures that are difficult in first-language acquisition tend to be difficult in second-language acquisition, so that they are acquired after more simple constructions in both cases. Nevertheless, he argued that the similarity between first- and second-language acquisition should not be taken for granted. His analysis of the Politzer and Ramirez data suggested that the developmental course in second-language acquisition differs from that observed in monolingual children. For the time being we shall defer judgment; a more detailed discussion of this topic follows in the next section. There are, however, other studies that bear on this issue.

Milon (1974) compared the developmental substages of negation in a 7-year-old Japanese boy's acquisition of English with those developmental stages observed by Klima and Bellugi (1966) in the acquisition of negation by monolingual, English-speaking children. As we saw in Chapter 2, Klima and Bellugi documented three stages in the development of negation. In the first stage, the negative appears outside the sentence nucleus (*Not cold, Not me*). In the second stage, the negative appears between the noun phrase and the verb phrase (*He no bite you, I can't catch you*). In the third stage, the adult pattern appears (*You don't want some supper, I not hurt him*).

Through video-tape recordings of 20-minute weekly sessions over a 7-month period, Milon gathered 244 negative utterances. Table 5.1 gives examples of the child's use of negative constructions. Of the child's first 47 negative utterances, 37 fit into Stage I, there were 9 *I don't know* constructions, and 1 anomaly. The *I don't know* construction probably was a phrase

TABLE 5.1
The Use of Negatives at Three Stages of Development
in a Bilingual Child's Speech[a]

Stage 1	Stage 2	Stage 3
No	I don't know what kind	I never saw yours
Not ocean	I no look	I never do
No more	He can not	I not saw
	Don't look Michael	You no go win
		You never cut yet

[a]From Milon, 1974.

borrowed in its entirety. The anomalous sentence was *I don't have a watch,* which occurred once, probably an exact repetition of a sentence heard from other children. Of the next 143 negative utterances, 90 fit into Stage 1 and 48 into Stage 2. There were five anomalous sentences, all of which were negative tag questions (a category not included in Klima and Bellugi's analysis). The final 131 negative utterances fit into all three stages with the majority still described by Stage 1 rules, but with Stage 3 rules emerging (9%).

Milon concluded that the child progressed through the same developmental stages in the same sequence as the children studied by Klima and Bellugi. This is not a priori predictable, since the negative in Japanese is formed by attaching a morpheme to the right of the verb stem. Thus one would expect utterances such as *I give not . . .* , where the negative structure follows the verb. Instead the child appeared to be replicating the developmental sequence (at least the first two stages) observed in monolingual, English-speaking children and not transferring the Japanese structure onto the English. Another interpretation of these data has been offered by Zobl (1980), and Hakuta and Cancino (1977) wondered whether there was evidence for developmental progression in Milon's data when all three sets of negatives were best described by Stage 1 rules.

Ervin-Tripp (1974) was impressed by the similarities between first- and second-language acquisition in the group of children she studied. Her sample was drawn from English-speaking children between the ages of 4 and 9 living in Geneva. She found evidence that the children, like children acquiring a first language, remember best the items they understand. Like Valette's (1964) child, they were capable very early of learning whole phrases because they knew their meaning.

Word order was related to meaning fairly early. The basic subject–verb–object strategy was used in interpreting sentences, even anomalous passive constructions (where the first noun was animate and the second inanimate). Although older children correctly interpreted English equivalents, they reverted to the subject–verb–object strategy and misunderstood the French passive. Similarly, indirect objects were often taken to be direct objects if English word order was followed—even though French marks indirect objects with a preposition. This again points to the predominance of the subject–verb–object strategy. In addition, other evidence, such as overgeneralization of lexical forms and the preference for simple sentence production heuristics, seemed to indicate that the process of second-language acquisition was similar to first-language learning.

Table 5.2 gives examples of English to French translations that occurred in the speech of the children in Ervin-Tripp's sample. As she pointed out, at first glance the children seem to be translating word-for-word. Yet this

TABLE 5.2
Examples of English to French Translations[a]

Stimulus	5-year-old child 9 months in Geneva	7-year-old child 9 months in Geneva
I see her.	Moi je vois elle.	Je elle vois.
She sees them.	Elle regarde eux.	Elle les voit.[b]
Why does she eat them?	Pourquoi il mange ça?	Pourquoi elle les mange?[c]
He gave her the carrots.	Il a donné les carottes.	Il a donné à elle les carottes.[c]
Who is she waiting for?	Qui elle attend pour?	Elle attend pour qui?
She's waiting for them.	Il attend pour eux.	Elle les attend.[b]
What pushed the door?	Quoi il poussait la porte?	Qu'est-ce qui a poussé la porte?[b]
What fell down?	Quoi il a tombé?	Qu'est-ce qui a tombé?
Why is he pushing her?	Pourquoi il pousse elle?	Pourquoi il elle pousse?
Where is the dog going?	Où le chien il va?	Où va le chien?[b]
Where is he going?	Où lui il va?	Où ils 'en va.[c]

[a] From Ervin-Tripp (1974).
[b] Correct.
[c] Colloquial, possible in native speaker's usage.

strategy of mapping the French onto the English word order and syntax was actually used in only a few sentences. The basic strategies seemed to be as follows:

- In declarative sentences, use subject–verb–object order. Very few children, for example, had acquired the separate rule for pronominal objects.
- In questions, give the question word then the nuclear word order, either subject–verb–object or subject–verb–locative. Although word-for-word translation would lead to inversion in these sentences, this rarely occurred.
- In a residual number of cases young children used a word-for-word translation strategy.

In short, it seems that children either have to relearn the heuristics they use in their first language when acquiring a second, or lose subrules governing indirect object, passives, and word order in questions when acquiring a second language. In either event their performance seemed similar to that of children learning the target language as their first language.

Cancino, Rosansky, and Schumann (1974, 1975) found some evidence, however, that suggests that different processes are involved in at least some aspects of second-language acquisition. They studied the speech of six Spanish-speaking persons: two children age 5, two adolescents ages 11 and 13, and two adult subjects. All were visited approximately twice monthly for an hour over a 10-month period. The data were based upon speech utterances, elicited imitations or negations of model utterances, and preplanned sociolinguistic interaction at parties, restaurants, museums, sport events, and the like. For none of the individuals did inverted *yes/no* questions precede inverted *wh-* questions, as is typical in the development of native, English-speaking children. Nor did the stages of acquisition of the negative correspond to those observed by Klima and Bellugi (1966) for native speakers.

Hakuta (1974a,b, 1975) also found evidence that second-language development differs in some ways from first-language development. He studied a 5-year-old Japanese girl acquiring English as a second language by recording samples of spontaneous speech for about two hours biweekly over a 60-week period. Analysis of the development of grammatical morphemes (Brown, 1973a) revealed an order that did not invariably parallel that of children acquiring English as a first language.

On the other hand, Kessler and Idar (1977) found a developmental order for four verb phrase morphemes that was identical to the sequence found in monolingual speakers (Brown, 1973a). Their subject was a 4-year-old Vietnamese girl observed over a 9-week period when the girl lived with an American family. Kessler and Idar pointed out that the developmental similarities do not reflect language similarities: comparison of the structures in the two languages predicts a different ordering for the two languages. Kessler and Idar concluded that their findings support the hypothesis that second-language acquisition follows the developmental path of first-language acquisition in English.

Note, however, that the Kessler and Idar study had a much shorter time span than did Hakuta's. Kessler and Idar also used a different, more limited set of morphemes in their study. These differences may explain why the results contrasted with each other. In addition, the first language of the child and the ways in which it differs from the target language may affect the course of second-language acquisition. In fact, the influence of the first language has been noted in a number of recent case studies.

In discussing the acquisition of negative constructions, Wode (1978) pointed out that utterances that reflect the child's first language may intrude in the developmental sequence. His data were based on the speech of his four German-speaking children acquiring English naturalistically. Constructions such as *I'm steal not the base, Marilyn like no sleepy* appear to reflect German word order and are not found in the speech of native, English-speaking children. Wode argued that children acquiring a second language may take what superficially looks like a step backward in their development, reverting to their first language, but that such "detours" are the result of the application of acquisition principles that may or may not be the same as those governing first-language acquisition.

Keller–Cohen (1979) examined the acquisition of English questions by three children, whose native languages were Swiss German, Japanese, and Finnish. Swiss German and Japanese are like English in that questions are frequently accompanied by rising intonation. Finnish, however, does not use rising intonation. Both the Swiss German and Japanese-speaking children used rising intonation as an early and persistent feature of their questions, whereas the Finnish-speaking child did not use rising intonation at all. This suggests that the first language of the child has an effect on what is learned in the second.

Another example comes from Lightbown's (1977) study of two 6-year-old English-speaking children learning French as a second language. She compared their acquisition with that of two French monolingual children. The two monolingual speakers differed in the extent to which their early speech conformed to native language word order. One child produced both transitive and intransitive utterances that were generally congruent with adult French usage; the other composed many intransitive utterances that deviated from adult French usage. In contrast, the two English-speaking children consistently produced both transitive and intransitive utterances that were congruent with the dominant French S-V-O word order. This suggests that the English-speaking children, having learned a language where word order is essential in determining grammatical roles, are more sensitive to word order than are children who learn a language where word order is less integral to sentence interpretation.

Lightbown (1980) also reported that while the order in which question forms emerged in her second-language learner's French was similar to that reported for monolingual children, the use to which questions were put was much broader. That is, the children used language forms they knew to express new functions. For example, one child used *où* to ask about time (*où est ton fête*), prior to learning *quand*. Similarly, Felix (1978) reported that *wo* (*where*) was learned early by two English-speaking children acquiring German and was also used to ask *why* and *how* questions. This is a tactic young monolingual children use as well, as Ervin–Tripp's (1970a) research on the development of questions demonstrated. The point is that older second-language learners make greater use of this strategy because they have more to say than do younger children.

There have been a number of other case studies of successive second-language acquisition in children (see Hatch, 1978; Wode, 1981), some of which will be mentioned in the discussion that follows. Table 5.3 summarizes the studies that have been discussed to this point. It is clear from this review that investigators differ in their assessment of the role of first language in second-language learning. Two aspects of this issue deserve more detailed treatment—the first concerns the effect of the first language on the sequence of second-language development, and the second relates to the question of interference from the first language in the second.

TABLE 5.3
Case Studies of Successive Bilingual Acquisition

Author	Languages	Age of child at time of study	Concerns of study[a]
Volz (Stern & Stern, 1907)	Malay-German	3 years, studied for a year	Sp S, Interf
Kenyeres (1938)	Hungarian-French	6 years, 10 months, to 7 years, 8 months	Sp S, Sem, Sy Dvlp Seq, Interf
Malmberg (1945)	Swedish-Finnish	4½ years	Sp S, Sy, Mor, W O, Dvlp Seq, Interf
Tits (1948)	Spanish-French	6 years	Sp S, Interf
Valette (1964)	English-French	3 years, 3 months, for a year	Sp S, Sem, Sy, Mor, Dvlp Seq, Interf
Francescato (1969)	Italian-Dutch	Two children, from 4th year	Interf
Ravem (1968)	Norwegian-English	6 years, 6 months, for 3 months	Sy, Mor, W O, Dvlp Seq, Interf
Ravem (1974)	Norwegian-English	3 years and 9 months for 10 months	Sy, Mor, W O, Dvlp Seq, Interf
Hernandez (Ervin-Tripp, 1970b)	Spanish-English	3 years	Sp S
Dato (1970, 1971)	English-Spanish	Son from 4 years, 1 month, for 9 months, and 6 other children between 5½ and 6½	Sy, Mor, W O, Dvlp Seq, Interf
Milon (1974)	Japanese-English	7 years for 7 months	Sy, Mor, W O, Dvlp Seq, Interf
Cancino et al. (1974, 1975)	Spanish-English	Two children, two adolescents, two adults for 10 months	Sy, Mor, W O, Dvlp Seq, Interf
Hakuta (1974a, b, 1975)	Japanese-English	5 years for 1 year	Sy, Mor, W O, Dvlp Seq, Interf
Wode (1978)	German-English	Four children	Sy, Mor, W O, Dvlp Seq, Interf
Kessler & Idar (1977)	Vietnamese-English	4 years for 1 year	Sy, Mor, W O, Dvlp Seq
Keller-Cohen (1979)	3 first languages acquiring English	between 4;3 and 5;6 for 8 months	Syn, Pragmatics, Interf, Dvlp, Seq
Lightbown (1977, 1980)	French-English	4 to 6½ years	Syn, W O, Interf, Dvlp Seq

[a]Abbreviations: Sp S = Speech Sounds; Sem = Semantics; Sy = Syntax; Mor = Morphology; W O = Word Order; Dvlp Seq = Developmental Sequence; Interf = Interference Phenomena.

LANGUAGE ACQUISITION PROCESSES WHEN A SECOND LANGUAGE IS ACQUIRED SUBSEQUENT TO A FIRST LANGUAGE

In Chapter 3 I discussed the literature dealing with the acquisition of second languages in childhood and adulthood. I argued there that the evidence does not support the assertion that children and adults acquire or learn second languages in essentially different ways. The child and the adult approach a second language in a manner consistent with their cognitive development, but the same processes seem to be involved in both cases. Cook's (1973) research suggests that adults learning a second language pass through essentially the same stages as a child does acquiring that language as a first language. Can the same be said of children acquiring a second language?

Developmental Features

Case studies.   Before discussing syntactic development, a few comments are in order about phonological and semantic development in the second-language acquisition of children. In the previous chapter we saw that *sound-system processing* in children exposed simultaneously to two languages is probably no different than it is when the child is exposed to a single language. The child most likely initially treats the input as part of a single system and only later distinguishes the two sound systems from each other. The amount of confusion between sound systems seems to depend on the way in which the two languages are presented to the child: if they are kept sharply differentiated with respect to persons and situations, interference will be reduced. Similarly, if the two languages are maintained in balance, interference is reduced.

What of successive acquisition of a second language? Unfortunately the data are skimpy. There is some evidence suggesting that the strategy employed in processing the sounds of a second language is similar to that used in processing the sounds of the first language. Children tend to acquire the more simple sounds of a second language earlier than those that are more complex (Hernandez in Ervin-Tripp, 1970b; Malmberg, 1945). The problem with this sort of evidence, however, is that it tends to be circular: sounds used later are defined as more difficult to acquire than those used earlier. What is needed is careful documentation of the sequence in which children learning given languages acquire the sound systems of those languages as a basis of comparison for examining the developmental sequence followed by children acquiring these languages as second languages.

Wode (1978) found that German-speaking children learning English used their knowledge of German phonology to acquire certain English sounds, substituting German phonemes for English phonemes. But this was not the case for all sounds. Some were acquired in a manner that could not be related to first-language phonological capacity. Instead, such sounds as the English /r/ followed the same developmental sequence as is observed in native, English-speaking children.

Hecht and Mulford (1982), in a study of a 6-year-old Islandic child learning English in a naturalistic setting, concluded that neither an explanation based on transfer from the child's first language nor one based on developmental processes in the second language could adequately account for the child's acquisition of the sound system in the second language. Predictions based on a transfer position were best supported when the relative difficulty of particular segments was examined, whereas the developmental position best accounted for which sounds would be substituted for difficult segments. Hecht and Mulford argued that a systematic interaction between transfer and developmental processes best explained phonological acquisition in their subject. Their analysis was limited, however, to fricatives and affricatives and may not apply to other aspects of phonology. Furthermore, as Hecht and Mulford pointed out, there are considerable individual differences in phonological production in English first-language speakers, so that any generalizations about developmental sequences must allow for individual variation.

Ervin-Tripp (1974), upon observing that young children playfully pronounced English words with a French accent, devised an elicitation test to determine what phonological principles were involved in this skill. She gave children of different ages stimuli in English, such as *knife, ride, winter, birthday,* and asked them to pronounce these words as if they were French. Even children with limited amounts of exposure to French seemed to have developed certain phonological rules. Younger children tended to reduce all words to a single syllable and to delete most final consonants. The uvular /R/ replaced the apical /r/, and nasal segments were converted to nasalized vowels. In contrast, older children tended to use more complex rules, including more complete /R/ replacement, a shift of stress to second syllables, vowel changes to the French vowel values, and correct nasalization.

These differences are not surprising in view of the fact that the older children have already discovered some basic principles of phonology. If they have learned to read a syllabic written language, they have acquired a fairly abstract knowledge of oral language phonology. Indeed, the greatest differences seemed to occur between children who could read and those who could not read.

Information about *semantic processing* is also relatively meager. Few researchers have concerned themselves with this topic (Hakuta, 1981). We know little, for example, about the occurrence of overextensions in the second languages of children—whether they occur and whether they resemble those that are found in first-language acquisition. A common finding is that the first words that children learn when placed in a milieu in which they must acquire a new language relate to greetings and to terms dealing with interactions. These utterances are usually learned as a whole without any syntactic differentiation. Words relating to the self also seem to be learned early (Table 5.4).

Ervin–Tripp (1974) pointed out that the second-language learner, like the child acquiring a first language, tends to learn best items that have meaning. Recurrence in meaningful situations provides the basic categorization device for building a lexicon. The child tends initially to prefer one form for one meaning and rejects two forms for what appears to be an identical meaning on the basis of the referential situation. Children acquiring French

Table 5.4
Spontaneous Speech Samples of Two English-Speaking Children[a]

Weeks in French-speaking environment	Speech sample	
	6;7-year-old child	
6	moi sanglier	(me boar) [claiming animal from comic book]
	au-revoir	(goodbye)
	je-ne-comprends	(I don't understand)
	à moi, lait, moi	(mine, milk, me) [gesturing he wants milk]
	allez-y	(hurry up, get going)
8	Nicolas dit non	(Nicholas says no)
	Nicolas dit pourquoi	(Nicholas says why)
	pousse-moi	(push me)
	ça Nicolas vélo	(that Nicholas bike)
	ferme la porte	(close the door)
	toi nez rouge	(you nose red)
	5-year-old child	
8	regarde	(look)
9	regarde, escargots	(look, snails) [for dinner]
	moi bébé	(me baby) [in play]
	moi poupée	(me doll)
	moi princesse	(me princess)
11	regarde, Anna	(look at Anna)
	le crayon bleu, c'est là-bas	(the blue pencil, it's over there)
16	pas moi, toi, moi là	(not me, you, me there) [directing play locations]
	ça moi, ça Alexandre	(that me, that Alexander) [possessions]
	moi, c'est grand	(me, it's big) [mine's big]
	ça va, ça va pas, Eric?	(that's okay, that's not okay, Eric?)
	pas lait là, pas lait, milk	(not milk there)

[a]From Ervin–Tripp, 1974.

in Ervin–Tripp's sample regularly treated *le* (the masculine article) and *la* (the feminine article) as synonymous, because they appeared to have identical meanings. One child reported that he had learned a new word, *Assiedstoi* (*sit down*), pronounced as though it were a single word. The next day he reported that this was a mistake and that the word was *Asseyez-vous*, again pronounced as though it were a single word.

Ervin–Tripp noted that older children have the advantage of possessing more efficient memory heuristics and greater knowledge than younger children. The older children learn word combinations faster than younger children and can map new vocabulary into storage more efficiently. The older child has a more developed semantic system in the first language and so merely needs to discover new symbolic representations. Because of these differences, Ervin–Tripp argued that the major changes that occur between learners of a second language at various ages tend to relate to semantics.

Most research concerned with developmental sequences in second-language acquisition has been directed at *syntactic processing*. There seems to be good evidence that many of the same strategies are employed in second-language acquisition as are used in first-language acquisition. For example, word-order regularities are of initial importance in both first- and second-language acquisition. In both cases children appear to work from simpler to more complex structures, to use meaning, and to prefer simpler word orders to more complex order strategies such as verb–subject inversions (Ervin–Tripp, 1974).

The research of Ravem (1974) on questions lends support to the hypothesis that second-language development in children progresses through stages similar to first-language development in monolingual speakers of the target language. The apparently conflicting evidence from Ravem's (1968) study can be interpreted in processing terms that are consistent with the general trend of research findings. That the Norwegian inversion pattern was retained in interrogative sentences but not in negative sentences may be attributed to a strategy, particularly important in *yes–no* questions, of inverting the subject of interrogatives so as to indicate meaning from the start (*Like you ice cream?*). This inversion may be relatively strong at 6 in the Norwegian-speaking child. However, in *wh-* questions, the tendency to invert is not so strongly established, and so the pattern observed in English-speaking children is found. In the negative, location is less important for meaning, and since a separate rule is used for modals and non-modalized verbs in Norwegian, the English construction is simpler and more likely to be adopted (Ervin–Tripp, 1970b).

As we have seen, Politzer (1974) expressed scepticism about the similarity between developmental sequences in first- and second-language acquisition. Although an initial analysis of the Politzer and Ramirez (1973) data showed a developmental trend that suggested a great similarity between first- and second-language acquisition processes, Politzer found that when the data were reanalyzed controlling for length of utterance and correct utterance, the bilingual children did not show the same developmental pattern as monolingual children.

The difficulty with Politzer's analysis is that the controls he employed were far too rigid. Their application does not so much yield different developmental sequences in bilingual and monolingual children as eliminate developmental sequences entirely. Controlling for length and correctness of utterance wipes out the developmental patterns usually found in the speech of monolingual children. No coherent pattern was found in either group. It is not surprising, then, that this analysis produced inconclusive results.

If we look at the earlier studies of successive language acquisition, we again find support for the hypothesis that first- and second-language learning involve similar processes. Stern and Stern (1907) reported that Volz's son at 3 years and 6 months built the past participle of German verbs in the same manner that the Sterns' son had at 2 years and 4 months (*ge* + infinitive). Furthermore, Volz noted that his son adopted the simplification strategy of using the infinitive as the verb in early sentences. Tits (1948) felt that the girl she observed passed through the same stages of development as a monolingual child although at a faster pace. Kenyeres (1938) also observed that her daughter processed sentences like a child acquiring a first language—by seizing on known and dominant words and using these words as clues for meaning.

Kenyeres maintained, nonetheless, that her daughter's development did not simply recapitulate early first-language development; nor did the child learn language as an adult would. Instead, she worked at the level of a child of her age, and her sentences were of the type spoken by children her age. This, however, does not contradict the hypothesis that first- and second-language acquisition involve similar processes. It is certainly the case that second-language acquisition makes use of the cognitive abilities of the child, but this is also the case for first-language acquisition (Ervin-Tripp, 1974). But this does not mean that intrinsically different processes are involved in first- and second-language acquisition.

This distinction is important. Politzer (1974) was doubtless correct in pointing out that the tendency to view second-language acquisition as similar to first-language acquisition depends on the conceptual perspective one adopts toward language acquisition generally. From a cognitive perspective, the experiences are obviously different. There is no evidence that the sequence of cognitive operations to which first-language acquisition is tied is repeated in second-language acquisition. The child, in acquiring a second language, does not have to build up knowledge of the world and of language from scratch. On the other hand, if one views language acquisition in terms of the processes involved and in terms of the strategies used in acquiring language, the similarities between first- and second-language acquisition become more pronounced. In process terms, language acquisition in both cases seems to involve the same operations, although the older child (and the adult) proceeds at a much more rapid rate of development.

Aside from the studies already mentioned, Ervin–Tripp's (1974) data support the contention that the process of second-language acquisition is developmentally like first-language acquisition. As we have seen, she found that children of various ages prefer a simple subject–verb–object strategy for all constructions, although they had already learned the appropriate constructions for passives and questions in their first language. Even when a preposition appeared after the verb, children often ignored the preposition and interpreted the noun following the verb as the object.

It should be noted, however, that the findings of Cancino, Rosansky, and Schumann (1974, 1975) and Hakuta (1975) indicated that there is individual variation in the way in which learners acquire structures of the second language. These authors did not find the kind of sequences reported by Ravem and Milon for negative and *wh-* questions, and it may be that Wode (1978) is correct in suggesting that children occasionally use first-language structures to solve the riddle of second-language structures. Reliance on first-language structures may be greater, the more intractable the structural problem.

In short, the case-study literature reveals that there is a high degree of correlation between developmental sequences observed in monolingual children acquiring the target language as a first language and in children acquiring the same language as a second. There are, however, instances where second-language learners seem to wander off the developmental path. Zobl (1980) argued that where there is syntactic congruity between structures in the two languages (Wode, 1978) or morphological similarity (Zobl, 1979), transfer of a first-language rule is more likely to occur.

Cross-sectional research. There is another line of research that bears on the question of developmental sequences in successive second-language acquisition. This research involves larger samples and compares children at different ages or levels of acquisition. For example, Natalicio and Natalicio (1971) studied the acquisition of English plurals by native, Spanish-speaking children in grades 1, 2, 3, and 10. Their sample included a control group of native, English-speaking children, and both groups were tested by a procedure similar to that used by Berko (1958) to study children's knowledge of morphological rules (discussed in Chapter 2). Both Spanish-speaking and English-speaking groups acquired the /-s/ and /-z/ plural allomorphs before the /-iz/, though the mean proportion of overall correct responses was lower for the Spanish-speaking group. These findings indicate that Spanish first-language structures are not transferred to the

English second language, since transfer from Spanish to English would predict that /-s/ be acquired first with /-z/ and /-iz/ acquired simultaneously (because Spanish plurals are all voiceless and voicing is the new feature English requires).

In a study of the acquisition of Welsh by 21 English-speaking children, Price (1968) found that the Welsh noun phrase constructions produced by the children reflected Welsh rather than English word order. The data were gathered by a classroom observer who took written notes on the children's utterances at various times during the day. Children followed Welsh word order in adjective-noun phrase constructions (*blodyn cock* for *flower red, cyw bach melyn* for *chick little yellow*) and in possessive-noun phrase constructions (*esgidiau Dadi* for *shoes Daddy* and *cadair y babi* for *chair the baby*). This indicates that the children did not follow their first-language word order, but it is not clear whether the developmental sequence the children followed was similar to that followed by monolingual Welsh children since the study did not deal directly with this issue.

Finally, there is a series of studies conducted by Dulay and Burt (1973, 1974a, 1974c) directly concerned with the question of the developmental sequences followed by 5- to 8-year-old children acquiring a second language (English). They began with Roger Brown's (1973a) finding that there is a common—"invariant"—sequence of acquisition for at least 14 "functors." Functors are little function words in English that have a minor role in conveying sentence meaning—noun and verb inflections, articles, auxiliaries, copulas, and prepositions such as *in* and *on,* etc. Dulay and Burt asked whether children who acquire English as a second language acquire these functors in the same sequence and whether this sequence is the same as that found in children who acquire English as a first language.

Dulay and Burt used an instrument called the Bilingual Syntax Measure (Burt, Dulay, & Hernández–Chavez, 1975), which consists of seven cartoon pictures and a series of questions. The questions are designed to elicit spontaneous speech that should contain most of the morphemes described by Brown. Using this instrument, Dulay and Burt looked at the accuracy order of eight morphemes in children's speech. This accuracy order was assumed to reflect acquisition order.

In one study Dulay and Burt (1973) elicited speech samples from 151 Spanish-speaking children living in California, Tijuana, Mexico, and New York City. Even though the three groups differed in amount and type of exposure to English, they showed roughly the same patterns in their use of the functors in obligatory contexts. The degree of acquisition was somewhat different for the three groups, reflecting differential exposure. Table 5.5 shows the "order of acquisition" of the functors for the three experimental groups and for native, English-speaking children. Note that the order of acquisition for the three second-language groups was clearly different from that of the first-language group.

TABLE 5.5
Order of Acquisition of Functors in First- and Second-Language Learners[a]

Functor	Native English-speaker	California sample	Mexican (Tijuana) sample	Puerto Rican (New York) sample
Present progressive (-ing)	1[b]	2	2	2
Plural (-s)	2	1	1	1
Irregular past (ate, took)	3	7	7	5
Possessive (noun phrases)	4	8	5	7
Article (a, the)	5	5	8	3
Third person singular indicative (-s)	6	3	6	8
Contractible copula (be + adjective or noun phrase)	7	6	4	6
Contractible auxiliary (be + verb + -ing)	8	4	3	4

[a]Table based on Dulay and Burt, 1973.
[b]The first column is the rank order of acquisition for these particular functors in Brown's (1973a) original list of 14 functors.

Dulay and Burt attributed this discrepancy between first- and second-language acquisition to the different cognitive abilities of children at different stages of their development. Since older children are more sophisticated than younger children with respect to cognitive and conceptual development, their pattern is different. Nonetheless, there does seem to be a common sequence according to which children acquiring a second language acquire certain structures.

In a subsequent study, Dulay and Burt (1974c) compared Chinese- and Spanish-speaking children's acquisition of 11 English functors to determine whether the order of acquisition of functors was the same across children with different language backgrounds. Examination of small corpora of speech from 60 Spanish-speaking children in Long Island and 55 Chinese-speaking children in New York City's Chinatown revealed that the sequence of acquisition of the 11 functors studied was virtually the same for both groups. Rank order correlations using various scoring procedures were remarkably high (averaging .94). Thus, although the grammar of the functors differs greatly in Chinese and Spanish, they were acquired in the same sequence in the second language. Dulay and Burt concluded that their research provided a strong indication that universal cognitive mechanisms are the basis for the child's organization of the target language and that the second-language system, rather than the child's first language, guides the acquisition process.

In the third study in this series, Dulay and Burt (1974a) discussed the nature of the universal cognitive mechanisms they thought guide second-language acquisition in children. Rather than examining developmental data in terms of linguistic complexity, they argued that analysis should focus on critical characteristics or features of syntactic structures that distinguish groups of structures in an acquisition hierarchy from one another. For example, one characteristic common to a group of structures may be that their acquisition involves a strategy of looking for exceptions to syntactic rules, which would mean that this aggregate would tend to be acquired relatively late. Another aggregate of structures might be characterized by some feature expressing a semantic relation. The learner probably uses the strategy of looking for semantic relations relatively early, and so this aggregate would be acquired earlier.

The main thrust of Dulay and Burt's argument is that it is not enough to consider simply the complexity of syntactic structures in linguistic description. Analysis in terms of complexity ignores the possibility that the child, in acquiring a language, organizes linguistic data in accord with certain cognitive strategies. Though their analysis was tentative, Dulay and Burt hoped that analysis in terms of distinctive features of aggregates of structures would provide clues about the actual strategies learners use in acquiring second languages. These strategies may be universal, but not enough is known about acquisition hierarchies in second languages other than English to postulate specific universal language-learning strategies in children.

Nonetheless, we are left with the inconsistency between the findings of Dulay and Burt and those of other investigators discussed in this chapter. Whereas the majority of studies indicate that the child acquiring a second language passes through the same stages of development as the monolingual child acquiring the target language as a first language, Dulay and Burt found that the acquisition sequence is different for first- and second-language learners. The order in which English functors were acquired by children with different first languages correlated relatively weakly with that found in English, monolingual children (the average correlation for different scoring methods was .41). There are several possible reasons for the discrepancy between these findings and those of other investigators:

- Dulay and Burt lumped together children with different amounts of exposure to the second language and measured acquisition sequence by examining the degree to which the functors were correctly supplied in speech samples. Their study was not a longitudinal study, as were most of the studies discussed earlier. They did not, strictly speaking, measure *acquisition sequence* but rather *accuracy of use,* since they measured the percent of times a subject correctly supplied a morpheme in an obligatory context. Longitudinal studies of individual children yield more direct information about the developmental sequence in the acquisition of functors and are more directly comparable to Brown's (1973a) original (longitudinal) data.

- It may be that acquisition of functors, as Dulay and Burt suggested, is especially reflective of cognitive abilities. That is, children acquiring the English functors as grammatical features of a second language bring different and more sophisticated cognitive abilities to this task than do children who acquire the functors as part of their first language (at an earlier age). In contrast, other grammatical structures, such as negative constructions and questions, may not reflect differential cognitive ability to the same extent.

Nonetheless, the morpheme research does suggest that there are common strategies that children second-language learners use regardless of their first language. This appears to be true of adults as well. Research with adults (Bailey, Madden, & Krashen, 1974; Fathman, 1975; Krashen, Sferlazza, Feldman, & Fathman, 1976; Larsen–Freeman, 1976a) indicates that despite differences in amount of instruction, exposure to English, and first language, there is a high degree of agreement as to the relative difficulty of the set of grammatical morphemes studied. Moreover, the relative degree of difficulty for the various morphemes found in adult second-language learners corresponded closely to the relative difficulty observed in children second-language learners for the same morphemes.

There is evidence that suggests that the principal determinant of accuracy order of the morphemes in second-language learners is the frequency of occurrence of these same morphemes in the input to which learners are exposed. Larsen–Freeman (1976a) showed that accuracy ordering in adult subjects correlated highly with the frequency of the morphemes in the speech of English-speaking parents reported by Brown (1973a). In a subsequent study, Larsen–Freeman (1976b) found high correlations between the frequency of the morphemes in the speech of ESL (English as a Second Language) teachers and her own morpheme accuracy data (average correlation .61) and Dulay and Burt's (1974c) data (average correlation .75). This suggests that the frequency of forms in input influences what the second-language learner produces (Wagner–Gough & Hatch, 1975).

Although these studies point to important variables in second-language learning, there are serious methodological difficulties with the morpheme studies (Hatch, 1983). One difficulty, for example, is that the morphemes may appear both in correct and incorrect contexts, so that a confusion matrix analysis (Hatch, 1977) might be the best way to determine the extent to which individuals use the morphemes appropriately. There is the further problem that grouping data may obscure individual variation in learning strategies and that group curves may in fact not reflect the accuracy ordering of any individual in the group (Andersen, 1978; Huebner, 1979; Rosansky, 1976).

Another critique of the morpheme research is that this approach does not adequately describe the process of second-language acquisition. Wode, Bahns, Bedey, and Frank (1978) have argued from data on four German-speaking children learning English that acquiring a second language involves decomposing complex structural patterns and rebuilding them step by step until target-like mastery is attained. This process cannot be captured, Wode and his associates maintained, by research that focuses on the accuracy of use of specific morphemes in large cross-sectional samples of second-language learners.

Furthermore, some research on morpheme acquisition does not support the conclusion of a universal order of acquisition. Hakuta and Cancino (1977) have argued that the semantic complexity of the morphemes may vary depending on the learner's native language. They cited research that indicated that where a second-language learner's first language does not make the same discriminations as the target language, more difficulty in learning to use these morphemes occurs than is the case for learners whose first language makes the semantic discrimination. Thus, Korean children, whose language has no article equivalents, performed more poorly on the articles in morpheme studies (Fathman, 1975) than did children whose languages, such as Spanish, contain articles. Similarly, Hakuta's (1976) Japanese-speaking child showed great difficulty with the definite/indefinite contrast—Japanese also being a language that does not make the same semantic discrimination as English.

In sum, both the case studies and the cross-sectional research lead to the conclusion that order of acquisition of syntactic and morphological structures involves an interplay of both developmental and transfer factors. The developmental factor may, as Dulay and Burt suggested, involve universal cognitive mechanisms and/or universal strategies of language acquisition (Slobin, 1973, 1977). Variables such as frequency and salience also seem to direct the sequence of acquisition toward a universal order, regardless of the child's first language. The transfer factor leads to deviations from this order in cases where there is confusion because of syntactic congruence or morphological similarity (Zobl, 1980). In such cases learners may use strategies that are specific to their needs in solving particular syntactic or morphological problems. In fact, the investigation of the different types of strategies that second-language learners employ is more important than resolving the debate about developmental versus transfer influences (McLaughlin, 1981).

Interference Between Languages

One argument against the hypothesis that first- and second-language acquisition involve similar processes is based on interference in second-language learning. Usually such authors as Haugen (1953, 1956) and Weinreich (1953) are cited as authoritative sources for the validity of the assumption that interference from the first language influences second-language acquisition. As Dulay and Burt (1972) pointed out, however, both Haugen and Weinreich were concerned with the relationship between the languages and dialects of speech communities in contact with each other and not with individual language development.

Nonetheless, for many years linguists believed that interference from the learner's first language was the major problem in acquiring a second language (Lado, 1964; Prator, 1969). It turns out, however, that the existence of interference between languages in the case-study literature is surprisingly scanty. Children acquiring a second language in a social milieu supportive of that language generally show few signs of first-language interference. Once the languages are distinguished, the child appears to keep them apart and does not impose first-language structures on second-language syntax. Huntsberry (1972) concluded on the basis of parental reports that children who showed the greatest amounts of interference from their first language in their second language were children who were either very young or who had little contact with children and adults speaking the second language. Similarly, the children in the study by Politzer and Ramirez (1973) seem not to have spoken English in their own community but learned and used it principally in the school.

The evidence suggests that when the learning conditions are such that the larger social milieu provides a supportive context, interference from first language is minimal in second-language acquisition. When, on the other hand, the second language is not the language of the child's larger social environment, interference tends to result from the imbalance in exposure and use. This seems to be the case when the second language is learned exclusively in the school and would account for the large amounts of interference observed by educators and those testing school children (e.g., Rivers, 1964; Senn, 1932; Stern, 1970; Vey, 1946).

Ervin–Tripp (1974) also thought that interference is maximized when the second language is not the language of the learner's larger social milieu. In such a case, the learning context is aberrant both in function and frequency of structure. That is, the learner in the classroom is exposed to a different language sample than is a learner in the natural milieu, and the language is learned in isolation without being tied to concrete situations. Presumably, situational specificity is an important factor in minimizing interferences between languages (as we saw in discussing simultaneous bilingual acquisition).

Ervin–Tripp speculated that the simpler the semantic task, the less the likelihood that the child will have recourse to first-language formations. When children attempt to communicate at a more complex level, they will tend to fall back on first-language structures. This may be one reason why more interference is apparently found in the classroom setting than is reported in case studies. In the classroom the child may be expected to communicate about fairly complex topics, whereas in the home or on the playground language may be simpler and more repetitive.

In recent years increasing attention has been given to attempts to systematically classify the errors that second-language learners make. This approach, called *error analysis,* aims at clarifying the strategies that learners employ (Burt & Kiparsky, 1972; Corder, 1967, 1975). Dulay and Burt (1972, 1974b) have concerned themselves specifically with errors children make in acquiring a second language. They cited the evidence from studies of syntactic development (e.g., Milon, 1974; Natalicio & Natalicio, 1971; Ravem, 1968, 1974) as evidence that errors in children's second-language syntax reflect first-language developmental errors.

In addition, Dulay and Burt (1972) analyzed data from Spanish-speaking children who were learning English as a second language. Table 5.6 gives some examples of the types of errors found in their data. The critical errors are those classified as interference errors, because such errors supposedly reflect the influence of Spanish constructions on English. These errors, Dulay and Burt argued, could just as well reflect overgeneralizations, which

TABLE 5.6
Errors Found in the Speech of Spanish-Speaking Children Learning English as a Second Language[a]

Type of error	Construction	Example
Interference	Possessive pronoun + noun agreement: not allowed in English, obligatory in Spanish.	Now she's putting her*s* clothes on.
	Omission of obligatory *how* in English; obligatory in Spanish.	I know to do all that.
	Use of infinitive for gerund: not allowed in English, obligatory in Spanish.	I finish to *watch* TV when it's four o'clock.
Developmental	Irregular plural treated as regular form.	He took her teeth*s* off.
	Two verbal words tensed; only one required.	I didn't wear*ed* any hat.
	Accusative pronoun with nominative.	*Me* need crayons now.
	Do-subject agreement missing.	Where does the spiders go?
	Object pronoun missing.	My mother can fix.
Ambiguous	Wrong *no* placement; *no-not* distinction; *do* missing.	It *no* cause too much trouble.
Unique	Substitutions for possessive pronoun.	*She* name is Maria.
	Overuse of *do*.	We *do* got no more book.
	-ing with modal.	Now we will talk*ing* about.

[a]From Dulay & Burt, 1972.

though not found in the speech of monolingual children acquiring the target language, correspond to strategies used by children acquiring the target language as a first language. That is, although errors such as *Now she's putting hers clothes on* are not found in the speech of monolingual children, such errors may be instances of overgeneralizing the possessive */-s/* from English. In contrast, overgeneralizations that reflect Spanish influence, such as *bigs houses* and *talls boys,* are not found in the data.

In short, Dulay and Burt argued that the interference errors do not provide unequivocal evidence that first-language structures interfere with second-language learning. Even sentences such as *I know to do all that* and *I finish to watch TV when it's four o'clock* may reflect overgeneralization from English verb-complement constructions (if *want* is substituted for *know* and *finish,* the result is a common construction in English). What the second-language learner appears to be doing is using a strategy similar to that used by monolingual children—namely, syntactic generalization.

In a subsequent study, Dulay and Burt (1974b) summarized and added to the evidence that there are common strategies used in second language acquisition by children with various language backgrounds. In this research, error analysis of English speech samples of Spanish-, Chinese-, Japanese-, and Norwegian-speaking children acquiring English as a second language indicated that the types of mistakes made by the children were strikingly similar. Dulay and Burt argued that the similarity of errors, as well as the specific error types, reflect what they referred to as "creative construction"—a process whereby children gradually reconstruct rules for the speech they hear, guided by strategies that derive from certain innate mechanisms that cause them to formulate certain types of hypotheses about the language system being acquired, until the mismatch between what they are exposed to and what they produce is resolved. The construction of linguistic rules is said to be creative, because no speaker of the target language models the kind of sentences regularly produced by children who are still acquiring the language.

The result of this "creative construction" process is a developing language often referred to as *interlanguage* (Richards, 1972; Selinker, 1972). By interlanguage is meant a separate linguistic system that results from the learner's attempted production of the target language norm. Selinker (1972) argued that interlanguage (in adults) resulted from five central processes involved in second-language learning:

- Language transfer: some items, rules, and subsystems of the interlanguage may result from transfer from the first language.
- Transfer of training: some elements of the interlanguage may result from specific features of the training process used to teach the second language.

- Strategies of second-language learning: some elements of the interlanguage may result from a specific approach to the material to be learned.
- Strategies of second-language communication: some elements of the interlanguage may result from specific ways people learn to communicate with native speakers of the target language.
- Overgeneralization of the target language linguistic material: some elements of the interlanguage may be the product of overgeneralization of the rules and semantic features of the target language.

Most adults, Selinker argued, never master a second language to the point where they are indistinguishable from native speakers of that language. Children, on the other hand, seem to be capable of going beyond interlanguage and achieving mastery in a second language, especially if the two languages are acquired simultaneously or if the child has environmental support for successive acquisition through family and peers. However, if the child's second-language acquisition is nonsimultaneous and if it occurs in the absence of peers who speak the second language, interlanguage is likely to result (Selinker, Swain, & Dumas, 1975). This is consistent with the previous comments about interference being maximized when the second language is not a part of the learner's larger social milieu and is also supported by research that suggests that non-developmental errors are found in the speech of school children who learn a language in the absence of native-speaking peers (Naiman, 1974).

To summarize, interference between languages resulting from language transfer is probably greatest in those situations where languages are learned in a classroom setting and where there is no daily contact with native speakers. When one is dealing with children who acquire a second language in a natural milieu where they have daily contact with native speakers, evidence for language transfer is more difficult to come by. It should be noted, however, that conclusions based on evidence from error analysis have been criticized on a number of grounds (Peddie, 1982). For example, Schachter and Celce–Murcia (1977) have pointed out that it is difficult to be certain what type of error a second-language learner is making or why the learner makes it. One and the same error can frequently be attributed to intralingual (reflecting developmental mistakes found in monolingual speakers) and interlingual factors (reflecting the influence of the learner's first language). Indeed, this may not be an either-or proposition: there is evidence that some errors are the result of the interaction of both factors (Andersen, 1978).

Hakuta and Cancino (1977) have argued that error analysis rests on the questionable assumption that an error is an appropriate unit of analysis. Research that indicates that a predominance of errors in a second-language learner's corpus are intralingual (developmental) usually involves coding the omission of high frequency morphemes—such as nouns and verb inflections and the verb *to be*—as intralingual errors. Since interlingual errors often involve large constituents or changes in word order, Hakuta and Cancino maintained that the relative opportunity of occurrence of the two types is not equivalent. Furthermore, it may well be that second-language learners simply avoid certain linguistic structures on which they would be likely to make errors (Schachter, 1974). It is conceivable that such avoidance tendencies reflect structural differences between their first language and the target language.

Another problem with the error-analysis research is that much of it—especially Dulay and Burt's work—rests on cross-sectional samples. There are relatively few studies that examine whether specific errors are prevalent at specific points in time or whether certain errors persist longer than others. There is some evidence that interlingual (transfer) errors appear primarily at the early stages of development (Taylor, 1975) and when learners are faced with particularly intransigent problems (Wode, 1978).

It is probably safe to say that transfer errors occur in all second-language learning situations. The important issue is to determine when and to what extent they occur in different situations (Wode, 1981). Like overgeneralizations and simplifications, transfer errors reflect general strategies used by second-language learners. Precisely what the nature of these strategies is and whether they relate to innate mechanisms, as Dulay and Burt suggested, are unresolved issues at the present time. Most likely the strategies that second-language learners employ reflect general cognitive abilities and linguistic information processing systems. In fact, as we noted in Chapter 3, errors that appear to result from language transfer can be viewed as reflecting the strategy of utilizing one's first language as a source of information to crack the code of the second language. From this perspective, interference is not transfer in the learning theory sense, but the result of a particular strategy.

This discussion ends on the same note as the previous discussion of developmental sequences in first- and second-language learning: it would seem to be more fruitful from a practical and theoretical point of view to direct research attention at the strategies that individuals use in acquiring a second language rather than to argue over the presence or absence of interference from the learner's first language. To do this, more detailed information is needed about the types of errors second-language learners make and about the extent to which these errors reflect the learning situation and the structural similarity between languages.

The evidence to date supports Corder's (1967) contention that similar processes are involved in first- and second-language learning for both adults and children. The influence of the learner's first language appears to be indirect and restricted because it must accommodate itself to the language learning process. But the influence of the first language is real, especially at some points in the learning process and for some learners. The important goal for future research is to determine how transfer structures conform to general abstract strategies for the induction of linguistic structures (Zobl, 1982).

Code Switching

Both Weinreich (1953) and Haugen (1953) noted that bilingual individuals occasionally make use of a separate code that includes structures from both languages for the sake of enriching their language and for affective purposes. This phenomenon has been found to be especially common in the speech of Mexican–Americans (Gumperz, 1970; Gumperz & Hernández–Chavez, 1972; Lance, 1969) and has been cited as an instance of interference between languages (Mackey, 1965). Here it is helpful to recall the distinction between *mixing* and *switching* codes. As we saw in Chapter 4, code mixing refers to changing language within sentences, whereas code switching refers to changing languages over phrases or sentences. Some bilinguals mix (or switch) codes for rhetorical purposes when communicating with members of their own bilingual community, but they are perfectly capable of separating codes without interference structures (switching to a single code) when dealing with members of a monolingual community.

In their analysis of the mixing phenomenon in Mexican–American speakers, Gumperz and Hernández–Chavez (1972) showed how the choice of speech forms is highly meaningful and serves definite communication needs. Speakers build on the coexistence of alternate forms in their language repertory to create meanings that may be highly idiosyncratic and understood only by members of the same bilingual speech community. For instance, the speaker may insert Spanish words into English sentences as identity markers:

Speaker A: Well, I'm glad that I met you. Okay?
Speaker B: Andale, pues (okay, swell), and do come again, mmm?

The use of Spanish expressions in this context was apparently intended to convey a sense of ethnic similarity. The speakers had been strangers and had met for the first time. By injecting Spanish in the farewell, Speaker B conveyed that since they shared the same ethnic identity, they should get to know each other better.

Another example of this use of mixing codes is the following exchange (Gumperz & Hernández–Chavez, 1972):

Speaker A: . . . I mean do some of the other people in the neighborhood have kids?

Speaker B: They don't associate with no children. . . . There's no children in the neighborhood. Well . . . si, hay creatures (There are children, yes) [p. 96].

Here the use of Spanish serves to single out Mexican children from others, and the speaker goes on to talk about this Mexican family.

Such mixing of Spanish expressions in the flow of English speech seems to be a normal part of Mexican–Americans' style in English. Speakers use such expressions when speaking to others of the same ethnic background in much the same way that American Jews use certain Yiddish expressions or Italians use certain Italian expressions to mark in-group identity. Often they are used by speakers who no longer have effective control of the first language.

In addition to mixing languages, switching from one language to another is often common in the speech of bilingual individuals. The speaker may switch codes because of the nature of the topic or because a topic is more intimate and personal. Such a practice seems to be fairly common among Mexican–Americans, who are often at a loss to explain why it is that they switch languages at certain points in their speech.

Children who live in a bilingual environment where they are exposed to a good deal of switching and mixing may find it difficult to separate the two codes in formal speech. In fact, interference can be thought of in terms of the inability of the child to discriminate between the two codes, rather than in terms of language transfer. The more the people around the child mix codes, the more difficulty the child will have in differentiating between them. It seems, however, that children also learn to mix languages for stylistic purposes (Lance, 1969).

Children—especially young children—seem initially to prefer a single referent or linguistic form to the two codes required in bilingual speech. Occasionally they confuse codes within a single word or phrase. For instance, the child may identify two morphemes because they have functions they share in common. This phenomenon Haugen (1955) referred to as a "diamorph." In the example of the development of the prepositional construction in the Swedish of a Finnish-speaking child described by Malmberg (1945), there was a systematic progression from the Finnish to the Swedish structure, with Swedish diamorphs gradually replacing their Finnish counterparts until syntactic restructuring was achieved. A similar phenomenon was observed in the development of a Swedish–Estonian, bilingual child (Oksaar, 1970).

Malmberg's analysis is valuable in that he showed the stages through which the child progressed in switching from one code to another. Such process descriptions are rare, however, and little is known about the conditions under which children adopt switching rules. It may be that such rules are situationally controlled (Ervin–Tripp, 1970b) but precisely how and to what extent remains to be clarified.

In any event, it seems useful to view the successive acquisition of two languages in the same way as we viewed simultaneous bilingual acquisition—as a process of learning to differentiate two linguistic codes. This task is probably no different in terms of the operations involved than is the task of switching codes within a single language. Such a perspective has the advantage of economy: no new processes need be postulated to account for second-language learning, and a similar development seems to be followed, though at a different rate.

CONCLUSION

Methodologically, the early literature on successive acquisition of two languages suffers from the same drawbacks as does much of the literature on simultaneous bilingual acquisition. Early case studies were mostly descriptive and almost anecdotal accounts of children's second-language acquisition. They dealt unsystematically with a broad range of issues and questions.

The recent literature, however, is characterized by a more systematic concern with specific topics. Ravem's (1968, 1974) examination of interrogative and modal constructions, Lightbown's (1980) work on negatives, and Dato's (1971) study of verb-phrase constructions are examples of the ways in which recent investigators have tackled limited areas of theoretical interest. The tendency has been to try to go beyond description to explanation. In addition, there has been a number of studies with larger samples directed at resolving specific questions. Natalicio and Natalicio (1971) conducted a comparative study of the acquisition of English plural forms by native and nonnative speakers; Dulay and Burt (1972, 1973, 1974a, 1974b, 1974c) have carried out a number of studies dealing with the analysis of errors and the developmental sequence of the acquisition of English constructions by non-English-speaking children.

The result of these systematic research efforts is that we have more answers to questions about second-language acquisition in the case where a second language is acquired after the first language is established than we do in the case where the two languages are acquired simultaneously. Some of the questions left unanswered at the end of the previous chapter can, at least tentatively, be answered with respect to the successive acquisition of two languages. For instance, I asked the question:

- What developmental stages do children exposed to two languages go through in acquiring specific syntactic structures such as negative constructions, interrogative constructions, relative clauses, and so on?

Research on successive acquisition of two languages has been directly concerned with this question. The work of Ravem (1968) and Dato (1971), as well as the evidence from the studies of Ervin–Tripp (1974) and Natalicio and Natalicio (1971), suggests that the developmental stages are much the same as those that monolingual children go through in acquiring the target language, probably because second-language learners recapitulate this process in acquiring the language.

Although the evidence seems to support the similarity between the developmental stages followed by first- and second-language learners of a given language, there are some findings that are not entirely consistent with this notion (e.g., Cancino, Rosansky, & Schumann, 1974, 1975; Wode, 1978). This brings us to the second question asked at the end of the previous chapter:

- Are these developmental stages always identical with those followed by monolingual children?

Dulay and Burt (1973, 1974a, 1974c) found that children who were speakers of different first languages learned English constructions in the same developmental sequence but that this sequence was different from that reported in studies of monolingual, English-speaking children. This appears to contradict other studies, but we noted that there are several possible reasons for this. The most interesting aspect of this research (and the point where it converges with other research) is that the children studied did not resort to the strategies of their first languages but used common strategies in approaching the second language, regardless of the nature of their first language. Nonetheless, there is evidence that in certain cases, children make detours from the developmental path (Wode, 1978). The challenge for research on developmental processes in second-language learning is to determine under what conditions learners resort to first-language structures (Zobl, 1980, 1982).

The next three questions dealt with interference phenomena:

- How do specific languages interact with each other phonetically, syntactically, and semantically?
- What regularities are to be found in semantic and morphological mixings?
- Do particular language combinations cause more retardation in individual language development than others?

The evidence from error-analysis studies appears to indicate that interference is by no means a main cause of error—except possibly when children learn a language in the school that they do not use outside of the classroom with family and peers. Many errors that appear to be interference errors might be errors brought about by overgeneralizing strategies learned from the second language itself (Dulay & Burt, 1972).

One of the most interesting findings in the error-analysis research is that children whose first languages were Spanish, Chinese, Japanese, and Norwegian all made the same types of mistakes when acquiring English as a second language (Dulay & Burt, 1974b). This suggests that interaction between different language combinations is a minor factor in second-language acquisition. We have seen, however, that such a conclusion needs to be tempered by recognition of the serious methodological problems involved in error-analysis research. Furthermore, a number of studies (Hakuta, 1976; Wode, 1978; Zobl, 1980) have shown that the learner's first language may, under certain conditions, play a role in determining what errors will occur. It is premature to rule out transfer; the important question is when and why transfer occurs and how this information helps us understand the strategies learners use.

There are a number of additional questions about second-language learning that should be added to our list, some of which have not been given much attention in research. These include:

- What are the differential aspects of simultaneous and successive acquisition of the two languages?
- Does successive acquisition lead to more or less interference than simultaneous acquisition?
- What is the developmental sequence of more complex grammatical constructions in a language acquired as a second language? Is this sequence similar to that observed when the language is acquired as a first language?

Some attention has been given to two other questions:

- Does acquiring a second language after a first language is established interfere with the first language, or does it facilitate further development in the first language?
- Under what conditions are first or second languages lost?

For example, Berman (1979) reported that her daughter had to relearn Hebrew on returning to Israel after a stay in the United States. What little information we have on this question suggests that children seem to forget languages more quickly than adults do (Hatch, 1983), perhaps because they have learned them less well or because their learning is more dependent on context. The issue of language loss is under-researched, but there has been some increase in interest in the topic lately (R. Lambert & Freed, 1982).

Finally, two questions have received a great deal of attention. These are:

- Is second-language learning more difficult for some children than for others? Why is this so (if true)?
- What are the effects of bilingualism on the child and on the adult?

The first of these questions is dealt with in the next chapter; the second in Chapter 7.

6 Individual Differences and Language Learning Strategies

One of the more robust findings in the literature on child language acquisition is that there are large individual differences. Some children pick up language rapidly and with apparent ease. One such case was Roger Brown's (1973a) subject, Eve, whose utterances averaged four morphemes at two years and two months. Other children make much slower progress. It took Brown's Adam and Sarah until three and a half years to average four morphemes per utterance.

Similarly, children differ in the rate and ease with which they learn second languages. Some observers believe that it takes about a year for young children learning a second language in a naturalistic situation to reach the level of their peers (Francescato, 1969), whereas other observers believe that even with very young children a year is not sufficient time to catch up with native-speaking peers (Valette, 1964). Of course, different observers may use different criteria for comparing second-language learners with native speakers, but careful comparison of children learning a second language naturalistically in similar circumstances clearly reveals a broad range of individual differences in rate and ease of second-language learning (Ervin-Tripp, 1974; Snow & Hoefnagel–Höhle, 1979; Wong Fillmore, 1976).

The interest in individual differences in first- and second-language development reflects a trend away from emphasis on universal and rule-governed aspects of language learning. This is part of a more general tendency on the part of researchers to devote more attention to the linguistic environment of the child (see Chapter 2) and to patterns of interaction that affect language learning. In this chapter I examine some of the research on first-language development that relates to individual differences, and then turn to studies of individual variation in children's second-language learning.

INDIVIDUAL DIFFERENCES IN FIRST-LANGUAGE DEVELOPMENT

There are two lines of research in recent literature on individual differences in language learning. The first consists of studies of individual variation in first-language development that reflect personal styles of language learning. This research has been carried out, for the most part, with children from mainstream, middle-class families. The second line of research concerns those studies of individual variation in first-language development that reflect differences in the input to which children are exposed. This research has been carried out with children from various social-class and cultural backgrounds. After discussing these two lines of research, I examine how individual differences in styles and strategies affect first-language learning.

Style Differences

Analytic and gestalt styles.   One of the classic studies in the literature dealing with first-language development is Ann Peters' (1977) study of Minh. Minh was the second of two boys in a family in which the mother had attended college and the father had a graduate degree. The mother was Vietnamese and had come to the United States at the age of 12. She spoke very little Vietnamese with her children, although she used it when speaking with friends and relatives. The father was born in the United States and was a native speaker of English. The family lived in Hawaii and the children were exposed primarily to Standard English, with some secondary exposure to Hawaiian English and Vietnamese.

Peters began studying Minh when he was seven months old. She recorded his speech on a fairly regular basis until he was two years and three months old. His first utterances (as distinct from babbling, around seven and a half months) appeared to be imitations of adult speech. At about a year, Minh displayed a few spontaneous utterances, but Peters was reluctant to call these intentional, because they were surprisingly complex. At about a year and a half Minh developed a frustratingly unintelligible style of speech that Peters labeled "mush mouth."

The child's speech sounded as if it should mean something, but Peters was rarely able to understand it, unless the child was naming pictures in a book. Gradually, Peters realized that Minh was actually producing two kinds of speech. The first she called *analytic*. This was the kind of speech usually found by researchers studying child language. It consisted of utterances that gradually increased in number and in closeness to the adult target. This style of speech shows a gradual progression from simpler one-word utterances to two-word utterances and, ultimately, to more complex strings or words.

The second type of speech Minh used Peters called *gestalt* speech. This speech began even earlier than analytic speech. It was characterized by utterances in which the combination of syllables, stress, and intonation gave a very good impression of sentencehood, although individual words were difficult to understand. That is, Minh captured in this style of speech the "melody" of adult speech and attempted to model it in his own. As Peters put it, he "learned the tune before the words." A musical child, Minh used the same strategy in singing or playing musical instruments; at twenty-two months he could produce a very creditable gestalt of a piano piece.

Once she listened to Minh's speech with a new set of expectations, Peters eventually determined that he was attempting to produce whole phrases or sentences before he had mastered the constituent words. At fourteen months, for example, Minh said *Open the door,* while pounding on the bathroom door and shouting to his brother on the inside. None of these individual words were in his repertory at this time, but he was able to produce (something like) the whole utterance. Given enough contextual information, Peters was able to identify a number of these gestalt utterances.

Some of Minh's early gestalt utterances contained "filler syllables" that functioned as place-holders to fill out not yet analyzed parts of a phrase. For example, he used *uh-oh, x x x* when something fell on the floor, presumably intending *uh-oh, fell down* or *uh-oh, what happened?* Another example was *Mommy, x x x* to express *Mommy, I want you* or *Mommy, come help me!*

In short, when Peters was able to overcome her tendency to look for short, single-word utterances in her subject's early speech, she found that "mush mouth" became much more intelligible. But was her child unique or is the gestalt strategy more widely used by young children learning language than is realized? A small, but growing body of literature now exists that suggests that Minh was not an isolated case, but that other children use a similar strategy to acquire language.

Related research. Peter's work with Minh challenged the view that language acquisition in childhood involves a relatively invariant progression through a series of stages (the one-word stage, the two-word stage, and multi-word utterances). Other research also pointed to the existence of large individual differences in the acquisition process. Rather than a single and uniform path to language acquisition, there seem to be several ways of learning a first language.

For example, Nelson (1973) studied eighteen children learning their first 50 words and reported that some children acquired a vocabulary that contained mostly general nominals (words referring to all the members of a category). Other children's early vocabulary was characterized by a greater number of personal or social expressions (words expressing affective states and social relationships). She called the first group *referential* children, because these children's orientation was more object-oriented. The second group she called *expressive* children, because these children seemed to be learning a self-oriented language.

At age two the ten referential children in Nelson's sample scored higher on measures of vocabulary development, while the eight expressive children were higher in measures of syntactic development. It is important to remember, however, that all the children had vocabulary items from both classes. What is at issue is the relative proportion—the strategy or learning style that predominates in individual children—of naming as opposed to using speech for social purposes.

Nelson found that the child's linguistic development related to the degree of correspondence between the style that the child adopted and the style that predominated in the mother's speech. If the child was working with the strategy that language was used to name things, it helped if the mother was using the same strategy. On the other hand, if the child adopted the strategy that language was for dealing with people, it helped if the mother provided lots of social expressions. Nelson found cases where children in mismatched pairs seemed to remain stationary in their language development, until the child revised the strategy he or she was using, bringing it into accord with the mother's language use. When this happened, greater progress was observed.

The variation that Nelson observed between referential and expressive styles seems related to Peters' distinction between analytic and gestalt styles. Indeed, in Nelson's discussion of the characteristics of the expressive style, she noted that the "personal-social" language that typifies this style included expressions such as:

Go away
Stop it
Don't do it
Thank you
I want it

that could be considered "preformed or stereotyped" (1973, p. 25) units that are not themselves analyzed. In children using the referential or analytic style, language acquisition proceeds one word at a time and language is used primarily for its labeling function. Children using the expressive or gestalt style tend to use whole utterances in a socially appropriate manner. Peters (1977) suggested that there is a continuum of children, varying from those who are very analytic from the beginning, to those who mix analytic and gestalt styles, to those who are predominantly gestalt in their orientation and who convert gradually to an analytic approach.

One of the children studied by Bloom (1970), Eric, appears to have been an example of the last type. At nineteen months Eric produced a large proportion of unintelligible utterances that were "extended strings of sounds with recognizable English sentence intonation patterns" (p. 102). In contrast to Minh, however, Eric did not seem to mind that his speech was nonsense; he seemed to be playing with speech rather than trying to communicate.

Bloom, Lightbown, and Hood (1975) reported that children have different ways of acquiring syntax. Some children they called "analytic" in that they used many different nouns to express semantic categories in their two- and three-word utterances. Other children they called "synthetic" in that they encoded a semantic category as a constant form using adverbs and pronouns as if they were affixes of the verb. In the terminology of another author, some children seem to be "noun-lovers" and others are "noun-leavers" (Horgan, 1980). The analytic, noun-lovers seem to correspond to the children Peters characterized as analytic; the synthetic, noun-leavers appear to correspond to Peters' gestalt style.

Further evidence for Peters' contention that there is a range of individual differences along the analytic-gestalt dimension comes from a study by Dore (1974) of two children, J and M. The speech of J was instrumental, more involved with other people—that is, more expressive—than was the speech of M. Dore called this speech style "message-oriented," in that it was intended primarily to manipulate other people. In contrast, M was more concerned with individual words and used speech more to label—that is, her speech was more referential. This style Dore called "code-oriented," because it was used mainly to declare things about the environment. J was more at the gestalt end of Peters' continuum in that he often used intonation alone in communicating. Language development for him was "prosodic development" more than "word development." In fact J and his mother did not participate in word-learning routines, whereas this was very much the case for M and her mother.

In summary, there are a number of indications in the literature on first-language development that there are individual differences in the learning styles or strategies that predominate in children's early speech. Investigators have observed two different extremes in the styles that characterize children's early language development. The parallels in terminology used by different authors are listed in Table 6.1. It is important to note that these labels are not meant to be evaluative. That a child used predominantly object or social words in early speech does not mean that the child is destined to be an introvert or extrovert. There is no evidence of a correlation between early speech and personality factors. Furthermore, it is possible for a given child to use one style for one situation and the other for other situations. Minh, for example, seemed to speak analytically when naming, but to use the gestalt style for social functions. Bowerman (1976) reported that her daughter, Christy, used some words in an expressive manner initially, but that eventually these words took on a referential character; similarly, words that were first used referentially could take on an expressive character. Bowerman made the important point that characterizing the child's approach to language means looking at how the child uses words in a variety of contexts.

Input Differences

Why is it that some children use a predominately analytic approach, while others use a more gestalt strategy? One answer to this question relates to the input to which the child is exposed. In a replication of Nelson's research, Klein (1980) video-taped children in 19 families. When the children obtained a 50-word vocabulary, their speech was analyzed using Nelson's referential-expressive distinction. In her sample, in contrast to Nelson's original report, mother's speech style generally corresponded to the child's style; mothers of referential children were found to use more common nouns and made more references to objects than did mothers of expressive

TABLE 6.1
Some Characterizations of First-Language Learning Styles

Author	Styles	
Peters (1977)	analytic	gestalt
Nelson (1973)	referential	expressive
Bloom et al. (1974)	analytic	synthetic
Dore (1974)	code-oriented	message-oriented
Horgan (1980)	noun-lovers	noun-leavers
Features (Nelson, 1981):	object words	social words
	nouns	pronouns
	two-word combinations	unanalyzed phrases
	clear segmental articulation	clear intonation

children. This suggests (in contrast to Nelson, 1973) that mothers' speech has an influence on the child's orientation from the beginning.

Della Corte, Benedict, and Klein (1983) looked at the speech of mothers of one-year-old referential and expressive children and found that mothers of referential children spoke more and used more descriptives, whereas mothers of expressive children used more prescriptives. In general, the mothers of expressive children in this study were less well-educated than were mothers of referential children. Because the mothers in this study were from middle- and working-class families, the findings point to the possibility that social-class factors may relate to the kind of input the child receives and to the strategies used to deal with that input.

Social-class differences. Nelson (1973) observed that there was a tendency for first-born children to adopt a referential style, whereas second-born children tended to be expressive. This relationship was not significant in her sample, but when she took the educational level of the parent into account, she found that all of the first-born children from families with college educations or more were in the referential group. If first-born children in highly educated families do in fact tend to use an analytic/referential strategy, it is not surprising that the literature on first-language development shows an orderly progression from the one-word to the two-word to multiword utterances (because almost all research in this field has been carried out with first-born children in highly educated families). It is possible, however that children from less well-educated families or children whose language development is strongly influenced by older peers use different strategies in learning language.

Ethnographically-based research on working-class families supports the notion that differences in the language environment lead to very different language-learning strategies. Heath (1983), in particular, has shown how the experience of children learning language in some working-class families can be quite different from the experience of children in middle- and upper-middle class families.

Heath's data are based on ethnographic observation of two communities, which she called Roadville and Trackton, in the Piedmont Carolinas. Roadville is a white working-class community where the principal occupation for four generations has been in a local textile mill. Trackton is a working-class black community whose older generations worked on the land but whose recent source of employment has been the textile mills. Whereas the children of Roadville receive much the same sort of input as children in middle- and upper-middle classes, the children of Trackton have a very different experience. As Heath put it, in Roadville adults teach children how to talk, in Trackton children learn to talk (see Table 6.2).

Table 6.2
Some Differences between Two South Carolina Communities
That Affect Language Learning Styles

	Roadville	Trackton
Physical Environment:	Working-class white families	Working-class black families
	Books, manipulable toys	Few books, manipulable toys
Language Input:	Speech to children modified	Rich speech environment, but not addressed to child
	Child's early speech interpreted	Early speech not inter- preted
	Bookreading, bedtime story routines	No bookreading or bed- time stories
Expectations:	Early sound are at- tempts to convey meaning	Early sounds are not attempts to convey meaning
	Children are conversa- tional partners from the beginning	Chidren are not conver- sational partners until can hold floor
	Children are taught to talk	Children learn to talk

Based on Heath (1983).

Roadville children are "taught" to talk through numerous kinds of adult–child interactions supplemented by many props, such as books, toys, stuffed animals, and so on. Even before the child can talk, adults use fictionalized speech:

But this baby wants to go to sleep, doesn't he?
Yes, see those little eyes gettin' heavy.

When the child grows older, adults immediately respond to word-like sounds, turn them into words, repeating them and expanding them into well-formed sentences. At a very early age children are taught to use politeness formulas, such as *Bye, bye* and *Thank you.*

Books are especially useful in this teaching process. There are dozens of books in the homes of Roadville children—stories about pets, nursery rhymes, simplified Bible stories. Adults use books to train children in vocabulary and to ask what-questions:

What's this?
Can you see the puppy?
What does the puppy do?

This is your ABC book. See the A.
You find the A on your blanket.

Bookreading serves to help children name basic items pictured in books, to retell stories in the words of adults, and to learn numbers and letters of the alphabet.

In contrast, children in Trackton live in a world devoid of teaching props. Their world is almost entirely human—there are no cribs, car-seats, mobiles, rattles, or books. The world around the child is one of constant human communication, verbal and nonverbal. Children are talked about and are kept in the midst of a constant stream of speech that flows continually past them. Little attention is given to their attempts to verbalize; cooing and babbling noises are ignored. No one interprets their early sounds.

Children sleep in their parents' bed until they are about two years of age. Their toys are pot lids, spoons, and occasional trucks, balls, baby dolls. They do not demand nor receive manipulable toys such as puzzles, blocks, take-apart toys, books, or letter games. There is no reading material in the house specifically for children, and parents do not sit and read to children. Because children are usually left to sleep whenever they fall asleep, there is no bedtime story routine.

Children learn to speak (between 12 and 24 months) by imitating the ends of overheard phrases or sentences. Heath described their early attempts as imitations of the tune or general "gestalt" of the complete utterance. They pick up and repeat chunks (usually the ends) of phrasal and clausal utterances of speakers around them. They seem to remember fragments of speech and to repeat them without active production. This Heath called the *repetition stage*—imitation of the intonation contours and general shaping of utterances. Adults seem to pay no attention to children's talk at this stage and often overlap their repetitions:

Mother:	(talking to neighbor with child nearby)
	But they won't call back, won't happen-
Child:	-call back
Neighbor:	Sam's going over their Saturday, he'll pick up a form-
Child:	-pick up on, pick up on
	(the child seems to have heard "form" as "on")

The second stage Heath called *repetition with variation*. In this stage Trackton children manipulate pieces of conversation they pick up. They incorporate chunks of language from others into their own on-going dialogue, applying productive rules and inserting new words for those used in adult speech. They also play with rhyming patterns and varying intonational contours.

> Mother: She went to the doctor again.
> Child: (in a sing-song fashion)
>   -went to de doctor, doctor, tractor, dis my tractor, doctor on a tractor, went to de doctor.

The child has created a monologue, incorporating the conversation he heard into his own talk as he plays. Again, this speech is largely ignored by adults.

Heath called the third stage *participation*. At this point children begin to enter into the ongoing conversations around them. They do so by attracting adults' attention with a tug on the arm or pant leg and they provide nonverbal reinforcements to help recreate a scene they want to describe to a listener. To get the floor children will make gestures, extra sounds, or act out some outstanding feature of the scene they are trying to describe. Much of their speech involves telling stories about things in their lives, events they see and hear, and situations in which they have been involved. Now adults respond directly to the child and accept their communicative efforts.

The differences between Roadville and Trackton children in their language development reflect differing sets of expectations about appropriate language use and acceptable language style. Heath noted that in middle-class families and in Roadville homes children are viewed as potential conversational partners from the beginning, even before they can take a conversational turn. Parents and older children modify their language when talking to young children, they expand their utterances, they teach young children labels, and contextualize speech.

In Trackton homes a very different set of assumptions operates. Children are not viewed as potential conversational partners until they have achieved enough skill to get the floor and maintain a topic. They are not spoken to nor are their early vocalizations attended to. They learn to talk by imitating the speech around them, not by being taught labels. Speech is not contextualized for the child, children have to figure out meaning by drawing parallels between items and events. There is no belief that children can be taught to talk; they "come up" on their own. When they have something to say they will say it. As one mother put it:

> Ain't no use tellin' 'em: 'learn this, learn that, what's this, what's that?' He just gotta learn, gotta know; he see one thing one place one time, he know how it go, see sump'n like it again, maybe it be the same, maybe it won't.

Cultural Differences.   The differences between Roadville and Trackton families reflect different expectations and patterns of behavior that exist in American working-class society. When we look to other cultures we find an even greater range of expectations and behavioral patterns. For example, Schieffelin (1979) reported that the Kaluli of New Guinea, like American middle-class parents—are very conscious of language development and deliberately try to teach young children to speak. But they go about this by direct instruction—by telling children appropriate things to say in specific circumstances. Furthermore, the speech they use, and expect the child to use, is normal adult speech. There is no such thing in their culture as "caretaker speech." Even young babies are thought to have their own identities, and it is the mother's job to help these identities emerge—first by speaking for their infants and then by instructing them how to interact in socially and linguistically appropriate ways.

Ochs (1980) noted that caretaker speech to children in Samoa contained no expansions of children's utterances. This is in contrast to the widespread use of expansions in middle-class American caretaker speech. Ochs compared Samoan and American beliefs about status, rights to speak, and capability to act intentionally, and concluded that Samoan caretakers do not expand their children's utterances because they do not believe that young children can communicate intentionally. Furthermore, it is not appropriate in Samoan society for higher-status caretakers to try to accommodate to a child's perspective by offering confirmatory checks on the child's speech.

We know very little about the effect of these cultural expectations and the behaviors they lead to on child language development. If one assumes that the language to which the child is exposed has an effect on the strategies that the child uses in early speech, one might predict that the language development in the Kaluli will be more like what is found in middle-class English-speaking families, whereas the Samoan pattern might be more like what was found in Trackton. But such generalizations must be made with caution, in part because we do not have enough information about the role older siblings play in the language development of younger children in these cultures, and in part because even within American middle-class society, there appear to be large individual differences (perhaps reflecting personality and/or neurological differences).

In reviewing the literature on variation among children learning their first language, Peters (1983) concluded that four factors explain many of the observed strategy differences. The first of these relates to the *function* of language for the child. If children see language primarily as a way of talking about things, they are likely to adopt a referential style; if they see language primarily as a way of interacting with others, they are likely to adopt an expressive style. Second, the type of *input* the child receives will affect how the child approaches language. Children in Trackton do not receive the modified "caretaker talk" that middle-class American children receive, and they appear to learn language by imitating multi-morpheme chunks of the language they hear adults use rather than by extracting single words. Third, the type of speech that the culture *expects* children to use has an effect on their language development. Thus, for example, the cultural expectation in Samoa is that babies' early vocalizations are of no consequence and that children achieve the right to participate in conversation only through age and status. Finally, there is the issue of *individual makeup*: it may be that personality and neurological factors influence how children approach language, even apart from how the culture or their parents speak to them.

In short, there is no simple answer to the question of why some children adopt one strategy in dealing with a first language, while other children adopt another. There are some factors that probably limit how far a child will be able to go in, say, adopting an analytic or gestalt strategy. If the child's approach is inconsistent with adult expectations and input speech (Nelson, 1973) or possibly for reasons that are less clear (Bowerman, 1976), the child may shift to another approach. What is more important than describing the learning styles that different children adopt is determining *how* the various strategies relate to the process of language development. I would like to discuss this topic briefly before turning to individual differences in second-language learning.

Individual Strategies and Language Development

Earlier in this book I argued for an approach to language development that emphasized the child's processing capacities and the strategies children employ in learning to communicate with others. An example, cited in Chapter 2, of such an analysis is Macnamara's (1972) discussion of the strategies infants use to determine early meanings and subsequent syntactic development. Another process model—one that is quite relevant to the present discussion—is Ruth Clark's (1978) account of the role of imitation in language learning.

The role of imitation.   Clark argued that imitation is a central process in language learning. She rejected the view that children build up syntactic competence as a result of interpreting and analyzing adult utterances. In her view syntactic competence develops from imitating not-fully-comprehended utterances. These utterances can be imitated overtly or recorded for delayed imitation. They constitute a repertoire of linguistic structures from which children only gradually extract information about the syntactic features of their language.

Clark denied that there are length constraints on children's speech and cited Braine's (1974) finding that corpora of young children's speech consistently reveal relatively long utterances that break through supposed length constraints. Braine argued that children, lacking complete command of the rules of adult grammar, use a strategy in speech production whereby they single out something pragmatically salient in the situation. Their utterances are limited, Braine maintained, not because of performance constraints but because of the child's use of the salient feature strategy for communicating semantic intentions within the limitations set by syntactic knowledge. Clark agreed with Braine that sentence production is not limited by length constraints, although like Olson (1973, see Chapter 2), she saw the speech of young children to be limited by operative memory.

According to Clark, imitations are retrieved as "stored fragments" (Cazden, 1968) that are combined or fused in simple ways. When these stored fragments are reproduced, they are subject to limitations on retrieval and will be reproduced in part or as they originally stood. Furthermore, they may be combined with other stored fragments as amalgams. The creative aspect of early speech, Clark argued, consists of novel utterances that are essentially simple modifications and combinations of imitations.

To illustrate this process, Clark (1974) cited the speech of her son, Adam. Just before his third birthday Adam often incorporated into his utterances whole strings from a preceding adult utterance:

Mother: That's upside down.
Child: No, I want to upside down.

Child: It's cold.
Mother: Isn't it?
Child: Isn't it? Isn't it dark too?

In addition, Adam used such utterances as *Sit my knee* to mean "I want to sit on your knee." These were interpreted by Clark as incompletely analyzed units. Because they were retained intact for several weeks without other lexical items being substituted, Clark saw them as functioning as units with limited internal structure. At this point in his development Adam's speech consisted of a number of routine unproductive sequences, coexisting with a few simple productive rules. The rules seemed to Clark to derive in large measure from invariable routines, used for some time with the original lexical items before new lexical items were inserted.

As the repertoire of stored fragments builds up, Clark argued, children assimilate sequences they hear to familiar sequences. They use their linguistic repertoire to generalize syntactic structures they know to new lexical items and to develop new structures. As time goes by, the repertoire of stored fragments becomes gradually analyzed for more elaborate information about syntactic structure, which will, in turn, be accumulated in the child's competence. This analysis suggests that language learning may involve the gradual "unpacking" of the content and structure of imitated sequences already in the child's repertoire. How frequent is such a strategy in early language development and what purpose does it serve?

The units of speech.   A problem that pervades all language learning is the problem of unitization (Peters, 1983). One of the most significant tasks for a learner is to identify what is a word. Words are not separated neatly from each other by pauses, but tend to run together. For children learning the first language the problem is intensified because the units have to be differentiated in real time. The child cannot go back and reread the text (Peters, 1983). Hence it is unreasonable to assume that children will extract units that coincide exactly with the words or morphemes in the adult system. When the child produces an utterance that contains several words from the adult language, this "package" may be only one unit to the child.

This helps to explain some of the findings in the individual difference literature. Certain children—such as Peters' Minh—may in part use a strategy of imitating phrases and using them as unanalyzed units in their early speech. Such children may appear not to be going through the one-word and the two-word stages of language acquisition, but may in fact be going through a *one-unit* and a *two-unit* stage, whole phrases being the linguistic equivalents of words for these children (Peters, 1983). This is consistent with the notion that the child is imitating poorly understood whole units from adult speech and only gradually analyzing them.

For many years, however, the belief prevailed that unanalyzed units impeded language development. While admitting that children were likely to imitate highly frequent utterances, Brown and Hanlon (1970) concluded:

> We suggest that any form that is produced with very high frequency by parents will be somehow represented in the child's performance even if its structure is far beyond him. He will find a way to render a version of it and will also form a notion of the circumstances in which it is used. The construction will become lodged in his speech as an unassimilated fragment. Extensive use of such a fragment probably protects it, for a time, from a reanalysis when the structure relevant to it is finally learned (p. 51).

This statement seems to imply that "unassimilated fragments" are separate from the rule-governed process and are not "unpacked" or analyzed as Clark (1974, 1978) and others (Carey, 1978; Olson, 1973) have argued.

Do imitated stored fragments provide the raw materials for linguistic analysis or are these fragments protected from analysis, as Brown and

Hanlon would have it? A number of recent authors have concluded that imitated fragments may indeed provide material for eventual analysis with the resulting pieces themselves becoming part of the growing linguistic system. The most thorough discussion of this process is Wong Fillmore's (1976) analysis of the use of "formulas" in the speech of five children learning English as a second language. As we will see shortly, Wong Fillmore provided convincing evidence that formulaic speech is broken down by children, first into formulaic frames with abstract slots representing constituent types, and eventually toward analysis of the syntactic features of the language.

Snow (1981) and Moerk and Moerk (1979) have also argued that imitations are used by children in developmentally progressive ways. Both of these authors pointed, in particular, to the role of deferred imitations in language development. They were able to show that in many cases the child's imitated chunk does not get reproduced immediately, but appears later (sometimes some days later) in the child's speech, first as unanalyzed, then as partly analyzed, and ultimately as fully analyzed forms. Their data, like Clark's, support the contention that imitations provide child learners with material that is susceptible to segmentation and further analysis. Peters (1983) also provided many examples from various studies that indicate a developmental sequence that begins with unanalyzed chunks, proceeds through a stage of more or less complete analysis, and concludes with refused but analyzed chunks.

Some children seem to rely especially heavily on the strategy of imitating and analyzing phrases. Heath's (1983) Trackton children were heard, not only imitating phrases, but playing with them, manipulating the parts in various ways. This "repetition with variation" appeared to be modeled in adult speech, because there was a great deal of repetition and paraphrase in everyday speech, in storytelling and in prayers.

In a linguistic environment such as Trackton the use of imitation is much more apparent than in middle-class American families. In middle-class families one seems to find—at least in first-born children—a gradual progression from one-word to two-word to multiword speech. But such an analytic approach does not rule out the possibility that all children eventually use a more gestalt strategy once some words are learned. Nelson (1973) reported that imitation correlated significantly with vocabulary level. This suggests that children are more likely to utilize imitated phrasal units once they are beyond the one- and two-word stage. That is, after children have developed some vocabulary, they are more likely to display superficially complex utterances such as:

I wanna see where the dolly is.
That a big car going over a little bear.
I come where the ball is.

These sentences seem well-analyzed, but may represent the conjunction of imitated unanalyzed chunks. This is what Clark (1974) referred to as "performing without competence."

What Clark, Snow, Moerk, and others are arguing is that all children, at some point or other, use the strategy of imitating unanalyzed chunks and use them in their productive speech. It is clear, however, that there are individual differences in the extent to which children imitate and use unanalyzed chunks productively. Bloom, Hood, and Lightbown (1974) noted that even within an individual child, there was great selectivity in what was imitated. The particular strategy that the child adopts seems to depend on individual cognitive style factors and on the child's early experience in conversational interaction with parents and other members of the immediate family circle.

To summarize, it is not surprising that, because the units of speech are so difficult to discriminate, children tend to rely to some extent on imitated chunks and unanalyzed forms. A number of authors have argued that these unanalyzed forms are gradually analyzed and become an important part of productive language. Such a strategy plays a large role in the speech of some children throughout the early years, and there is increasing evidence that this strategy is used, with considerable individual variation, by all children at the multiword stage.

INDIVIDUAL DIFFERENCES IN SECOND-LANGUAGE LEARNING

Researchers investigating second-language acquisition in children have been greatly impressed by the variation they have observed between individual children. This is true both for studies of children learning two languages simultaneously and for investigations of successive second-language acquisition. In both cases, it is obvious that there is no simple and sovereign path to bilingualism.

The Evidence for Variation

In the discussion in Chapter 4 of simultaneous bilingualism and in Chapter 5 of successive second-language acquisition, we saw that various studies report large differences in the success that children achieve in maintaining their languages in balance and in avoiding interference between languages. In some cases of simultaneous bilingualism, the two languages seem to develop in parallel and unproblematically. In other cases, one language begins to predominate and there are intrusions from the lexical or syntactic system of one language onto the other. It was suggested in Chapter 4 that variation in the degree to which children succeed in simultaneously learning two languages relates to differential opportunities for language use and different conditions of presentation. Only if there are equal opportunities to use both languages and if the conditions of presentation are such that children receive the same quality and quantity of input in both, are the optimal effects likely to occur.

Similarly, research on successive second-language acquisition suggests that children take different paths to learning a second language depending on their first language, their age, and possibly certain learning style tendencies. In Chapter 5 we saw that children are likely to experience more interference between first and second languages when there is syntactic congruity or morphological similarity between the two languages (Wode, 1978; Zobl, 1980). Now I will look at one additional aspect of individual differences in second-language learning—one that relates to the preceding discussion of individual differences in first-language development—that is, the question of differences in learning styles among child second-language learners.

Differences in learning styles. Vihman (1982a) compared three Estonian-English children and concluded that different children take different routes to bilingual competence. She focused mainly on her son, Raivo, who was exposed from birth to Estonian and English. The primary language of the home was Estonian, but Raivo's older sister, Virve, brought home playmates who spoke English and Raivo spent his weekday mornings in an English-speaking daycare center from 6 months on. Raivo's early lexicon was mainly Estonian, though about a quarter of his first 500 words were English. When he first began to combine words, at 20 months, he drew on both languages indiscriminately, so that as many as 34% of these early combinations were mixed. By two years, however, only about 4% of his utterances were mixed.

Vihman described Raivo's morphological development as characterized by a "whole-word" approach. He seemed to have adopted the strategy of avoiding functors not expressed by whole words. Thus in his early speech (around 1:10) Raivo preferred to use postpositions to express location in Estonian rather than use inflectional case markers:

puu peal	for "on the tree"
auto sees	"in the car"
isa 'juurde	"to father"

Some nouns did appear during this period with locative case markers, but these were in all likelihood imitations of expressions or routines that were of relatively high frequency in the language he heard.

Similarly, Raivo's preference for what Vihman called "memory work" as opposed to "system building" was reflected in his preference for irregular over regular forms. In the past tense of verb forms, for example, Raivo's early speech showed mainly irregular forms until about two years and two months, when the regularized versions began to appear. In English he showed a similar pattern, learning irregular verbs first and avoiding the regular forms. When he was about 3-years-old, Raivo adopted a strategy of using *did* to mark the past tense in English:

And they did run away.
Because I did take my clothes off at school.
I didn't be there.
Nicholas did give a key to me and I did put it in my pocket.

In contrast to Raivo, two other Estonian children observed by Vihman did not show the same tendency to avoid inflections. Both children (who had less exposure to English) made productive use of various inflected forms before their second birthdays. As Vihman pointed out, it may be that Raivo avoided inflectional morphology because he was dealing with two languages to a greater extent than was true of the other children. At the point where Raivo began to form multiword utterances his lexicon was mixed and so it may have been difficult for him to systematize the endings he heard in the two languages. To lessen the cognitive load, the child may have resorted to rote memorization in preference to system building.

There is some evidence in the literature on simultaneous bilingualism that bilingual children do avoid system building and hence show a delay in morphological development. For example, Leopold's daughter, Hildegard, was apparently slow in learning the German inflectional markers (Leopold, 1949a) and Murrell's daughter, Sandra, also showed a delay in acquiring English morphological affixes (Murrell, 1966). On the other hand, Burling's son, Stephen, had no problems in acquiring inflectional morphology in Garo (Burling, 1959), although his mastery of English morphology was rather primitive. Other studies (e.g., Imedadze, 1967; Ronjat, 1913) suggest that under certain conditions children experience little morphological delay as a result of bilingual presentation.

One possibility is that the child's approach to solving morphological riddles does not relate to bilingualism per se but to a more general cognitive style. Raivo's whole-word approach to morphology may have been part of a tendency to grasp a whole gestalt, rather than pay attention to details. Like Peters' Minh, Raivo seemed to have taken a global approach to the acquisition of morphology (and phonology, Vihman, 1981). He seemed to use delayed imitation in place of analysis and to prefer prefabricated units to minimal meaning-bearing units.

In contrast to Raivo, his sister Virve proceeded in a remarkably systematic fashion to assimilate new segments and new phonological elements one after the other. In terms of our previous discussion, Virve was an analytic child, whereas Raivo was more gestalt in his approach. Other research in the second-language literature seems to point to a similar dichotomy in learner styles.

In a study of 51 English speakers (including 19 children) learning Dutch naturalistically, Snow and Hoefnagel–Höhle (1979) tested various aspects of language proficiency at three points during the first year in the second-language environment. The tests reflected abilities in pronunciation, auditory discrimination, morphology, syntax, vocabulary, comprehension, fluency, and metalinguistic judgments. A factor analysis of the test results yielded two major factors: control of vocabulary and grammatical skills and control of phonological skills. Although the factor analysis was performed with the data from all 51 subjects, even young children were found to differ on the two factors.

Snow and Hoefnagel–Höhle hypothesized that their findings relate to the research of investigators studying individual differences in first-language development. Conceivably, learners who do well on tests of pronunciation and auditory discrimination are more likely to adopt a wholistic and imitative strategy to language learning and are more likely to do less well on tests of grammatical ability. Snow and Hoefnagel–Höhle cautioned that any such conclusions require a research strategy in which information about both the process of acquisition (the nature of the strategies used by the learner) and the product of acquisition (what the learner knows at any one time) are available.

At this point, attempts to work out a typology of second-language learning styles are necessarily tentative. Vihman (1982a) made the interesting point that Raivo's use of early vocabulary would classify him as a referential child in Nelson's sense, whereas Virve was somewhat more expressive than referential. Because Raivo approached language more wholistically and Virve more analytically, it may be misleading to infer a correspondence between Peters' analytic and gestalt styles and Nelson's referential and expressive speech. As Vihman (1982a) pointed out, a great deal more data is needed before we can begin to resolve the present constellation of partially coherent characterizations of styles and strategies into a single objectively definable set of labels.

Variation within developmental stages.   A somewhat different approach to the investigation of individual differences in child second-language learning has been taken by a number of European investigators. In particular, Meisel and his associates (Clahsen, 1980; Meisel, 1980; Meisel, Clahsen, & Pienemann, 1979; Peinemann, 1980) have argued that there are different types of learners, with different communicative needs and motivations, who employ different strategies and develop language in different ways. Meisel and his colleagues concluded from their research on the acquisition of German by immigrant workers and their children that there is no single path to second-language acquisition. They advocated a multidimensional model in which groups of learners form different paths to the target language.

In this model, the learner's position relative to the target language is defined by two dimensions: the learner's *developmental stage* and the learner's *sociopsychological orientation* (Table 6.3). The developmental stage can be defined in terms of linguistic criteria, but within these stages learners can differ because of their sociopsychological orientation. Specifically, Meisel (1980) proposed that learners vary along a sociopsychological continuum that ranges from a segregative to an integrative orientation, depending on how favorably they are disposed toward speakers of the target language.

In Table 6.3 individuals 1 and 4 are at the same developmental stage (as defined in terms of the grammatical complexity of their speech), and both are at a higher developmental stage than individual 2 and at a lower stage than Individual 3. Individual 1, however, is located in Group A—the group with the most favorable (integrative) orientation to the target group. Individual 4, on the other hand, is located in Group C—the group with the least favorable (segregative) orientation to the target group. Learners in Group C are thought to be most "fossilized." That is, they are less likely because of their attitudes and motivation to advance toward the target norms. Learners in Group A are least fossilized and, in comparison, have the best chance to learn the target language well.

According to Meisel (1980) most, if not all, second-language learners employ two strategies of simplification: restrictive simplification and elaborative simplification. Restrictive simplification involves the omission of elements and morphology, making the structure of the language more

TABLE 6.3
A Multidimensional Model of Second Language Acquisition

Developmental Stage	Orientation		
	Integrative		Segregative
	Group A	Group B	Group C
IV			Individual 3
III	Individual 1		Individual 4
II		Individual 2	
I			

Based on Meisel, Clahsen, & Pienemann, 1979.

easy for the second-language learner to handle. Elaborative simplification occurs at a later stage and involves the formulation of hypotheses about the rules that are used in the target language, with subsequent overgeneralization of these hypothesized rules. Learners with segregative orientation (Group C) are more likely to retain restrictive simplification longer, whereas learners with integrative orientation (Group A) employ elaborative simplification more.

Although most of the research by Meisel and his associates has involved adult second-language learners, there has been some work on children learning a second language in an untutored situation. Pienemann (1980) studied the acquisition of German by three 8-year-old Italian girls and found evidence for uniform acquisitional stages in the development of syntax in affirmative sentences. Within stages, however, there was variation. For example, at the point where the children were beginning to link words into longer utterances, they showed the same sequence of occurrence of verb forms. They differed in *how* their language developed. One child, Luigina, was not concerned with conforming to the target language and chose the quickest and easiest way to express herself; the second, Concetta, tended to avoid all deviations from target norms; and the third, Eva, was somewhere in between, trying to communicate but not without regard to the demands of the target language system.

Pienemann saw these differences as evidence for the multidimensional model. Luigina's language was marked by restrictive simplifications. She lived in cultural separation from the German community and was not making much progress toward target language norms. Concetta, in contrast, was growing up in a social climate where there was a great deal of contact with the German community. She was much more motivated toward conformity with the target language norms and her language development was marked by a greater use of elaborative simplifications that served to bring her language closer to the target.

Another German researcher, Wode (1981), has taken a slightly different approach to the question of variation in a detailed analysis of the acquisition of English by his four German children during a six month visit to America. Like Meisel and his co-workers, Wode found evidence for ordered developmental sequences, both in the acquisition of negative constructions and in phonology. Within developmental sequences there were variations in structural types. Not all children employed the same structural types and even when two children had the same alternative structures they tended to favor different ones in their actual use. For example, Wode's son, Lars, showed different morphological preferences than his daughter, Inga. Lars' speech showed occasional instances of *not* + verb, whereas this was rare in Inga's speech. On the other hand, there were no instances of Lars using *no* + verb, though this structure was common in Inga's early negative constructions.

While acknowledging that not enough is known about the types and ranges of individual variation in second-language learning, Wode proposed that there exist universal developmental principles or strategies that set limits to the amount of variation to be found in language learning. One such principle is "Free forms are acquired before bound forms." This principle predicts that a free form, such as *no* would be acquired before a bound form, such as *-n't*. Thus utterances such as *no drink* or *no celery* are predicted to occur before utterances such as *don't* or *can't*. This does not rule out the possibility of some variation, in that other free form negatives besides *no* could appear as, for example, Lars' *not*. It is Wode's view that the direction of research should be toward identifying acquisitional regularities and the developmental principles that underlie them so that the limits of individual variation can be defined. While structural variation among individual learners was quite extensive in his data, Wode remained convinced that the range of individual variation is limited relative to the formal properties involved in the target structure.

In short, European work on individual differences in child second-language learners has been concerned with variation within regular developmental sequences. Researchers have been impressed with the regularity in second-language acquisition but have noted that there is variability within the developmental sequence. Wode has been less willing to speculate on the source of this variation than Meisel and his colleagues, who have developed a sociopsychological model that predicts the extent to which different simplification strategies will be used by different groups of learners. The emphasis on groups of learners contrasts with American research, which has been concerned with distinguishing dichotomous language-learning styles that form a continuum characterizing individual learners.

Formulaic Speech

As we saw earlier in this chapter a number of authors have argued that because the units of speech are so difficult to discriminate, the utterances of first-language learners are likely to contain imitated chunks and unanalyzed forms. The extent to which children rely on such pre-packaged forms varies considerably, depending to a large degree on the input to which the child is exposed and, conceivably, on stylistic differences in the way individual children approach language. Some children rely extensively on imitated chunks and unanalyzed speech, and, as we have seen, it may be that this strategy is used by most first-language learners when they begin to form multiword utterances.

There is now convincing evidence that untutored child second-language learners make considerable use of unanalyzed or formulaic speech—though here again there are probably individual differences. In fact, the use of formulas has been called the hallmark of child second-language learning (Vihman, 1982b), and research on formulaic speech in second-language learning—especially that of Wong Fillmore (1976)—has stimulated much of the recent work on the role of imitation and unanalyzed chunks in first-language learning.

The use of formulas in child second-language learners. As Vihman (1982b) pointed out, the first study to report the use of formulaic speech in child second-language learners was that of Kenyeres (1938), who noted that her Hungarian-speaking daughter's early French contained utterances that were strikingly formulaic. For example, the child attempted to make up with her mother after a quarrel by saying, *Maman, s'il vous plaît, qu'est-ce que c'est, voulez-vous?* that is, 'Mother, please, what is it, would you like?' Another memorized string was *Où sont les mamans?* for 'Where are the mothers,' which was probably based on a sentence learned at school, *Où sont les ciseaux?* for 'Where are the scissors?' We saw in Chapter 5 that Kenyeres was of the opinion that her daughter deliberately memorized words and phrases, consciously analyzing the language to determine the underlying rules.

Studies of formulaic speech in other child second-language learners, however, suggest that the use of such expressions is a spontaneous strategy that children often employ for communicative purposes. Huang (1970, cited in Huang & Hatch, 1978) was one of the first recent researchers to note the widespread use of formulaic speech in succesive second-language acquisition. His subject, a 5-year-old Chinese boy, Paul, was capable of imitating amazingly complex sentences in English almost from the time he started learning the language. Among the first things the child said in English was *Get out of here,* an expression he heard at play-school and which he muttered to himself, without being able to explain its meaning. A day later, when he was bothered by another child, he said, *Get out of here,* but when asked by Huang what these words meant separately, he said he did not know. It seems that they functioned as an unanalyzed unit, were stored in memory as a global unit, and were used in what the child considered an appropriate situation.

Among Paul's early expressions were the following:

Get out of here.
It's time to eat and drink.
Let's go.
Don't do that.
Don't touch.
It's time to go home.
You shut up.

It seems clear that the child was repeating utterances that appeared with great frequency in the teacher and peer language to which he was exposed, and that he used these utterances without fully understanding what they meant. Initially, Paul used his unanalyzed units in highly constrained situational contexts. For example, he learned the expression, *I'm finished* when painting and used it only in this context for some time. Ultimately, he was capable of using the expression appropriately in many different situations.

Paul was so talented in imitating the speech he heard and in using it in appropriate contexts, that it appeared that he could understand everything that was said to him and that he could use English productively. There was a limit, however, to how far rote imitation could take him, and in time Paul adopted a new form of speech, which involved two-word utterances with a distinct pause between them. This was seen to be the beginning of the development of a differentiated syntactic system that depended on both imitation and rule formation (Huang & Hatch, 1978).

In his study of a 5-year-old Japanese girl learning English, Hakuta (1974b, 1976) noted that his subject was able to construct *where-* questions from the first sample taken:

Where's purple?
Where is potato?

She also formed *how-* questions of the following sort:

How do you make it bread?
How do you play this?
How do you put it on?

Hakuta argued that in many such instances the child was relying on what he called a prefabricated pattern.

Hakuta (1974b) analyzed three such patterns, those using the copula, the string *do you* in questions, and the string *how to* in embedded *how-* questions. His analysis revealed that although the child's utterances were well-formed on the surface, they were in fact memorized without internal analysis. For example, *do you* functioned as a question marker and appeared to indicate productive mastery of the structure, except that errors such as

What do you do it, this froggie?
What do you doing, this boy?

indicated that the child had not mastered the form when it involved a third person subject. Hakuta argued that prefabricated patterns enabled learners to express functions that they are as yet not able to construct from their internal, rule-governed linguistic system. As the learner's system of linguistic rules develops over time, the externally consistent prefabricated patterns become assimilated into the internal system.

The analysis of formulas. The most detailed treatment of the use of prefabricated or formulaic expressions is Lily Wong Fillmore's dissertation (1976), based on a study of five Spanish-speaking children ages five to seven, acquiring English in a bilingual school situation, in which both Spanish and English were used as the media of instruction. Second-language acquisition was naturalistic in the sense that the children received no explicit instruction in English. The main source of data in the study consisted of weekly tape recordings and observations of each child playing with a monolingual (in one case, bilingual) friend.

Wong Fillmore argued that there were three (sometimes overlapping) stages in the second-language acquisition process. Each stage represented a different primary concern of the language learner. The first concern of the learner was to establish social relationships with speakers of the second language. At this point exchanges with other children were mainly oriented toward interaction rather than toward information. There was heavy reliance on formulas to achieve interactional goals in the play situation that Wong Fillmore observed. The children used such expressions as

Lookit
Wait a minute
Shaddup your mouth
Whose turn is it?

as fixed formulas appropriate to specific contexts. There was no evidence, however, that the children had analyzed these formulas or understood the words as separate units. The expressions seemed to be learned through non-verbal cues and by associating certain critical sound patterns with specific situations.

In the second stage the child's concern was to communicate messages. At this point the children began to create more novel utterances and combined parts of formulas with newly acquired lexical utterances. There was a tendency in some cases to mix languages—to pull out lexical items from either language—to get the message across. The children seemed more interested in getting their point across than at getting it correct. It is at this stage that formulas began to be analyzed and separate elements began to be freed from the intact expression.

In the third stage the child's concern was to achieve "native-like" competence. The children seemed to be working on the finer details at this point, deriving from the analysis of formulas already in their repertory grammatical rules that form the basis for productive speech. That is, once the children discovered that constituents of formulaic expressions were interchangeable and could be freed from the original pattern, they had at their disposal an abstract structure consisting of a pattern or rule by which the construction of a novel utterance became possible.

Wong Fillmore's analysis is reminiscent of Ruth Clark's. As we saw earlier in this chapter, Clark argued that her son, Adam, acquired his first language by relying on incompletely analyzed units that were retained intact for several weeks without other lexical items being substituted and that only gradually were "unpacked" and used as the basis for more productive speech. The value of Wong Fillmore's analysis is that, with a richer data base, she was able to go into more detail in demonstrating how children unpack formulaic speech.

Wong Fillmore argued that, in order to use language in social situations, second-language learners need some special *social strategies* directed at two major issues: how to get along for a while without a common language, and how to get your friends to want to help you learn their language. In addition, second-language learners need some special *cognitive strategies* directed at the major cognitive tasks confronting the language learner: how to understand an unintelligible language, how to gain entry into the language, and how to figure out how the pieces fit together. Wong Fillmore specified three social strategies and five cognitive strategies (Table 6.4). The strategies were phrased as maxims and were thought to be interwoven, because it was not possible to separate them totally.

The first social strategy Wong Fillmore saw to be the one that gets the learner into a position to learn the language:

Social Strategy I:
Join a group and act as if you understand what is going on, even if you don't.

Unless children can succeed with this strategy, they are unlikely to receive the kind of input they need to become successful second-language learners. Wong Fillmore made the point that learners must somehow give the impression they are worth talking to before speakers will allow them to join the group. This means that they have to behave as if they understand, even though at the early stages of language acquisition, they in fact understand little.

The effect of following this strategy is that the native speakers include the learners in their conversations. Wong Fillmore pointed out that, although the native speakers believed that the learners could understand, they realized that this understanding was limited. They adjusted their speech ac-

TABLE 6.4
The Social and Cognitive Strategies of Second-Language Learners

Social Strategies	Cognitive Strategies
I. Join a group and act as if you understand what's going on, even if you don't.	
	I. Assume that what people are saying is directly relevant to the situation at hand, or to what they or you are experiencing. METASTRATEGY: Guess!
II. Give the impression—with a few well-chosen words—that you can speak the language.	II. Get some expressions you understand, and start talking.
	III. Look for recurring parts in the formulas you know.
III. Count on your friends for help.	IV. Make the most of what you've got.
	V. Work on the big things first; save the details for later.

Based on Wong Fillmore (1976).

cordingly, and thereby provided the learners with the kind of input that they needed to make an entry into the language.

Associated with the first social strategy was a cognitive strategy:

Cognitive Strategy I:
Assume that what people are saying is directly relevant to the situation at hand, or to what they or you are experiencing. METASTRATEGY: Guess!

As Wong Fillmore put it, the first social strategy constitutes the learner's motivation for making the effort to figure out what is being said; its related cognitive strategy constitutes the plan that enables the learners to begin comprehending the language around them. To carry out this strategy the child needs to rely on situational cues and to link up utterances with specific situations. Although this is not always easy to do, there are many speech routines that lead to the formation of situation-utterance associations. Wong Fillmore gives the following examples of speech routines that are situationally determined and readily interpretable:

Who's buying lunch in the cafeteria today?
It's time to clean up now.
Let's see which table can sit up the straightest.
Let's line up for recess.

By watching what other children are doing, the learner can interpret with a fair degree of accuracy what is being said.

The next social strategy relates to what the second-language learner has to do once social contact has been established:

Social Strategy II:
Give the impression—with a few well-chosen words—that you can speak the language.

It is the second-language learner's responsibility to give evidence of being able to speak well. It is not enough for learners to show that they can understand the language; they have to give the impression that they can use it, so that native speakers will keep trying to communicate with them.

The way this is done is through the second cognitive strategy:

Cognitive Strategy II:
Get some expressions you understand, and start talking.

This is where formulaic speech comes in. The learner is not in a position to use the target language productively at this point. Instead, the learner must rely on unanalyzed wholes or formulas to give the impression of being able to speak the language. Wong Fillmore found a striking similarity among the five students she studied in the acquisition and use of formulaic expressions. In fact, her subjects were so good at creating the impression that they could speak the language, that native-speaking children often showed annoyance at the learners when they did not understand or could not speak.

Table 6.5 lists some categories of formulas observed in the early speech of Wong Fillmore's subjects. The formulas learned tended to be the most useful to the child. They helped the child to appear to know what was going on, to participate in games, and to request information or clarification from others. As Wong Fillmore pointed out, this kind of language was extremely important because it permitted the learners to continue to participate in activities that provided contexts for learning new material. Not only did the children make guesses as to the conditions under which particular utterances could appropriately be uttered, but they also were able to test their conclusions by using these formulas and receiving feedback that told them whether their guesses were right or wrong.

The central thesis of Wong Fillmore's research is that the strategy of acquiring formulaic speech is central to second-language learning in children.

TABLE 6.5
Formulaic Speech in Second-Language Learning
Children: Some Categories and Examples
(Based on Wong Fillmore, 1976)

Category	Examples
Attention Callers	Oh teacher
	Hey stupid
Name Exchanges	What's your name?
	I'm ...
Greetings and Leave Takings	I see you
	I gotta go
Politeness Routines	I'm sorry
	Thanks
Language Management	I don't understand you
	I don't speak English
Conversation Management	You know what?
	What is it mean?
	You shaddup
Comments and Exclamations	Man
	Oh crazy
	All right you guys
Questions	Who has the ...?
	Can I have one?
Response to Questions	I don't know
	I don't care
Commands and Attention Callers	Hey look
	Let me see
	Knock it off
Play Management	Me first
	My turn
Wannas and Wannits	I wanna get these
	I don't wanna do nothing
Miscellaneous	Get the Anacin
	Time to clean up

She argued that it was this step—acquiring formulas and using them in speech—that puts the learner in a position to perform the analysis that is prerequisite to acquisition. Formulas constituted the linguistic material on which a large part of the children's analytic activities were carried out. Because the formulas were so situationally bound, they could be learned without the child having to understand anything of their internal structures. Once in the repertory, they could be compared (without any conscious effort on the child's part) with other utterances in the repertory and with the speech of native speakers.

The next step involved another cognitive strategy:

Cognitive Strategy III:
Look for recurring parts in the formulas you know.

The analysis of language that Wong Fillmore described began when the child noticed (at some level): (1) *how* parts of formulaic expressions used by others vary in accordance with changes in the speech situations in which they occurred: and (2) *which* parts of these expressions are like parts of other utterances. Wong Fillmore gave the example of one of her subjects, Nora, who had in her speech repertory two related formulas:

> I wanna play wi' dese
and I don' wanna do dese.

Perhaps because of the similarity of these expressions she was able to discover that the constituents following *wanna* were interchangeable, so that she could say

> I don' wanna play wi' dese
and I wanna do dese.

What she was doing, in essence, was discovering that formulas could serve as formulaic frames with analyzed slots:

> I wanna X/X = VP
and I don' wanna X/X = VP.

Wong Fillmore argued that by figuring out which parts of the formula in their speech repertories could be varied, the children were able to free recurring parts from the original intact formula. The formulas then served as formulaic frames with abstract slots representing constituent types. These constituent types could be derived from other freed formulas or from newly learned lexical items. Parts of formulas that had been freed could function in other constructions either as formulaic units or as wholly analyzed items. The last stage in the process occurred when all of the constituents of the formula have been freed from the original construction, and the learner is left with an abstract structure consisting of a pattern or rule by which like utterances can be constructed.

To clarify this process, let us look at one of Wong Fillmore's examples—in this case, Nora's freeing of the word *how* from her original formula, *How do you do dese.* The developmental course of this expression went through at least three stages:

Stage 1: Fixed Frame

How do you do dese?

Stage 2a: Adding Elements

How do you do dese flower power?
                              little tortillas?
                              in English?

Stage 2b: Adding "Did"

How did you lost it?
              make it?

Stage 3a: Freeing "You"

How do cut it?
How do make it?
How did dese work?

Stage 3b: Freeing "How"

Because when I call him, how I put the number?
How you make it?
How will take off past?

The examples in Stages 2a and 2b and in Stages 3a and 3b occurred in the same time period, hence at least chronologically, these are not regarded as separate developmental stages.

Note that the sentences in 3b are not more grammatical than those in Stage 1, yet, Wong Fillmore's analysis showed that Nora had made great strides. In Stages 2a and 2b the formulaic frame was acquired and provided the child with the means to gain information of various sorts. In the Stages 3a and 3b the child freed up the question word from its formulaic use completely and used it productively in accord with her present tactics for forming questions. Those tactics were quite rudimentary, but certainly demonstrated an advance over reliance on imitated formulas.

We come now to the fourth cognitive strategy:

Cognitive Strategy IV:
Make the most of what you've got.

The evidence that the children used this strategy comes from overgeneralizations, such as using *sangwish* to refer to food in general or *Wha' happen*? and *Wha'sa matter*? to serve for all questions. Such overextensions of individual words or formulas helped the child seem fluent in the early stages, even though the utterances may have been semantically empty.

A further example of how the learners tried to make the most of what they had comes from Nora's use of the word *anyway* in a great many sentences, such as

Nora: Anyway I making a fitching.
Observer: A what?
Nora: Anyway a fitching.

Another child: What is that anyway?
Nora: Anyway a flower. That what is that anyway.

Another child, Alej, had a similarly idiosyncratic pattern:

C'mon me you house.   (I'll come to your house)
C'mon me the shoe.   (Won't you give me the shoes?)
What time you my house? (What time are you coming to my house?)

Wong Fillmore argued that what Alej had done was to devise a pattern with a pronoun representing either a subject or indirect object preceded by a predicate that was generally a formulaic utterance of some sort or other. This rather awkward pattern helped the child to get by in English before he actually knew very much about the language.

This relates to the final cognitive strategy:

Cognitive Strategy V:
 Work on big things first; save the details for later.

Obviously, learning a language is a challenging task and the learner cannot deal with everything at once. None of the children Wong Fillmore studied had mastered the details by the end of the year. They had, through their use of formulas, learned some of the big things, but the details of grammar and grammatical relations eluded them. Thus, Nora's *how* questions were still grammatically ill-formed at Stage 3—she had not begun to master the rules for the auxiliary *do*. But Nora had begun to grasp the structural features of the language and it was just a question of time before she would sort out the details.

The final strategy is a social one:

Social Strategy III:
 Count on your friends for help.

Here Wong Fillmore made two points. First, because the learners were successful in creating the impression that they understood what was said and could actually say something themselves, their native-speaking friends talked and interacted with them in ways that guaranteed further learning. They used non-verbal cues, they simplified their speech, and—most important—they included the learners in their activities. Second, their friends provided needed encouragement for the second-language learners in the study. They expected the learners to communicate with them and they did not give up on them. They helped by providing contextual information—verbal and non-verbal—and they restricted their language to the here and now. The effect of this support was that the learners were able to get the input they needed to acquire the language.

Formulas and the language-learning process. From the preceding discussion it can be seen that it was Wong Fillmore's (1976) view that formulaic speech plays a critical role in the second-language learning process. As she put it:

> [Formulas] are indeed among the first things learned in the new language, and it is through the analyses of these units that the learner eventually figures out the form and meaning of the component parts. What the learner derives from the analysis of formulas already in his own speech repertory are grammatical rules, and these rules, which form the bases for productive speech, gradually free him from his early dependence on formulaic speech (p. 300).

From this perspective formulas constitute the linguistic material on which the children's analytic activities are carried out and from which rules are derived.

The early speech of Wong Fillmore's subjects was primarily formulaic in nature. Using only the clearest cases in her calculations, she found that from 52% to 100% of the utterances of the children in the early stages were formulaic, to a low of more than 37% in the most advanced learner at the end of the year. In fact, two children were almost completely dependent on formulas even at the end of the year.

Some authors, principally Krashen and Scarcella (1978), have argued that the kind of second-language learning that Wong Fillmore described was atypical. These authors maintained that in Wong Fillmore's study the children's need to communicate before they had achieved competence and the predictable nature of the daily routines of the school environment led to a heavy reliance on formulaic speech. Krashen and Scarcella (1978) asked whether this is the way second languages are generally acquired, and concluded it was not, because

Clearly, the sort of early output demands Wong Fillmore's subjects had imposed on them, and the routinized predictable input are not present in most language acquisition situations (p. 295).

Perhaps Krashen and Scarcella were thinking primarily of adult second-language learning, but I believe that it can be argued that for children in naturalistic, untutored situations, the kind of situation that Wong Fillmore's children found themselves in is by no means atypical. Much successive second-language acquisition in childhood occurs in play situations with other children where the input is routine and repetitive and where there are definite demands on the child learner to talk. Children's motivation to speak is extremely high in such situations, otherwise they are kept out of the interaction—something most children will do anything to avoid, even speak a new language.

Furthermore, there is evidence that formulaic speech can occur in situations other than those Krashen and Scarcella described as leading to formulaic speech. Vihman (Vihman & McLaughlin, 1982) observed the heavy use of formulaic speech by her daughter, Virve, especially in the early stages, as she learned her second language, English, from one year, nine months on. In Estonian she had made no use of unit-phrases or formulas, but by this time her experience in combining words had apparently been sufficient to lead her to look for and retain longer chunks in English. What is important in the present context is that the child used formulaic speech even though she was not subject to the pressure of "peer and school situations that demand linguistic interaction before competence is attained the 'slow way' " (Krashen & Scarcella, 1978, p. 292). In fact, Virve rather rarely spoke at all to her peers or even, at first, to English-speaking adults. A shy child, she reserved her conversation for the home environment, where for a brief period shortly after her second birthday she began to make considerable use of English in addressing her parents, despite their efforts to encourage her to use only Estonian. Remarks such as *That's good* and *That's yours* were used at home and had all the characteristics of formulaic speech. As Vihman noted, they could not be said to have been produced under pressure to communicate, because her Estonian was more than adequate to that task in that context.

In short, it seems that the use of formulas in second-language learning can result from situational demands as well as from stylistic preferences of the child. Be that as it may, Krashen and Scarcella were not convinced that this was the normal route to second-language learning. In fact, they maintained that reliance on formulaic speech was fundamentally different from "creative language." Although creative language was not defined by these authors, it presumably refers to the capacity of human beings to produce and understand sentences they never heard before:

To say that humans are creative with respect to language means that they do not simply imitate what they hear. In fact, they often use sentences they have never heard before. This central aspect of language acquisition is believed to be rooted in innate and universal structural properties of the mind (Dulay, Burt, & Krashen, 1982, p. 11).

Can the use of formulas be creative in this sense? Wong Fillmore, Ruth Clark, and others would answer this question affirmatively. According to these authors, larger units of speech are broken down into smaller units, unpacked and analyzed, in such a way that parts of formulas are freed to recombine with parts from other formulas or new lexical items in a productive fashion. Rules are learned through the analysis of formulas and serve as the basis for creative language.

Krashen and Scarcella (1978) argued that no such interactive process is possible:

> The available evidence indicates that routines and patterns are essentially and fundamentally different from creative language . . . that the creative construction process is independent of routines and patterns (p. 298).

Krashen and Scarcella acknowledged that in some instances prefabricated routines could serve as intake for the creative construction process, but regarded such intake as insufficient for successful language acquisition. In their view formulaic speech is a dead end as far as creative language is concerned.

Wong Fillmore, on the other hand, maintained that formulas and formulaic frames evolved directly into creative language and were, in her subjects, necessary ingredients of the creative process. She saw formulaic speech as leading to and interacting with the acquisition of creative language. Krashen and Scarcella did not deny the validity of Wong Fillmore's analysis, but they regarded the kind of learning that occurred in her subjects as atypical. As we have seen, however, the situation in which the children in Wong Fillmore's study found themselves is by no means unusual for young second-language learners. Her research is strong evidence for a language-learning process that involves a dynamic interplay between formulaic speech and the emergent rule system. Krashen and Scarcella seem to have minimized the evidence from Wong Fillmore's research because they wanted to make a (valid) pedagogical point about *adult* language learning (that excessive reliance on formulaic "pattern drills" is counterproductive).

There is another argument against Krashen and Scarcella's position. A number of authors have noted that all speech involves the interplay of formulaic expressions and creative language. This point was made by Vihman in her discussion (1982b) of the role of formulas in her daughter's second-language acquisition. On the basis of her data and data from other research, she argued that it is likely that both unanalyzed units and creative construction play a role in sentence formation in first- and second-language acquisition and use. She quoted Goldman–Eisler (1968):

> In the flow of normal speech voluntary and automatic activities are closely interlaced, symbolic behaviour alternates with habitual verbalization, the construction of propositions with emotional expression and with the use of ready-made phrases, choice in fitting words to meaning takes turns with submission to the routine course and to constraints of learned sequences. . . . Normal spontaneous speech might be viewed as a highly integrated blend of processes at both levels where results of practice alternate with spontaneous creation (p. 9).

If this is true, if adult speech typically alternates between creative construction and the use of ready-made formulas, then the use of formulas by children learning a second language is not so different from what must occur in first-language learning and in ordinary language use.

Sources of Individual Variation

When we consider how it is that children learn second languages, it becomes obvious that many factors have to be taken into consideration. There is the question of the age of the child, the conditions of presentation, the opportunities for language use, the social context, the languages to be learned, the personality and learning style of the child. All of these variables contribute to individual variation in child second-language learning. At the risk of simplifying the complexity involved, I would like to conclude this chapter by discussing briefly three sources of individual variation: learning style variables, personality variables, and sociopsychological factors.

Learning style variables.   We have seen that the descriptors of the learning style used to characterize first-language learners have been carried over to second-language learners as well. Krashen and Scarcella thought that Wong Fillmore's subjects used a "gestalt" route to language learning because of the complexity of the input and the conversational demands that were imposed on them. Yet as we have seen, other children can be typified as gestalt in their orientation, even though the input to them is simplified and there are few conversational demands (Vihman, 1982a).

The case of Virve Vihman is especially interesting in this connection because the child seemed to have employed one style in learning her first language, Estonian, and another style in learning her second language, English. Her Estonian was learned in a systematic fashion, with new segments and new phonological elements assimilated one after another (Vihman & McLaughlin, 1982). Virve's English, on the other hand, was learned in a gestalt fashion, with heavy reliance on formulaic speech.

One possibility is that certain languages predispose children to one approach or the other—a heavily inflected language, such as Estonian, predisposing the child to an analytic approach. The problem with this interpretation is that Virve's brother, Raivo, learned his Estonian in a global manner, preferring to approach the language through prefabricated units rather than through systematic analysis of morphological elements. Furthermore, Stephen Burling (Burling, 1959) learned Garo—a language with a very complex morphological system—in what appears to have been a gestalt manner:

> At one year and seven months, I began to notice a few utterances which, from an adult point of view, consisted of more than one morpheme . . . It seemed likely that all were learned as entire phrases . . . [He] apparently always used the construction first in certain specific examples which he learned as a whole and by rote (pp. 56, 59).

Another possibility is that older children tend to adopt a gestalt strategy because they are more capable of stringing words together than are younger children. As we have seen, once children's vocabularies have expanded somewhat they are more likely to use imitated phrasal units in their first language development. It may be that older children, with their superior memory capabilities and vocabulary, are developmentally predisposed to a gestalt approach. It should be noted, however, that some young children, like Minh and Raivo Vihman, also adopted a gestalt strategy. Nor have all older children learning a second language been reported to have employed a gestalt approach.

There are also considerable neurological differences between individuals that in all likelihood influence how languages are learned (Peters, 1983), but aside from the lack of exact knowledge about how neurological differences affect learning styles, the evidence that children, like Virve Vihman, can switch styles suggests that neurological factors alone do not in themselves determine the strategies learners use. Neurological factors may influence learning style preferences, but these preferences most likely interact with a number of other variables, including cognitive and developmental variables, situational factors, and personality variables.

Personality variables.   There has been a great deal of research on the relationship between personality variables and language learning in adult second-language learners (H. D. Brown, 1980b). It has proven rather difficult, however, to define the characteristics of "the good language learner." There are considerable methodological problems with research in this area (Oller, 1981) and the assessment technology for measuring personality variables is still quite primitive (McLaughlin, 1980). Nonetheless, many researchers remain convinced that some people are better than others at learning a second language and that this difference relates to personality factors.

There has been relatively little research on the relationship between personality and language learning in young children. Wong Fillmore (1976) argued that the individual differences she observed in the five children she studied had to do with the nature of the task, the sets of social and cognitive strategies they needed to apply in dealing with it, and certain personal characteristics. Although this research did not involve measuring personality variables, Wong Fillmore's observations suggested that among the critical factors were language habits, motivations, social needs, and habitual approaches to problem solving.

In Wong Fillmore's study, one child, Nora, was quite remarkable in her success as a language learner. She was gregarious and outgoing, highly motivated to associate with English-speaking children, whom she sought out to a much greater extent than any of the other children in the study. She was constantly engaged in dramatic play activities that involved the taking of roles and working out of relationships. She and her friends pretended to be teachers and students, fathers and mothers, boyfriends and girlfriends. They thought up problems and situations that needed to be argued over and resolved. Through these activities Nora received the input she needed and the opportunity to practice her new language skills.

Like Nora, one other child, Ana, was outgoing and communicative in her approach to language learning. Ana, however, was less concerned with communicating with her peers and more concerned with communicating with adults. Because the adults—teacher and aides—that Ana interacted with had to deal with many children and could not be constantly interacting with her, the input she received was more limited than the input Nora received. This may have been one reason why Ana's progress was slower than Nora's.

The three boys in the study, Juan, Alej, and Jesus, were more inhibited about using the new language than Nora and Ana were. Their second-language learning progressed slowly and in a manner that reflected their personality dispositions. Jesus was stubborn, slow to change his mind. This rigidity expressed itself in his language development: he learned formulas, but was slow in experimenting with them and in finding structural patterns and possibilities. Alej seemed to lack confidence in his language learning abilities: he tended to mumble what he had to say as if he were embarrassed or not sure of himself. Juan was more confident, but very cautious: he tended to work on one kind of construction at a time, and seldom used anything until he was quite certain that he was correct.

In general, the boys in Wong Fillmore's sample tended to limit themselves almost exclusively to talk that had to do with the activities they were involved in at the moment. Even in Spanish, the boys tended not to engage in conversation as such. Their language was mainly short responses, comments, and sound effects that carried little informational weight. This contrasted dramatically to Nora, who experimented and played with her new language in a totally uninhibited manner. These observations led Wong Fillmore to conclude that personality factors—in interaction with the nature of the task and the application of required strategies—play a crucial role in determining the rate of second-language learning.

In one of the few studies dealing with personality factors in child second-language learners, Strong (1982) examined the relationship between personality variables and second-language learning in kindergarten children. The 13 children in this study were native speakers of Spanish, learning English as a second language in an untutored situation. They were followed over the course of a school year, their behavior was observed, their friendship patterns examined, and samples were taken of English language skills.

Strong found that three variables based on long-term behavioral observations showed significant relationships with communicative language skills. These were talkativeness and responsiveness in Spanish and gregariousness in both languages. Other personality variables based on questionnaire data (assertiveness, extraversion, and social competence) and on sociometric information (popularity) were not related to language learning, although it was found that successful language learners, once they had achieved a certain level of competence, were rated as more popular on sociometric indices.

In Strong's study, actual contact with English speakers correlated only modestly with communicative language skills in English. None of the children he studied seemed to be highly motivated to interact or identify with Anglo children in the way Nora was. Observations of behavior at recess and the sociometric data showed that the target children were more oriented toward other Spanish-speaking children than toward monolingual English children. Because the faster learners in his study did not interact more with native speakers, Strong concluded that they simply made better use of what English input they received than did the poorer learners. In this research it was not contact with English speakers specifically as much as a propensity to initiate and respond to verbal intercourse with anyone and everyone that was most likely to lead to speedy acquisition of English.

An obvious problem with research on personality factors in child second-language learning is that one has to take into account the interaction between personality factors and a number of other variables, such as situational context, cultural background, learner styles, and the language demands placed on the child. No one study can explore all of these parameters. Each study requires the caveat that the results obtained applied to this case, but in other situations, with older or younger children, with children from another cultural background, with speakers of other languages, the relationship between specific personality variables (such as gregariousness and outgoingness) and language learning may be different.

Sociopsychological factors. We saw earlier in this chapter that Meisel and his associates have argued that learners vary along a sociopsychological continuum that ranges from segregative to integrative orientation, depending on how favorably they are disposed to speakers of the target language. It was assumed that learners with a strong integrative orientation are more motivated to learn the language and in fact use different strategies of "simplification," elaborating the language more and testing out hypotheses about the language to a greater extent than do learners who have a segregative orientation.

This theoretical perspective works well in explaining the difference between Nora and the other children in Wong Fillmore's study. Nora, as we have seen, was strongly motivated to be associated with the English-speaking children and she sought them out for play to a much greater extent than any other children in the study did. In each of the contexts Wong Fillmore observed—in the cafeteria, on the playground, in the classroom—Nora was with English-monolingual children. Because half the children in the kindergarten class were Spanish-speakers or bilingual, this was more than a coincidence and testifies to Nora's strong desire to identify with English speakers. By the end of the year Nora considered herself an English not a Spanish speaker.

In Strong's study none of the children seemed to have had the intense integrative motivation that Wong Fillmore observed in Nora. These children preferred to play with Spanish-speaking children and none of them went out of their way to interact with monolingual English speakers. This may explain why amount of contact with English speakers did not predict degree of second-language learning in his study, because the children were relatively homogeneous in this regard.

Strong's research indicates that sociopsychological orientation may be relatively equivalent within members of a group and therefore may not be predictive of differences between members of the group. Between groups, however, and within some groups, it is likely that there will be differences in sociopsychological orientation that will predict differences in language learning. The children of guest workers in Europe or of migrant workers in the United States have little incentive to learn the language of the host country if they do not need to interact with native-speaking children in these countries and know that they are returning to their own country. Children of immigrants, on the other hand, are likely to be more highly motivated to learn the language of their new country, especially when they must interact with monolingual speakers.

Once again, however, it is important to note that sociopsychological factors are only one component of the multiple regression equation that predicts individual differences in second-language learning. At this point we do not know how much of the variance is predicted by this component and how much by other components, such as learning styles, personality, situational factors, age of the learner, language factors, and the like. Part of the problem is the inadequacy of our measurement instruments and part is simply due to the unpredictability of human behavior.

In conclusion, we have seen in this chapter that there are large individual differences in first- and second-language learning. A number of factors contribute to the differences observed in learning—age of the learner, the languages involved, learning strategies, situational, personality, and sociopyschological factors. Although there has been some interest in personality and sociopsychological factors, researchers have focused on learning style differences and on strategies that learners use to crack the code of the target language. Wong Fillmore's research is especially important in this context, with its emphasis on learners' cognitive and social strategies, and on the role of formulaic speech in language learning. The impact of Wong Fillmore's work has been to make researchers more aware of the pervasiveness of formulas in normal speech and of the interplay between formulaic and creative speech in the language learning process.

7 The Effects of Early Bilingualism

We come now to the question of what effect bilingualism has on the individual. This has been a topic of empirical investigation for quite some time, and there are literally hundreds of studies in the literature. In this chapter, I restrict the discussion, for the most part, to studies investigating the effects of early bilingualism—that is, bilingualism in preschool children.

The question of the effects of early bilingualism is of more than theoretical interest. It is a pressing practical issue for many people. Parents in an increasing number of families have to deal with the question of whether to raise their children in a bilingual or monolingual environment. In some cases parents who have learned a second language for educational purposes may wonder about the advantages or disadvantages of raising their children bilingually. In many families husband and wife have different first languages and may wish to give their children access to both languages by using both in the home. In other cases the parents may have immigrated to a new country and may want to maintain the language of the old country while at the same time providing the conditions in the home for the children to learn the language of the new country.

How advisable is it to raise children bilingually? What consequences are there to bilingual upbringing? As we have seen, Jules Ronjat (1913) reported that his son Louis showed only positive consequences from having been raised in a bilingual, French-German home environment. According to his father, Louis learned to speak both languages as a native-speaking child would—he showed very few signs of interference between languages; nor did his bilingualism have a deleterious effect on his cognitive development. His development seems to have been quite normal and it has been reported that by the age of 15 he had equal fluency in both languages (Vildomec, 1963), preferring French for technology and German for literature. There was no evidence that the extreme nationalism and anti-German feeling in France at the time of the First World War had any effect on his bilingualism.

Many other researchers after Ronjat have come to the same conclusion—that early bilingualism has positive consequences for linguistic and cognitive development. A number of investigators (e.g., Imedadze, 1960; Leopold, 1949a) have suggested that early bilingualism can accelerate the separation of sound and meaning and can focus the child's attention on certain aspects of language. Vygotsky (1962) has argued that being able to express the same thought in different languages will enable the child to "see his language as one particular system among many, to view its phenomena under more general categories, and this leads to awareness of his linguistic operations" (p. 110).

These positive consequences are not the inevitable results of childhood bilingualism, however. Skutnabb–Kangas (1978), describing the experience of immigrant Finnish children in Sweden, reported that many of these children knew neither Finnish nor Swedish well. She observed that their Finnish pronunciation was often heavily influenced by Swedish, so that they were unable to differentiate between long and short phonemes, a crucial distinction in Finnish. On the other hand, their Swedish was also limited, especially in vocabulary. Skutnabb–Kangas described these children as "semilingual," in the sense of not knowing either of their languages properly, at the same level as monolingual speakers of the same age.

She characterized one such child, a 5-year-old Finnish boy living in Sweden, as follows:

> He couldn't count to more than three in any language, after that he said: many. He didn't know the names of any colours in any language. He didn't know the names of most of the things around him, either at the daycare center or outside . . . in any language. In Finnish he used only the present tense, in Swedish present and past (p. 226).

Skutnabb–Kangas argued that this child is no rare exception and that many immigrant children are like him in that they do not know either of their languages at a level appropriate for their age.

There has been a great deal of controversy about the notion of semilingualism, the principal issue being whether the bilingual's range of abilities across two languages is equivalent to that of a monolingual. It may be that the performance of some bilingual children in either language will lag behind that of monolingual speakers of that language; nonetheless, the bilingual child may possess a total vocabulary and total linguistic repertory that is quite similar to that of monolingual speakers (Baetens Beardsmore, 1982). In any event, this is not to say that the phenomenon that Skutnabb–Kangas and others describe is not real. The notion of semi-lingualism is a useful way of characterizing those cases where, through social deprivation, children do not learn to function well in their second language, and at the same time fail to develop their first language.

What are the differences between the experience of Ronjat's child and the immigrant children that Skutnabb–Kangas described? Why is it that for some children a bilingual experience is positive or "additive" (to use Lambert's (1977) terminology), whereas for other children it is a negative or "subtractive" experience? What conclusions can be drawn from research about the consequences of a bilingual experience on children?

There have been two major areas of research concern: (1) the effects of early bilingualism on linguistic development; and (2) the effects of early bilingualism on cognitive and intellectual development. In both of these areas there are important methodological issues, as well as theoretical implications that follow from what the research tells us. After summarizing the research findings I discuss, in some detail, methodological and theoretical issues, because research can only provide answers to the practical concerns of parents and educators if it is well-grounded methodologically and theoretically.

LINGUISTIC CONSEQUENCES

What does the literature tell us about the effects of early bilingualism on the language development of the child? Does learning two languages simultaneously influence the development of either one? For example, if an American parent speaks both English and Spanish to her child, how will the child's English be affected? Is it better for language development to speak only English than to use both languages? Early research on this question dealt with the so-called "bilingual handicap." Recent research has addressed more specific issues, especially with regard to lexical and syntactic development.

Early Research

We saw earlier that it appears to be difficult for an individual to maintain two languages in perfect balance. The environment is rarely perfectly bilingual, and usually the individual will need to use one language more than the other in daily life. Does this mean that one language inevitably suffers?

What evidence is there that bilingualism has a detrimental effect on one or both of the speaker's languages?

In a review of early research on this question, Jensen (1962) reported that some authors concluded that the bilingual child encounters many problems in language development. According to these authors, the child's active and passive vocabulary is smaller because the child must learn two words for each referent. Even the total number of terms was seen to be less than the total number for the monolingual child. Bilingual children were found to use fewer different words and to develop a confused, mixed vocabulary because of lexical borrowings and the tendency to hyphenate words. They were seen to use shorter sentences, more incomplete sentences, fewer compound and complex sentences, fewer interrogative and more exclamatory sentences than monolingual children. According to these authors, confused structural patterns, unusual word order, and errors in agreement and dependency characterize the speech of bilingual children. They were found to make many errors in the use of verb and tense, connectives, prepositions, nouns, pronouns, and articles (especially indefinite articles).

To a large extent these conclusions were based on research by Smith (1933, 1939) who studied preschool children in non-American families in Hawaii. A major confounding factor that limits the degree to which this research can be generalized is that pidgin English was quite common in Hawaiian communities at that time, and the main reason why the children appeared to perform so poorly may have been that they used this variant of English as their standard.

Other research, as Jensen noted, pointed to the conclusion that bilingualism is beneficial for the development of language skills. Some authors argued that bilingualism helps individuals become more sensitive to the nuances of language, aids them in their first language, enables them to manipulate languages more effectively, and helps them learn additional languages more easily. Anastasi and de Jesus (1953) found that a group of bilingual, Puerto Rican preschool children in New York City actually excelled a comparable group of monolingual children in mean sentence length and in maturity of sentence structure in English. Totten (1960) reported that his observations had led him to believe that vocabulary is increased in the bilingual child. Spoerl (1944) concluded that at the college level, bilingual students had no significant language handicap and even possessed some advantages.

The early literature varies so greatly in quality that almost all general statements are suspect. The usual procedure was to seek out two groups of children, one monolingual and the other bilingual, to test them in the language common to both, and to compare results. Very rarely was socioeconomic status or the children's intelligence controlled. Furthermore, the measures of language development used in the early studies were crude and yielded very rough estimates of linguistic ability. With recent advances in the field of language acquisition, researchers have been able to focus more specifically on various aspects of lexical and syntactic development.

Lexical Development

In contrast to the monolingual child, the bilingual child has to learn two words for a single meaning. Some authors argue that this involves no particular problems. For example, Imedadze (1967) contended that bilingual children face no additional difficulties in the acquisition of meaning, since they merely extend to a corresponding word in the second language the word meaning they have isolated and come to associate with a particular real world object in the first language. Her Georgian-Russian bilingual subject used the Georgian word *ball* to denote a toy, a radish, and stone spheres at the park entrance, and then transferred the same set of denotations to the Russian word equivalent. In this early stage, Imedadze (1967) remarked, "differences in shades of meaning of corresponding words do not play an essential role" (p. 3).

Later, however, the bilingual child has to learn that the meanings of some words have different extensions in the two languages that are being learned. For example, the English word *brush* can be used for a clothes brush, a shoe brush, and a paint brush, but the German word *Bürste* does not extend to paint brush—instead *Pinsel* is used. In such cases the child must learn to utilize a somewhat different set of feature markings for corresponding lexical items in the two languages.

One might expect to find mis-extensions of various kinds based on ill-matched lexical areas across the child's two languages, and case studies of bilingual children indicate that such mis-extensions do occur. For example, Leopold, in his careful treatment of lexical extension (1949a), mentioned a likely instance of such cross-linguistic interference, where the German *alle* was used (at 1;7-1;11) to mean *all gone* with reference to persons, as in *Mommy alle*. Standard German does not allow this because *alle* does not mean the same as the English *all gone* when applied to persons.

Until bilingual children have determined the different extensions words have in their languages, they can have problems being understood. Thus, the 3-year-old Raivo Vihman argued with his English-speaking friends that he could read and demonstrated by counting—the Estonian *lugema* is used for both "to read" and "to count" (Vihman & McLaughlin, 1982). Other instances of lexical mis-extensions have been reported by Rūķe–Draviņa (1967).

In the process of differentiating the lexical systems of the two languages, the child may make lexical selections on phonological grounds. Leopold (1947) suggested that the bilingual child's choice of vocabulary from one language or the other "might be explained by a consciousness of articulatory difficulties" (p. 267). Celce–Murcia (1978) emphasized this mechanism in her daughter's avoidance of French or English words, and Vihman noted it as well in her Estonian-English-speaking child's language (Vihman & McLaughlin, 1982). Another form of non-differentiation is the use of blends, a phenomenon reported by Leopold (1939), Murrell (1966), Oksaar (1970), and Vihman (Vihman & McLaughlin, 1982), whereby bilingual children settle on a single phonological shape to express the same concept in either language, the adult words bearing some phonological similarity in most such cases.

In reviewing their own data based on two sisters acquiring Italian and German and Leopold's (1939) data on his daughter Hildegard, Volterra and Taeschner (1978) proposed a three-stage developmental sequence in bilingual lexical development (see Table 7.1). In the first stage the child builds up a vocabulary repertory that involves a single lexical system with utterances containing mixtures of words from both languages. This completely non-differentiated stage is followed by a second stage in which the child possesses two lexical systems with mixed utterances continuing because corresponding words are learned at different times and each word tends to be tied to the particular context in which it is learned. Finally, in the third stage, two differential lexical systems are acquired. A similar developmental sequence was proposed by Nygren–Junken (1977) based on the speech samples of four French-English children.

The question that many parents would like to have answered is how long it takes the child to reach the third stage in the development outlined in Table 7.1. Does bilingual exposure lead to any retardation in normal lexical development? Is there a bilingual handicap in vocabulary development? Monolingual children have been observed to go through a period of very rapid vocabulary development somewhere between 26 and 30 months. Some authors argue that this vocabulary spurt occurs later in bilingual children because the recurrent pattern of association between speech noises (words) and objects and events is less uniform for the bilingual than for the monolingual child (M. Taylor, 1974). Swain (1972) agreed that bilingual children

TABLE 7.1
The Stages of Lexical Differentiation

Stage 1:	Single lexical system with mixtures of words from both languages
Stage 2:	Two lexical systems but undifferentiated, marked by mixed utterances
Stage 3:	Two lexical systems but differentiated

Based on Volterra and Taeschner (1978).

lag behind monolingual children in vocabulary development, but she also pointed out that the total conceptual vocabulary of the bilingual child usually exceeds that of the monolingual child. Furthermore, if there is such a lag, it seems to be of brief duration. There may be some delay during the second stage in Table 7.1, when the child continues to strive to make a single unit out of the bilingual presentation. But as bilingual children become aware that they are being presented two different languages, they begin to use the appropriate word in both languages (Leopold, 1939). When the child attains this metalinguistic insight, there is a spurt in vocabulary development in both languages with no apparent negative long-term consequences to either.

As we saw in Chapter 4, authors differ with respect to the point at which they see the bilingual child becoming aware of speaking two different languages. Ronjat (1913) believed that his son had this awareness at one year and six months; Pavlovitch (1920) also put the date of awareness relatively early—at two years. Other authors (Elwert, 1960; Geissler, 1938; Imedadze, 1967) set the date somewhere in the third or fourth year. The reason for this discrepancy is probably that there are degrees of meta-linguistic awareness: Leopold (1949a) saw some signs of awareness on the part of his daughter at two years, but it was only at three years and six months or so that the child had a good feeling for the differences between the two languages.

Does this mean that mixing persists until the age of three and a half? The evidence suggests that it may, but that mixed utterances represent a small proportion of the child's total utterances. Swain (1974) observed the linguistic interaction of a French-English bilingual child over a nine-month period beginning at 3 years and 1 month and found lexical mixing to occur in only 4% of the child's utterances. Half as many lexically mixed utterances occurred at 3 years and 8 months as at 3 years and 1 month, indicating that the child was progressing markedly during this period in differentiating the two languages.

Other authors report even less mixing of languages in bilingual children. Lindholm and Padilla (1977) found that only 2% of the utterances produced by five Spanish-English bilingual children ranging in age from two to six years contained mixes. In another study of 18 children in the same age range Lindholm and Padilla (1978) found about the same amount of mixing. This research bears upon some theoretical issues, which will be discussed in more detail subsequently.

Syntactic Development

Is the acquisition of grammatical structures by bilingual children the same in its basic features and in its developmental sequence as for the monolingual child? There is evidence that structural features of the two languages of the bilingual child are not necessarily acquired simultaneously. As Slobin (1971) noted, the syntactic realization of semantic relations (such as locative or possessive) can occur at different times within the two languages of the bilingual child, reflecting the perceptual salience of the features needed to mark the relationship in the two languages. Thus, we saw in Chapter 4 that Serbo-Croatian-Hungarian bilingual children (Mikeš, 1967) demonstrated locative relations in Hungarian (where the locative marker is expressed by noun inflection) earlier than in Serbo-Croation (where noun inflection and preposition are needed to express the locative). Mikeš (1967) pointed out, however, that the order in which various syntactic structures are acquired by bilingual children is the same as for monolingual children. The Serbo-Croation locative construction is also acquired relatively late by monolingual speakers of that language. Mikeš concluded that bilingual presentation has little effect on syntactic development.

This does not mean that there is no period of confusion in the syntactic development of the bilingual child's two languages. As we saw in Chapter 4, a number of authors reported that the children they observed went through periods of syntactic mixing and confusion (Carrow, 1971; Kessler, 1972; Rūķe–Draviņa, 1967). For example, Oksaar (1970) reported that her child used Swedish morphemes with Estonian endings in the home, where Estonian was spoken; but with Swedish-speaking playmates the Swedish forms predominated. Burling (1959) found morphological and syntactic mixing, although his son seemed aware that he was mixing the two languages.

Swain and Wesche (1975) found instances "in which the grammatical structure is French but the lexicon is English, and a few in which the structure is English but the lexicon is French" (p. 20). French negative constructions, with the negative element following the verb appeared in lexically English sentences. Similarly, to express possession, Swain and Wesche's subject used both French structure with English words and English structure with French words, suggesting that at this point both systems had been internalized, but their linguistic allocation was not yet under control.

Volterra and Taeschner (1978) found that the two children they studied initially developed a single syntactic system that was applied to the lexicon of both languages. This syntactic system appeared to be different from that of either language. They argued that children begin by fashioning a unique system; then the system of the language with the more simple syntactic structures becomes dominant and mixing of syntactic structures from both languages occurs; finally, the two syntactic structures become differentiated. Thus, the development of syntax in bilingual children was thought to parallel quite closely the stages hypothesized for lexical development (see Table 7.1).

Vihman (1983), however, found no evidence in her son Raivo's speech for the first of Volterra and Taeschner's stages. In her son's early word combinations there was a high proportion of mixings from the start, despite the presence of synonyms that might have been used to create single-language (in this case, Estonian) utterances. That is, Raivo's early word combinations were not based on a unique system with complementary terms from the two languages; instead, the child seems to have begun at stage two.

Thus it is unclear whether the three-stage process of a unitary system, mixing, and differentiation is a universal process characterizing syntactic development in bilingual children. There does seem to be a differentiation process that occurs as the child sorts out the two languages, and this process appears to be slower for syntactic than for lexical development. Swain (1974) reported that lexical consistency precedes structural consistency: at 3;9 her subject's lexicon was differentiated but the child's grammatical system remained essentially undifferentiated. Leopold (1949a) argued that syntactic differentiation cannot occur prior to lexical differentiation because the child does not yet "use the two languages as separate instruments" (p. 186). Until this process of differentiation is complete there is mixing of syntactic structures, although this stage seems to be of relatively short duration in most of the reported studies.

Methodological Issues

There are a number of methodological problems with the research that has been discussed to this point. One problem is sampling bias. Most of the case studies were done with children from upper-middle or upper-class families. In almost all instances the parents were highly educated and intelligent. For children from such families there may be a brief "bilingual handicap," but they quickly catch up in linguistic ability with monolingual children of the same age. In fact, there are a number of reports in the literature of an unusual interest in language by bilingual children. Thus Vihman's daughter invented words with fanciful definitions at three years; at four years and eight months she compared Estonian, French, and English sounds. Slobin (1978) reported that his daughter asked how to say certain words in other languages and seemed to be struck by the arbitrariness of language as early as age 3. At four she was able to comment on the grammaticality of her utterance and could answer questions about language.

To what extent does the concern about language shown by these children represent the proclivities of psycholinguists' children and to what extent do they reflect bilingual experience? There is some evidence that the benefits of a bilingual experience can be less positive for children from lower-socioeconomic and less well-educated families. For example, in a study of lower- and middle-class Mexican-American children aged three to ten Carrow (1971) found that there were specific areas where the children studied were, as a group, significantly delayed when compared to a control group of English-speaking children. In particular, the comprehension of pronouns, negatives, and some tense markers caused difficulty for children in the bilingual group.

Cornejo (1973) investigated the language development of 24 five-year-old Mexican-American children of lower-middle-class background and found a high degree of transfer, borrowing, and language mixture in the language samples. Transfer from Spanish to English was most prominent at the phonological level, whereas transfer from English to Spanish was most noticeable at the lexical level.

In addition to these studies there is Skutnabb–Kangas' (1978) contention that for many lower-class immigrant children bilingual exposure can lead to a state of "semilingualism":

> Many of the children do not know any language properly, at the same level as monolingual children. The language tests and estimates show that they often lag up to four years behind their monolingual peers in language tests in both languages (p. 229).

Regardless of what position one takes on the semilingualism issue, it is clear that for many immigrant children learning a second language is a difficult task that takes a long time and may interfere with the development of the child's first language.

That bilingual exposure can have different consequences for different children suggests that there are important intervening variables that have to be considered in research in this area. One such variable relates to the manner in which the child is exposed to two languages, which I refer to here as the conditions of presentation.

Conditions of presentation.   The child bilingual can be exposed to two languages in a number of different ways (Vihman & McLaughlin, 1982). Let us assume that the child experiences two basic distinguishable environments—"home" and "community." If we make the further simplifying assumption that three types of language use can be distinguished—one person-one language; mixed use by each person; and environment-bound language, with one language at home and another in the community—we have the following possibilities:

In the home:

    (a) parents and other members of the household each present one or the other of two (or more) languages (one person-one language);

(b) each member uses both languages;

(c) the home is essentially monolingual, with members of the outside community introducing a second language to the child.

In the child's community:

(a) different persons each use one of the child's languages, but not the other;

(b) members of the community tend to use both languages (a code-switching community),

(c) a monolingual community in which most persons know only one of the two languages the child is acquiring.

Combining the various possible situations in home and community, we arrive at a matrix with nine possibilities. Table 7.2 lists some representative studies that illustrate the possibilities of bilingual presentation. A few comments are in order on the range of actual usage represented by the cases cited in the various slots. One person-one language, for example, was the policy in both the home and the community in the case of Louis Ronjat. The family lived in France but had frequent contact with both French and German-speaking families. Thus, the child's world outside the home was bilingual, with the one person-one language formula carrying over to the community as well. In the Leopold case, on the contrary, exposure to one of the two languages, German, was virtually non-existent outside the home, except when the family travelled to Europe.

Fantini (1974) reported that his son was raised in a monolingual (Spanish-speaking) home in the United States. Because he made frequent trips to Bolivia and Mexico, however, it seemed appropriate to consider his outside

TABLE 7.2
Bilingual Presentation: Language Use at Home and in the Community

	Community		
Home	One Person— One Language	Monolingual Usage	Mixed Usage by Some
One Person— One Language	Ronjat, 1913	Leopold, 1939, 1947, 1949a, 1949b	——
Monolingual Usage	Fantini, 1974	Oksaar, 1970	——
Mixed Usage by Some	Murrell, 1966	Celce-Murcia, 1978	Lindholm & Padilla, 1977

environment bilingual, with separation of language by person. In contrast, Oksaar's (1970) children did not appear to have had any extensive contact with speakers of their home language outside the home.

Finally, there are the cases of mixed language input. Murrell (1966) spoke a mixture of English and Swedish to his daughter, who learned Finnish and Swedish—from different persons—outside the home, and Swedish only from her mother. Thus, the child received mixed input at least from her father at home, but separate languages according to the speaker in the community and with her mother at home. In the Celce–Murcia (1978) case, the child's father spoke with her mainly—but not exclusively—in French, whereas her mother spoke with her mainly—but not exclusively—in English. The outside community was monolingual English-speaking.

Perhaps the most frequently reported situation is the one in which both the parents and the community mix languages to some extent (Burling, 1959; Padilla & Liebman, 1975; Tabouret–Keller, 1962). In many families and communities, bilingual speakers use a separate code that includes mixing structures and vocabulary from two languages. This phenomenon has been found to be especially common in the speech of Mexican-Americans (Gumperz, 1970; Lance, 1969). As we saw in Chapter 5, Gumperz and Hernández–Chavez (1972) showed how the use of mixed expressions in the speech of Mexican-Americans is highly meaningful and serves definite communication needs. Speakers build on the coexistence of alternate forms in their language repertory to create meanings that may be highly idiosyncratic and understood only by members of the same bilingual speech community.

The problem for the child learner is that, the more mixing of languages occurs in adult speech, the more difficult it becomes to differentiate between the two languages. For example, Burling (1959) reported that his son's bilingual acquisition showed some mixing of Garo and English—Garo words being given English morphology and syntax. This was not too surprising, because all of the English-speaking adults around the child used Garo words in their English speech. Similarly, the Mexican-American child may find it difficult to differentiate Spanish and English if the adult input is mixed. Thus, the conditions of presentation can have an effect on how easy it is for the child to keep the two languages apart.

In addition to differences in bilingual presentation in the home and in the community, there are likely to be changes in the child's linguistic environment over time. Once the child is old enough to enter the community of other children or to attend nursery school, the child's linguistic input may change quite drastically. At the latest, entry into grammar school may effect the change—in the United States at least—marking the imminent disuse by children of a family language that may have been their sole means of expression for four or five years (Vihman & McLaughlin, 1982).

Another possibility is that the family moves from one community to another. Burling (1959) gives a poignant account of his son's shift from Garo to monolingual English after the family left the Garo Hills when the child was 3;6. Or the parents may change their home language policy, with or without such a change in locale. Thus, Major (1976) reported that he and his wife used Brazilian Portuguese exclusively in addressing their child until she reached 1;2, at which point the family moved to the United States, where they switched to a one-person-one-language policy. By 2;8 the child had begun to respond in English even when spoken to by monolingual Brazilian children.

In short, there may be any number of complexities and vicissitudes affecting the child's acquisition of two languages. Conditions of language presentation have important consequences for language differentiation, and must be taken into account in making generalizations about the effect of bilingual experience on the linguistic development of the child. Attaining bilingual competence is likely to be more difficult the more mixing the child is exposed to, although mixed exposure does not lead to permanent retardation in either language. In fact, researchers sometimes mistake mixing in the child's speech for confusion and language interference, when the child is actually using (or trying to use) mixed utterances rhetorically for sociolinguistic purposes, just as adult speakers in the child's linguistic environment do (Gumperz, 1970). More serious consequences for language differentiation follow from imbalanced presentation. This brings us to the next issue.

Active and passive bilingualism. For many children attaining bilingualism may be a more passive than active process. That is, the child may be exposed to a second language before being required to use it actively. The child's comprehensive abilities in the language may develop much faster than productive abilities. This is the case, for example, for many Spanish-speaking children in the United States for whom English is the dominant language of the larger social environment, but who have little opportunity to use English before entering school. For these children Spanish is the dominant language before school, but upon entering school emphasis is shifted to English. Throughout this process the input is imbalanced, first in favor of Spanish, then favoring English.

Children who acquire a second language passively by exposure and not by using it actively have a different bilingual experience than do those children who grow up speaking two languages. Passive bilingualism is also a different process from learning a second language after a first language is established. On the one hand, the child is not learning two languages equally, because there is such a strong imbalance in favor of the language that is being used actively. On the other hand, the child is not a novice when it comes to learning the second language, since there has been considerable exposure to that language.

Arnberg (1979) reported that one of the mothers she studied in Sweden used English with her child even though the child consistently spoke Swedish. Once the child became motivated to speak English on his own, while attending a day camp during a visit to an English-speaking country, his progress in English was quite rapid. Several other parents in Arnberg's study commented that their children spoke English fluently when visiting English-speaking countries merely as a result of having heard it spoken in the home.

Riley (1977) studied a five-year-old child who had grown up in Germany and who was beginning kindergarten in a California school. The child had never spoken English before, but had been exposed to English through his American father while in Germany. He was immediately able to speak English in kindergarten, although there were numerous mistakes—both developmental and transfer errors. When asked by his parents how it was that he could speak English, he replied (in German) that he could speak it at school, but when he came home he forgot. The child's progress in English was extremely rapid and within a few months his speech was indistinguishable from that of his English-speaking peers.

There is, however, the possibility that children who have achieved some bilingual proficiency through passive exposure may not have the same grasp of the language as do those children whose use of the language has been active from an early age. Often children from language-minority families acquire some knowledge of the language of the dominant culture in a more passive, imbalanced manner. Upon entering school, they may appear to be making fairly rapid progress in the majority language. This can be an instance of the "linguistic facade" (Cummins, 1979; Skutnabb–Kangas, 1978), whereby children give the appearance of being rapid learners of a language because of their surface fluency, when in fact they have not mastered the language to the extent of being able to use it effectively in school-related tasks.

Failure to distinguish active and passive bilingualism creates a methodological issue for research on the effects of bilingualism on language development because the consequences of the two forms of early bilingualism can be quite different. Although there has been no research specifically on this point, it may be that the child who has learned a second language through passive exposure needs to have the opportunity to use the language extensively before achieving mastery (in spite of surface fluency in the language). At this point we know very little about how passive comprehension skills transfer to active production skills when the learner becomes motivated to speak the language. We do know, however, that the transfer is not automatic—many adults have the experience of understanding a second language and being motivated to speak it, without being able to do so.

Defining differentiation. A final methodological problem for research on the consequences of early bilingualism on language development relates to defining language differentiation. We noted that authors differ with respect to the point at which they see the bilingual child becoming aware of speaking two different languages, and argued that the reason for this discrepancy is that there are degrees of awareness. The awareness that Imedadze (1967) saw to be necessary to enter the stage of discriminated language systems (at about 1;8) is obviously quite different from the awareness of the separateness of language that Dimitrijevic (1965) described as occurring between the fifth and sixth year. Unless some greater clarity is achieved in defining degrees of awareness of language differentiation, this debate will never be resolved.

One attempt to provide a more precise definition was made by Swain and Wesche (1975), who distinguished between language mixing and spontaneous translation as evidence that the child was aware of the separation between the two languages. Lexically mixed data was taken to indicate that the child did not differentiate the two languages, whereas spontaneous translation was seen to show that the child was aware of speaking two different languages. As Arnberg (1981) pointed out, however, this approach is not without its critics:

> Other researchers disagree, however, stating that in lexically mixed material there is a high degree of "grammaticalness" (Cornejo, 1973) and that structural consistency of the utterance is maintained (Lindholm & Padilla, 1977, 1978). Word order is preserved, and the forms do not overlap in meaning (Padilla & Liebman, 1975). For example, the child would not say *"es un* a baby pony" because the use of the English article would be redundant. For this reason, these utterances cannot be taken as evidence of failure to distinguish between the languages (Bergman, 1976) (p. 23).

The root of this disagreement is the contention on the part of some investigators (e.g., Bergman, 1976; Lindholm & Padilla, 1977, 1978; Padilla & Liebman, 1975) that bilingual children use a dual language system *from the beginning.* Their research and that of other investigators (e.g., Garcia, 1980; Huerta, 1977) shows little evidence of interference between languages. Most of what passes for interference, they argue, is code mixing or switching that represents a dialectical pattern, especially in Spanish-American communities in California and the Southwest.

According to these authors, the bilingual child is able to differentiate the two languages from an early age. When the lines between the two languages are clearly drawn, the argument runs, the languages of the bilingual child develop independently of each other and mirror their acquisition by monolingual children (Bergman, 1976). How then is lexical mixing to be explained? These authors content that lexical mixing is not due to failure to distinguish between languages, but to the absence of the appropriate term in the child's vocabulary, memory lapses, salience factors (e.g., frequent use of a particular word on television), or language mixing by those who provide the child with input.

Redlinger and Park (1980) challenged this argument and criticized studies showing little interference for not presenting a distributional analysis of code mixing for single subjects in a systematic fashion. Their own data on four 2-year-old children growing up bilingually in a German-speaking environment showed an initial higher rate of language mixing that diminished with growth in language development. Children at Stage I (Brown, 1973a) had 20%–30% mixing levels; this decreased to 12%–20% at Stage II, to 6%–12% at Stage III, and to 2%–6% at Stage IV and Stage V. Redlinger and Park concluded that language differentiation in bilingual children is a gradual process that can, in part, be traced through decreasing code mixing. They rejected the dual language theory in favor of the view that bilingual children initially process language through a single system that eventually is differentiated into two systems.

There is other evidence against the dual system notion. The example given by Volterra and Taeschner (1978) of a child using the German *da* and the Italian *la* with different meanings suggests that the child is striving to develop a single system. Leopold's (1939) data also indicated that Hildegard initially used only a single word for a particular concept, adopting the strategy of giving things one name only. This was followed by a period of competition, with both words occurring and one being preferred. The competition ceased and Hildegard managed to use the appropriate words in both languages only when she achieved some realization that there were two languages in her environment.

What this realization involves needs to be more closely researched. The argument that the bilingual child separates the languages when he or she is aware that there are two systems in the environment is circular unless some criterion is provided for assessing what is meant by this awareness—other than that the child separates the languages. Most likely the awareness that the child achieves of the separateness of the two languages will differ with different conditions of presentation, but even in the clearest case—the one person-one language situation (Ronjat, 1913)—identifying words with the language spoken by one parent or the other does not necessarily indicate that the child has some awareness that the two languages are different, because young children are greatly influenced by the context in which words are first used.

There is an obvious need for an analysis of the *different levels* of awareness through which the bilingual child passes. The one attempt of this nature in the literature is that of Vihman (Vihman & McLaughlin, 1982). In her son's case, language differentiation was seen to begin at about age two; awareness of the fact that words could be labelled by language and translated appeared to come slightly later, while consciousness of the bilingual situation as a whole seemed to dawn only at the end of the fourth year, with explicit awareness of the child's own bilingual capacities being acknowledged a few months later. Although this approach is promising, clearly defined criteria are needed for each of the different levels of awareness.

Theoretical Implications

I would like to conclude this section on the effects of early bilingualism on linguistic development by briefly discussing two theoretical issues: (1) what early bilingualism tells us about the language learning process: and (2) what conclusions can be drawn about the manner in which the bilingual child stores and processes the two languages.

Early bilingualism and the language learning process.   Are there any differences in the language learning process bilingual children go through that distinguish them from monolingual children? Using cognitive network theory (Rumelhart, Lindsay, & Norman, 1972), Taylor (1974) argued that initial words are "labels" linked with concepts through a process of associative learning. Because the recurrent pattern of association between speech noises (words) and objects or events is less uniform for the bilingual than for the monolingual child, bilingualism was predicted to lead to a delay in the onset of the vocabulary spurt that marks the acquisition of the "label" metaconcept.

In a test of this notion, Doyle, Champagne, and Segalowitz (1978) found that French-English preschool bilingual children were not delayed in reported age of first word, but did score significantly lower than monolinguals on vocabulary attainment in the dominant language on the Peabody Picture Vocabulary Test. Doyle et al., however, did not attribute these lower scores to the delayed acquisition of the "label" notion, but rather to the lack of variety of linguistic input in the dominant language.

A number of other investigators (e.g., Carrow, 1957; Skutnabb-Kangas, 1978; Smith, 1949, 1957) have also reported lower vocabulary scores for bilingual children, but as Carrow pointed out, the "bilingual handicap" may be due more to the family environment than to bilingualism per se:

In homes where there is a language atmosphere that is favorable to wide experience in both languages and where good speech models are present, the bilingual child may not experience any problem in either language (p. 378, cited in Arnberg, 1981).

It is to be expected that families that present a stimulating and diversified linguistic environment will promote language development in children—whether monolingual or bilingual. Wells (1981) reported that there are interaction patterns in the family that relate strongly to language development and success in school. One particular process is that of "negotiating meaning" (Wells, 1981)—that is, collaborating in conversation to express one's needs, ideas, and intentions. Wells' research indicated that there is a clear association between the quality of adults' contributions to conversation and their children's rate of oral language development in the preschool years.

Wells (1981) cautioned, however, that there is no necessary connection between social class and oral language development. A simple class-based distinction is not as enlightening as an approach that stresses the pattern of interaction between parents and children. In all likelihood there are differences between parents that are related to their perception of their role as the child's first teachers. These differences, in turn, affect the way in which parents interact with children and the extent to which they make meanings explicit.

In short, there seems to be nothing unique about the language learning process in bilingual children. We have seen that the developmental process mirrors that observed in monolingual children. Even if Taylor's argument concerning the delay in acquiring the "label" metaconcept holds for bilingual children, this does not mean that the language learning process is any different for them than for monolingual children. It would simply indicate that the process is more complex for bilingual children. What appears to be most important is how the languages are presented to the child. If children experience a rich and balanced language environment, they will develop verbal proficiency in both languages. To the extent that the language environment is unstimulating and noncommunicative, language learning will be impeded.

Two systems or one?   How does the bilingual child store and process the two languages? As we have seen, there are two positions on this issue. According to some authors (e.g., Swain, 1972) separate sets of rules for both languages would be inefficient in terms of memory storage. It is more efficient for the child to employ a common core of rules with those specific to a particular language tagged as such through a process of differentiation. Swain's data indicated that the rules acquired first in the acquisition of *yes/no* questions by French-English bilingual children aged 2;1 to 4;10 were those that were common to both languages. Rules that were language-specific or more complex were acquired later.

A different position was taken by Bergman (1976), who argued that each of the bilingual child's languages develops independently of each other. According to this dual system position, the two lexicons of the bilingual child and the systems of rules that characterize the two grammars are kept separate from a very early age. What seems like interference is seen as the result of the code mixing and code switching to which the child is exposed (Lindholm & Padilla, 1977; Padilla & Liebman, 1975).

We have just seen, however, that research with bilingual children does not support the notion of a dual language system (Redlinger & Park, 1980; Volterra & Taeschner, 1978). Furthermore, research on adult bilingual subjects generally favors the view that there is a single system for the semantic representation of words in memory and that the language tag is also stored in some way so that it can be correctly applied in output (Liepmann & Saegert, 1974; Lopez, Hicks, & Young, 1974). The single system hypothesis regards the bilingual child's two languages as separate linguistic codes, analogous to the separate codes of a monolingual speaker. There seems to be no reason to argue that the task of switching languages involves additional processes over and above those used to switch codes in a single language. Each code can be thought of as part of a single system with some means of discriminating lexical entries and syntactic forms characteristic of a particular code (or language).

Nonetheless, some research on memory in adult bilingual subjects suggests that a more complex model is called for. For example, Tulving & Colotla, (1970) presented trilingual subjects with lists of words that were to be recalled verbatim. The lists were of varying length and contained words from one, two, or three languages. They found that subjects were better at recalling words from unilingual lists than from bilingual lists and better with bilingual than with trilingual lists. They concluded that this probably reflected the trilingual's separate storage of three languages: the organization of lists of words in memory appeared to be more difficult between different languages than within a single language.

In order to account for such findings, Paradis (1978, 1980) proposed a model in which bilinguals were thought to possess one memory store corresponding to their knowledge of the world. This store contains mental representations of things and events, properties, qualities, and functions of objects. In addition, bilinguals were thought to have a language store for each of their two languages, both of which are connected to the conceptual store (Paradis, 1978). In these language stores units of meaning are grouped according to the conceptual features they possess in each language:

> Units of meaning in each language group together conceptual features in different ways. Thus the English unit of meaning "ball" is connected with conceptual features such as "spheric," "bouncy," "play," etc. . . . The French unit of meaning that corresponds to "balle" shares these features, but it is also

connected to "small." If it is too large to hold in one hand, it is no longer "une balle," but becomes "un ballon," a distinction which is irrelevant in English. A big ball is still a ball. Some units of meaning such as ball/balle share most of their features. Others share only a few (p. 2).

Thus, in Paradis' model there are three stores, a conceptual store and two language stores. The three-store model is not incompatible with the single system notion, because it is possible to think of both of the lexical stores as existing within a single system. Like the rules of the two languages, the lexical stores can be conceived of as part of a single system with those specific to each language tagged as such during the process of differentiation. At this point, however, much more research is needed to validate Paradis' (or any other) model.

COGNITIVE AND INTELLECTUAL CONSEQUENCES

How does early bilingualism affect a child's cognitive and intellectual development? There are two separate research traditions: (1) research on the effect of bilingualism on cognitive development; and (2) investigations of the effect of bilingualism on intellectual functioning. Again, this research needs to be read cautiously. We will see that there are serious methodological problems that limit the theoretical usefulness of much of this research.

Cognitive Development

Vygotsky (1962) believed that language brings about restructuring of cognitive processes both for social use and as a tool for thought. One might predict that two languages are better than one, that a second language gives the child a greater symbolic system and so enhances memory, perception, and creativity. Or does a second language interfere with competent cognitive functioning, confusing the child and producing a lack of clarity? As we saw at the beginning of this chapter, Vygotsky maintained that bilingualism has positive benefits, enabling children to see their language as one particular system among many, and this leads to awareness of linguistic operations.

Noting her child's precocious attention to speech at the end of her third year, Imedadze (1967) concluded that bilingualism

can thus be looked upon as a factor which accelerates the appearance and development in the child of the ability to consciously recognize (objectify) words and speech (p. 15).

A similar argument was made by Leopold (1949a), who believed that one gain of bilingualism was that the normal childish habit of clinging to a single wording (e.g., in rhymes, songs, or bedtime stories) seemed to be missing in Hildegard. From an early age, she would render a story freely in both of her languages. When memorizing rhymes or songs, she would often destroy the rhyme with her own insertions of meaningfully related vocabulary. She readily accepted new names for objects already denoted in one language and asked to be given the name in the second language. Leopold attributed this looseness of the link between the phonetic word and its meaning to the fact that the bilingual child hears the same thing constantly designated in two different phonetic forms, so that form and conceptual meaning are not rigidly identified with each other.

This, however, was not Burling's (1959) experience. He describes his son, Stephen, as "obsessional" in his identification of phonetic form and meaning:

> When we read to him, he instantly protested the slightest alteration in any familiar text. This was true even though we read to him in his second language, English, where one would suppose the form and meaning to be least rigidly identified. It must have been an idiosyncratic trait rather than bilingualism that freed Leopold's daughter from insistence upon stereotyped wording (pp. 67–68).

Was Hildegard Leopold an exception or was Stephen Burling? To answer this question, researchers have looked at samples of bilingual children under experimental conditions.

Studies of cognitive flexibility. Ianco-Worrall (1972) tested Leopold's hypothesis that bilingual children possess greater cognitive flexibility than do monolingual children by comparing the responses of Afrikaans-English bilingual children and matched control groups of monolingual English- and monolingual Afrikaans-speaking children. In one experiment she gave children a semantic vs. phonetic preference test, a two-choice test on which similarity between words could be interpreted on the basis of shared meaning or shared acoustic properties. For example, the child was asked, "I have three words: *cap, can,* and *hat.* Which is more like *cap—can* or *hat*?" A response of *can* was interpreted as indicating a phonetic preference, and the choice of *hat* was seen to indicate a semantic preference.

Ianco-Worrall found that in her bilingual groups, 4- to 6-year-old children responded predominately on the basis of semantic meaning, whereas monolingual children of the same age tended to respond on the basis of phonetic meaning. For older children, aged 7 to 9, both monolingual and bilingual children responded mainly on the basis of semantic meaning. Table 7.3 shows the percentage of children in each group whose choices reflected semantic or phonetic preferences.

In a second experiment, Ianco-Worrall had the children perform three tasks:

Give explanations for names:
   (Why is a dog called "dog"?)

Tell if names could be interchanged:
   (Suppose you could make up names for things, could you call a dog "cow" and a cow "dog"?)

Interchange names in play:
   (Let's play a game. Let's call a dog "cow").

and answer questions about the properties of the object:
   (Does this "cow" have horns? Does this "cow" give milk?)

There were no differences on the first task—both bilingual and monolingual children of different ages gave the same types of explanations for why things have specific names (perceptible attributes, social convention, functional attributes, arbitrary justification, etc.). On the second task, less than 20% of the monolingual children but more than 50% of the bilingual children consistently answered that names of things could be interchanged. Finally, responses to the last task indicated that older children were more willing to interchange the names of objects in play and scored higher in cor-

TABLE 7.3
Preferences for Semantic and Phonetic Dimensions Among Monolingual and Bilingual Children

Test and Age	Group	No. of Subjects	Choice	
			Semantic	Phonetic
English:				
4 to 6 yrs.	Monolingual	12	46%	54%
	Bilingual	13	68%	32%
7 to 9 yrs.	Monolingual	16	60%	40%
	Bilingual	17	67%	33%
Afrikaans:				
4 to 6 yrs.	Monolingual	13	49%	51%
	Bilingual	13	60%	40%
7 to 9 yrs.	Monolingual	17	64%	36%
	Bilingual	17	66%	34%

From Ianco-Worrall (1972).

rectly answering questions about the properties of the object than younger children, but there were no significant differences between monolingual and bilingual children on this task.

Ianco–Worrall interpreted her findings as indicating that Leopold's observations were valid. She argued that it was particularly impressive that in her sample, 54% of the bilingual children consistently (across all trials) chose to interpret similarity between words in terms of the semantic rather than the phonetic dimension. Of the monolingual children, only one English-speaking child and no Afrikaans-speaking children showed the same choice behavior. Although bilingual children did not perform better than monolingual children on tasks where names were conceived to be aspects of things, they did perform better when the task required the formulated concept that names are arbitrarily assigned to things.

Cummins (1978a) also conducted a number of experiments to determine whether bilingual children have greater conceptual flexibility than do monolingual children. He studied third- and sixth-grade Irish children on three tasks: (a) meaning and reference; (b) arbitrariness of language; and (c) nonphysical nature of words. In the first task the children had to state whether words used to refer to animals, imaginary (*flimps*) and real (*giraffes*), cease to have meaning when the last of that type of animals dies. Bilingual Irish-English children showed superior performance when compared to monolingual English children on this task, with differences for sixth-grade children reaching statistical significance. On the second task children were asked whether you could call the sun *the moon* and the moon *the sun*. Almost 70% of the bilingual children compared with 28% of the monolingual children answered that the names could be interchanged. On the third task children were asked questions such as "Is the word *book* made of paper?" On this task there were no significant differences between bilingual and monolingual children at either age group in the percent correctly answered. Cummins concluded that, in general, his research supported the hypothesis that bilingual children surpass monolingual children in conceptual flexibility.

There was one puzzling finding in Cummins' research, however. About as many bilingual as monolingual children asserted that if a cat were called *dog* it would bark, in spite of the fact that pictures of a cat and a dog were in full view. This makes one a bit cautious in asserting that bilingual children have freed the phonetic word from its conceptual meaning.

Studies of symbol substitution and cognitive functioning.   Ben Zeev (1977) reported that monolingual children aged five to eight performed more poorly on a symbol substitution task than did Hebrew-English bilingual children. In this task the children were asked to substitute one meaningful word for another in a fixed sentence frame, including instances where the substitution resulted in a violation of the obligatory selection rules of the language. For example, the child was told that "in this game, the way we say *I* is to say *macaroni.*" The children were then asked to tell how to say "I am warm," a correct response being, "Macaroni am warm."

The superiority of bilinguals in such a task was interpreted by Ben Zeev as indicating that bilinguals develop a more analytic orientation toward language than do monolinguals as a means of overcoming interference between languages. Ben Zeev's argument was that bilinguals, because they need to deal with two languages rather than one, habitually exert more processing effort in making sense out of verbal stimuli than do monolinguals. Bilinguals were thought to be more aware of the structural similarities and differences between their two languages and to develop a special sensitivity to linguistic feedback from the environment. This more developed analytic strategy towards linguistic structures is transferred, the argument runs, to other structures and patterns associated with different cognitive tasks. Hence bilinguals were seen to have cognitive advantages that monolinguals lack.

A similar argument has been made by a number of other authors. For example, Feldman and Shen (1971) found that bilingual 5-year-old children were better than their monolingual peers at re-labeling objects and using labels in simple relational sentences. Landry (1974) found that sixth-grade children in a foreign language program performed significantly better than monolingual children on a test of divergent thinking ability that measured such aspects of cognitive functioning as fluency, flexibility, and originality. Balkan (1970) found that bilingual 11- to 17-year-old children demonstrated greater cognitive flexibility than monolingual counterparts in a series of tests.

This research was interpreted to mean that bilingual children have greater cognitive flexibility than do monolingual children. Landry felt that bilingual children have learned to overcome the negative transfer of their first language in learning their second, and this experience makes them less susceptible to negative transfer generally. As a result, bilinguals acquire a "flexibility set," that is beneficial in divergent thinking tasks requiring inventiveness and originality. The child is thought to have developed an adaptability in learning a second language that can be used profitably in other cognitive tasks.

How valid is this argument? As we shall see shortly, there are sufficient methodological problems with this research to make one cautious about accepting the argument without scruple. Indeed, it seems premature to assume that bilingualism leads to greater cognitive flexibility. I will return to this issue after discussing research on the effects of early bilingualism on intelligence.

Effects on Intelligence

Does being bilingual have any effect on a child's intellectual development? A number of contemporary authorities have argued that it has a positive effect, enhancing the child's intelligence. This contrasts with the findings of older studies that concluded that bilingualism has a permanent negative effect on intellectual development.

Some early authors were quite convinced that bilingualism has a permanent negative effect on intellectual development. Weisgerber (1935) saw bilingualism as capable of impairing the intelligence of a whole ethnic group and crippling its creative ability for generations. This was a position shared by many German authors at the time, who saw it to be their patriotic duty to find evidence for the negative effects of bilingualism, especially of German-speaking people (Porsché, 1975).

The situation was somewhat the same in America where bilingualism was also negatively valued in the 1920s and 1930s. Here investigators were more "objective" than their German counterparts, whose evidence was usually based on personal intuition. American investigators typically employed "scientific" pencil-and-paper tests designed to measure differences in intellectual functioning between groups of monolingual and bilingual subjects.

In many such studies the conclusion was drawn that bilingualism had a negative effect on intellectual development (e.g., Manuel & Wright, 1929; Mitchell, 1937; Rigg, 1928; Seidl, 1937; Smith, 1939). According to these and other authors, bilingual children often must think in one language and speak in another with the result that they become mentally uncertain and confused. Bilingualism was thought to be a mental burden for children, causing them to suffer mental fatigue. Bilingual children were seen to be handicapped on intelligence tests, especially those demanding language facility.

In a summary of 32 studies carried out in the United States, Arsenian (1937) noted that 60% of the studies reported evidence that bilingualism is an intellectual handicap; 30% reported that the handicap, if it exists, is a minor one; and 10% found no ill effects of bilingualism on intelligence. Many of these studies, however, lacked adequate controls. Arsenian noted that there is no way of knowing whether the obtained results were found because of the children's bilingualism or because the children in the bilingual groups were disadvantaged socially and economically relative to the children in the monolingual groups. Such studies allow no conclusions to be drawn about the effects of bilingualism on intelligence. Bilinguals may, in fact, have been intellectually disadvantaged relative to monolingual children; but, if so, this need not have been due to their bilingualism.

In an attempt to avoid some of the problems of previous research Arsenian (1937) correlated the mental ability, age-grade status, and socioeconomic background of 1152 Italian and 1196 Jewish bilingual, American-born children, aged 9 to 14 in New York City. He found no significant impact of bilingualism, as measured by a test of bilingual language skills, and found no difference between "high" and "low" bilingual children with respect to mental development.

It should be pointed out, however, that Arsenian's results, though often cited, have been criticized because of the tests of intelligence he employed (Darcy, 1953). In an effort to avoid contamination from verbal ability in the bilingual's second language, he used nonverbal tests of intelligence—the Pintner Nonlanguage Test and the Spearman Visual Perception Test. The validity of these tests was not established and the Spearman test was not standardized.

Some of the classic work on the relationship between bilingualism and intelligence has been carried out in Wales with children bilingual in Welsh and English. Like the American research, these studies at first suggested that bilingualism has a negative effect on intelligence, but subsequent investigations challenged this conclusion. This line of research began with D. J. Saer's (1923) study of 1400 children, aged 7 to 14, in five rural and two urban districts of Wales. He found the following mean IQs:

	Urban	Rural
Monolingual	99	96
Bilingual	100	86

The inferiority of the rural children was attributed to the fact that these children learned their second language in the school; whereas most urban children had learned their second language earlier, through contact in play with English-speaking children. Saer felt that the urban child was able to resolve the conflict between the two languages earlier and with less inner turmoil, whereas the rural child had to expend "mental energy" to learn a new language in school and consequently suffered intellectual retardation in other areas.

Other research on the rural-urban difference has supported Saer's finding that rural children score lower on intelligence tests than urban children. When the analysis is carried further, however, and children are grouped according to the occupational status of their parents, rural-urban differences disappear (Morrison, 1958). Welsh studies in which socioeconomic class has been controlled reveal no differences between bilingual and monolingual children, whether urban or rural, in nonverbal intelligence.

Saer also tested bilingual university students and found that those from rural areas were intellectually inferior to monolingual individuals from the same areas, whereas no such differences were observed between monolingual and bilingual students from urban districts. On the basis of these findings, he concluded that the mental confusion due to bilingualism appears to be of a permanent nature, because it persists in students throughout their university careers. Doubt has been thrown on the validity of these findings, however, because a reanalysis of the data showed the difference between rural monolingual and bilingual students to be statistically insignificant (Jones, 1966).

Subsequent research with monolingual and bilingual children in Wales (Barke, 1933; Jones, 1952, 1966), in which both verbal and nonverbal types of intelligence tests were used, has indicated that the inferiority of bilingual children is a function of the type of material used: if nonverbal materials are used, no differences between the two groups are found; if the materials are verbal, the monolingual children usually score higher. Bilingual children tested in their second language are at a definite disadvantage in intellectual tests with a verbal factor because of their inadequate reading ability and because of inability to deal conceptually in their second language with the degree of fluency and accuracy that monolingual children possess. Bilingual children are especially disadvantaged if the tests emphasize speed of responding.

Research in the United States supports these findings. In reviews of the early research, Darcy (1953, 1963) concluded that apparently contradictory findings arise largely from methodological differences between the various investigations and from the absence of an agreed definition of bilingualism. Investigators have often failed to separate the bilingual factor from environmental factors by not controlling for socioeconomic class. The general trend in the literature indicates that, whereas bilingual children suffer from a language handicap in verbal tests of intelligence, there is no evidence of similar inferiority relative to monolingual children when bilinguals' performance is measured on nonverbal tests of intelligence. Nor is there evidence that bilingualism negatively affects intelligence in the broader sense of basic, universal, cognitive structures.

Indeed, some research has been interpreted as indicating that bilingualism can have a positive effect on intelligence as measured by intelligence tests. Peal and Lambert (1962) compared French-English bilingual children with French monolingual children, matched for age, sex, and socioeconomic status. The children, 164 in all, were 10 years of age and were selected from a larger pool on the basis of measures of bilingualism. All children were given an intelligence test with verbal and nonverbal subsections. Bilingual children were found to score significantly higher than monolingual children in nonverbal intelligence and in total intelligence (verbal plus nonverbal).

These findings can be questioned, however, since Peal and Lambert chose their bilingual subjects on the basis of bilingual ability as measured by tests in French and English. Children were chosen for the bilingual groups whose English (the second language) matched their French. It seems likely that only more linguistically gifted and intelligent French-Canadian children are capable of acquiring, by the age of 10, a command of English equal to their command of French (Macnamara, 1966). Thus, the method of selection may have produced a sample of children who were more intelligent to begin with than the monolingual comparison group. This brings us to the topic of methodological issues in research on the effect of bilingualism on cognitive functioning.

Methodological Issues

We have just seen that many of the early studies on the effect of bilingualism on intelligence suffered from lack of appropriate controls. It has become apparent in recent years that there are also serious methodological deficiencies in the research that has been carried out on the effects of bilingualism on cognitive development. I would like to discuss these problems briefly and then turn to some theoretical implications that can be drawn from our knowledge at present.

General methodological issues.   One general problem of research on the effects of bilingualism on cognitive development relates to *research design*. Most research in this area employs the following design:

Groups	+	*Independent Variable*	——	*Dependent Variable(s)*
Group X		Monolingual experience		Cognitive variable(s).
Group Y		Bilingual experience		Cognitive variable(s).

In the best studies, Groups X and Y are matched on relevant variables, especially socioeconomic status and intelligence. But even when intelligence and socioeconomic status are controlled, there remains the question of whether Groups X and Y are equivalent. There are possible differences in motivation, in parental attitudes toward bilingualism, school experience, ethnic identity, and so on.

Another methodological approach to investigating the effect of bilingualism on cognitive functioning is to study the longitudinal effects of bilingualism on cognitive variables. That is, rather than comparing monolingual and bilingual groups of children at one point in time (once-only design), it is possible to see what effect bilingualism has on a group of children over an extended period of time by measuring the cognitive variables in question repeatedly. This design, which can be called a matched group, repeated measures design, can be illustrated as follows:

| Matched   + | Matching   + | Independent   —— | Dependent |
Groups	Variables	Variable	Variable(s)
Group X	Cognitive	Monolingual	Cognitive
	variable(s)	experience	variables(s)
Group Y	Cognitive	Bilingual	Cognitive
	variable(s)	experience	variable(s)

Here the groups are matched on all relevant variables and on the cognitive variable or variables in question. Subsequent measures of the cognitive variable(s) should indicate whether there is some effect of the bilingual experience on these measures of cognitive functioning.

Studies using this design have not shown positive consequences from bilingualism on intellectual or cognitive functioning. For example, yearly retesting of students in a Canadian bilingual program (Lambert & Tucker, 1972) revealed no differences between bilingual and matched monolingual subjects on measures of intelligence or on measures of creative thinking. Other Canadian studies also reveal no differences between bilingual and monolingual subjects in intellectual functioning (Barik & Swain, 1974) or cognitive flexibility (Bruck, Lambert, & Tucker, 1974).

Another general issue is whether *the measures used to determine balance are related to the dependent variables used to assess cognitive functioning.* Is there some relationship between producing words in a word association test (a measure used in many studies to assess degree of proficiency in the bilingual's two languages) and the ability to list uses for common objects (often taken as a measure of divergent thinking)? If so, then there is a confounding between the independent and the dependent variable. In one such study, Cummins (1976) argued on correlational grounds that no such relationship existed in his data, but as MacNab (1979) pointed out, Cummins did not include non-balanced children in his sample, so that the low correlation between association test scores and divergent thinking may have been spurious.

Then there is the question of *the dependent variables* themselves. A wide variety of measures of cognitive functioning and intelligence have been used, so that comparability between studies is usually impossible. Interpreting the meaning of some studies is difficult: Cummins (1978a) noted that children can give a "correct" response without understanding the principle behind their response. As we have seen, the bilingual children in his study were more willing to call a cat a *dog,* but as likely as monolingual children to assert that if cats were called *dogs,* they would bark. This suggests that results from such studies should be interpreted cautiously until the cognitive processes underlying performance on this sort of task are better understood.

Determining the direction of causality.   We have seen that research on the effects of bilingualism on intelligence has raised the issue of the direction of causality. This is an issue for all research on bilingualism and cognitive functioning: Does bilingualism cause improvement in cognitive functioning or is the direction of causality from cognitive functioning to bilingualism? The second possibility has been posed by MacNab (1979), who reviewed research findings and concluded that there is no evidence in the literature that becoming bilingual leads to cognitive enhancement. Studies that show some positive consequences are, according to MacNab, questionable because of the criterion of "balance" demanded of bilinguals.

MacNab (1979) argued that by choosing "balanced" bilinguals a selection factor might be introduced that affects the results. As MacNab put it, most research with positive findings has been done on children who:

> tend to come from homes where there is an open cognitive ambiance and where there is encouragement of learning in general and language learning in particular. In this environment the brighter, more able child picks up the second language and becomes bilingual, the less able child is less apt to become fully (or balanced) bilingual, in part because he has other options open and does not have to spend energies becoming fluently bilingual if that is difficult for him (p. 251).

That is, the argument is that the non-balanced child is likely to be slower to begin with and so will score lower on most measures of cognitive functioning than will children who have achieved a balance in their bilingualism (see also Macnamara, 1966).

If this is the case—that is, if research has tended to confound independent and dependent variables—then we are at an impasse with respect to the issue of the direction of causality. One way around this problem is to use stepwise regression procedures to test the alternative causal models. This was the strategy used by Hakuta and Diaz (in press), who studied a sample of 123 Spanish-dominant bilingual children in kindergarten and first-grade classes. The children were administered a test of nonverbal intelligence (Ravem) and several tests of language ability in Spanish and English. More balanced children (those with higher scores in English) scored higher on the test of nonverbal intelligence, with age and Spanish ability partialled out. A stepwise multiple regression indicated that a model that claimed that degree of bilingualism affected nonverbal intelligence was more consistent with the data than a model that described the direction of causality as going from intelligence to bilingualism. It should be noted, however, that the relationship between degree of bilingualism and nonverbal intelligence obtained in this study, while significant, was relatively small ($r = .267$), so that there is a great deal of the variance in intelligence that was not accounted for by bilingualism (about 93%).

Type of bilingualism.   Another methodological issue that has frequently been ignored in research has to do with *the manner in which* the child achieved bilingual fluency. Bain (1976) studied groups of 22–24-month-old French-Alsatian children raised according to the principle "one person-one language" or in a family where the practice was to mix both languages. In his study children had to find a marble under a cup or tumbler in each of four instructional situations:

1. *Verbal-immediate,* in which the parent (using the language normally used with the child) instructed the child, "The marble is under the tumbler. Find the marble."
2. *Verbal-delay,* in which there was a 10 second delay between the indication of where the marble was and the instruction to find the marble. During the delay the experimenter diverted the child's attention. "The marble is under the cup. (10 second delay) Find the marble."
3. *Verbal-repeat-change-immediate,* in which the child was given three trials as in the verbal immediate condition, but on the fourth trial the position of the marble was changed. "The marble is under the cup. Find the marble." (3 trials) "The marble is under the tumbler. Find the marble." (4th trial)
4. *Verbal-repeat-change-delay,* where the first three trials were the same as in the verbal-delay condition, and the fourth trial involved changing the position of the marble, again with a delay between the indication of where the marble was and the instructions to find the marble. "The marble is under the tumbler. (10 second delay) Find the marble." (3 trials) "The marble is under the cup. (10 second delay) Find the marble." (4th trial)

Bain found that there was a progression in task difficulty for the two bilingual groups and the monolingual group he tested (Table 7.4). The verbal-immediate task was the easiest and the verbal-repeat-change-delay was the most difficult for all groups. What was particularly interesting in the data was that the bilingual group in which the parents mixed their languages indiscriminately was not different in their performance on this task from the monolingual subjects, whereas the bilingual children raised according to the "one person-one language" principle performed best of all (although the difference was not statistically significant). These findings do raise the question of whether the positive effects of bilingual experience are limited to children raised in a situation in which it is easy to differentiate the two languages. Clearly, similar investigations are needed with other groups and with children of different ages (see Bain & Yu (1980) for some research in this direction).

In addition to the manner in which bilinguals acquire their two languages, there is the question of *the age of acquisition.* Conceivably, the cognitive

TABLE 7.4
Percent Correct Responses of Bilingual and Monolingual Subjects to Four Verbal
Instructional Situations

	Group		
Instructional Strategy	Bilingual "One Person—One Language" (N = 15)	Bilingual Mixed Pre-sentation (N = 17)	Monolingual (N = 16)
Verbal-immediate	84%	63%	65%
Verbal-delay	72	58	57
Verbal-repeat-change-immediate	64	52	53
Verbal-repeat-change-delay	59	47	48

Based on Bain, 1976.

consequences of early bilingualism (simultaneous acquisition) are different from those of late bilingualism (successive acquisition). For example, Balkan (1970) administered several tests of nonverbal abilities that purported to measure cognitive flexibility to monolingual and bilingual children. The bilingual group performed significantly higher than the control monolingual group on several of the measures of flexibility. The results were statistically significant, however, only for children who had become bilingual before the age of four. For children who had become bilingual later, the results favored the bilinguals but did not reach statistical significance.

Lambert and Rawlings (1969) tested French-English bilinguals who had acquired their bilingualism either early (before 6) or late (after 6). The task was to search for core concepts in a mixed-language set of associations (e.g., to search for a word such as *table* when presented with the words, *chaise, food, desk, bois, manger,* etc.). Lambert and Rawlings found that the task was more difficult for the late bilinguals than for early bilinguals, presumably because the task was more confusing and distracting for the late bilinguals whose languages were more functionally separate.

On the basis of a series of experiments comparing bilinguals who had acquired their languages before the age of 4 with those who had acquired their languages later, Vaid (in press) concluded that early onset of bilingualism predisposes the subject to a semantic mode of processing linguistic input, whereas late onset of bilingualism leads to a greater sensitivity to surface features of the input. In one experiment, for example, subjects were asked to decide, as quickly as possible, whether successively presented words rhymed

or were from a common semantic category (e.g., *nose: rose/legs*). Early bilinguals performed better on the semantic task than late bilinguals or monolingual subjects. Vaid hypothesized that the relative salience of meaning for
early bilinguals may arise from their early exposure to different forms conveying a single referent. In contrast, late bilinguals were proficient in determining whether words rhymed—a task that requires attention to surface
features. The relative salience of surface features for late bilinguals was
thought to have developed as a byproduct of a tendency to keep their two
languages apart (surface features being better markers of the language-of-
input).

At this point, there is very little research on the effects of early versus late
bilingualism. The research that exists does suggest that there are behavioral
differences between subjects who acquire their two languages early and
those who acquire a second language after the first is established. This
research underscores the need to keep this distinction in mind in any discussion of the effects of bilingualism on the individual.

Theoretical Implications

What theoretical conclusions can be drawn on the basis of research on the
cognitive consequences of bilingualism in early childhood? The first to be
discussed here relates to the issue of the validity of Cummins' (1979)
threshold hypothesis. The second relates to the question of how the consequences of early bilingualism on cognitive functioning—if there are such
consequences—can be thought to come about.

The threshold hypothesis.   To account for the possibility of negative as
well as positive consequences from bilingualism, Cummins (1979) put forth
the "threshold hypothesis," arguing that the positive or negative effects of
a bilingual experience are a function of an intervening factor, the level of
competence bilingual children achieve in their two languages:

> Specifically, there may be threshold levels of linguistic competence which bi-
> lingual children must attain both in order to avoid cognitive deficits and to
> allow the potentially beneficial aspects of becoming bilingual to influence their
> cognitive growth (p. 229).

The threshold notion assumes that some limited knowledge of the second
language must be attained before any of the positive benefits of bilingualism are achieved. Similarly, there must be a minimal proficiency in
the first language, especially in linguistic minority children whose first
language is threatened by the acquisition of a second language.

Cummins proposed that there are in fact two thresholds (Table 7.5). The first is the lower threshold that children must attain if they are not to suffer negative consequences from bilingualism ("subtractive" bilingualism). The higher threshold must be attained if the child is to experience positive benefits from bilingualism ("additive" bilingualism). Children who are above the lower threshold in their proficiency, but who have not attained the higher threshold (proficiency in both languages) are likely to be dominant in one language, and their bilingualism has neither positive nor negative consequences. The thresholds (Cummins, 1979) cannot be defined in absolute terms, "rather [they are] likely to vary according to the children's stage of cognitive development and the academic demands of different stages of schooling" (p. 230).

What support is there for the threshold notion? In one of the most direct tests of the hypothesis, Duncan and De Avila (1979) found that minority-language children who had developed high levels of first- and second-language proficiency, as measured by the Language Assessment Scales (LAS), performed significantly better than monolinguals and other subgroups of bilinguals (partial and limited bilinguals on the LAS) on a battery of cognitive tasks. This suggests that the proficient bilinguals had achieved high enough levels in both languages to experience positive cognitive effects.

Again, however, there is the problem of the direction of causality. In the Duncan and De Avila study, it may simply have been the case that the less

TABLE 7.5
The Threshold Hypothesis

		Type of Bilingualism	Cognitive Effect
		1. Additive Bilingualism	Positive
		High levels in both languages	
Higher threshold			
	↑	2. Dominant Bilingualism	Neither Positive nor Negative
			Native-like level in one of the languages	Cognitive Effects
Lower threshold			
	| ↑	3. Subtractive Bilingualism	Negative
			Low level in both languages	

Based on Cummins 1979.

intelligent children were less successful at acquiring a second language (hence were less likely to belong to a "balanced" group) and scored lower on measures of cognitive functioning. In contrast, it could be that the more intelligent children were more successful in learning the second language and scored higher on measures of cognitive functioning.

What evidence is there for the lower threshold? In support of this notion Cummins (1979) cited the Swedish research of Skutnabb–Kangas and Toukomaa (1976) that indicated that some groups of minority-language and migrant children show less than native-like skills in both languages, with detrimental cognitive and academic consequences. Presumably, these are children who did not reach the lowest threshold in linguistic ability and so experience subtractive bilingualism.

But does linguistic ability alone predict what consequences bilingual experience will have? Lower SES children are likely to be discriminated against socially, and these social and economic factors, rather than language per se, may have accounted for their poor showing on language tests in the Swedish research. MacNab (1979) argued that the minority-language child is

> forced to learn the second language, no matter what the cost in other learning. This demand for second-language skills may be especially difficult for average and duller children because slowness in learning the language cuts into time needed for other learning and because they do not have the opportunity to specialize in other subject areas where they might find learning easier. In addition, the subtractive environment is a stressful one because the child's cultural heritage is denigrated by the society (p. 251).

In MacNab's view, positive and negative consequences of bilingualism can be explained by a model that stresses the child's opportunity for exposure to the second language, innate differences in learning ability, and differential rewards for learning the second language.

Although MacNab contrasts his model to Cummins' threshold hypothesis, it should be noted that Cummins (1979) was careful to include social and motivational variables in his larger "interaction" model. Both Cummins and MacNab would agree that some children—those raised in "subtractive" environments—require special educational treatment if their bilingual experience is to be a successful one.

To summarize, Cummins' hypothesis is appealing in that it provides a way of accounting for differential outcomes of bilingual experience. It may, however, be an oversimplification to define the threshold levels on the basis of purely linguistic criteria. There are also social and motivational factors that have to be considered to explain why some children fail to profit from a bilingual experience.

Language and cognition. There have been a number of proposals to explain claims of cognitive advantages for bilingual children. For example, Cummins (1976) and Ben Zeev (1977) have suggested that the cognitive advantages of bilinguals could be explained by the bilingual's need to become aware of and manipulate linguistic structures. As we have seen, Ben Zeev argued that in order to avoid linguistic interference, bilingual children need to develop greater awareness and sensitivity to linguistic cues.

But is there a cognitive advantage for bilingual children? That is, has the bilingual child acquired an analytic frame of mind, a way of thinking about experience, that the monolingual child lacks? The findings of research on sound-meaning differentiation, in which the child is asked which of two words, *can* and *hat* is more like *cap,* are questionable because the original findings (Ianco–Worrall, 1972) were not replicated (Cummins, 1978b). Research on the interchangeability of words ("Can you call a dog *cat*?") is also questionable because bilingual children do not show better understanding of the underlying principle than monolingual children do (Cummins, 1978a).

The superior performance of bilingual children on word substitution tasks, especially ones that require violation of syntactic selection rules (*macaroni* for *I,* as in Ben Zeev, 1977) can be explained on linguistic rather than cognitive grounds. As Aronsson (1981) has noted, the bilingual child has more crucial experiences concerning syntactic form than a monolingual child has. Bilingual children not only know that something can be said in a variety of ways (active vs. passive modes)—as all children do—but they come to understand that there are different formal means of realization in the two languages.

The underlying assumption of many investigators in this area is that bilingual children acquire some insight into the arbitrariness and complexity of language due to their bilingual experience, and that this sense of relativity generalizes to other cognitive tasks. Yet even monolingual children have to deal with lexical arbitrariness. As Aronsson (1981) put it:

> For instance, there is not really any reason to believe that the parallel existence
> of e.g. BOY:POJKE (English:Swedish) would assist the child's thinking more
> than the exposure to relative synonyms (e.g. BOY:GUY in American English)
> (p. 12).

It may be that the bilingual child's advantage comes more from a sensitivity to the formal aspects of language, than from any more general cognitive insights.

At this point we do not know enough to make any definitive statements about the effects of early bilingualism on cognitive development. As we have seen, there are serious methodological problems with almost all research in this area, and statements about the positive (or negative) effects of early bilingualism on cognitive functioning should be viewed with scepticism. Until we have longitudinal studies with adequate controls (through random selection or via statistical procedures using multivariate techniques), no definitive statements are possible.

CONCLUSION

It is possible to distinguish two positions or stances on the issue of the consequences of early bilingualism: a "maximalist" and a "minimalist" position. Those who take a *maximalist* position hold that early bilingualism is essentially a positive experience for children. Not only do children acquire two languages, they do so with ease (whereas older children and adults need to exert considerable effort to learn a second language). In this view, there is no such thing as a "bilingual handicap." Studies such as Ronjat's or Leopold's are cited as evidence that children can learn two languages at once without one interfering with the other. Furthermore, the argument is made that early bilingualism leads to an analytic attitude toward language and toward cognitive tasks. Bilingual children are seen to be more cognitively flexible than their monolingual counterparts. Parents are urged to raise their children bilingually because of the linguistic and cognitive advantages that are thought to follow from such an experience.

The *minimalist* position holds that early bilingualism has little—or even a negative—effect on children. Although the older notion that early bilingualism leads to linguistic and cognitive confusion is usually rejected, advocates of the minimalist position point out that most case studies were done by linguists with their own children. Studies based on immigrant workers' children throughout the world do not show positive benefits from bilingualism. In fact, many of these children seem to have learned both of their languages poorly. The advice of some educators is that such children should attain mastery in one language before being taught a second.

There is an *intermediate position* possible between the extreme maximalist and the minimalist ones. According to this position what matters in determining the effects of early bilingualism on children is *how* the languages are presented to the child. If the two languages are clearly differentiated in adult speech, the child will be more able to keep them apart and avoid mixing their lexicons and syntaxes. Children who have only passive exposure to one of their languages are less likely to deal successfully with that language: a critical predictor of success in mastering two languages is how active the child is in using both languages in conversation with adults and peers.

It seems clear that the child who has mastered two languages has a linguistic advantage over the monolingual child. Bilingual children become aware that there are two ways of saying the same thing. But does this sensitivity to the lexical and formal aspects of language generalize to cognitive functioning? There is no conclusive answer to this question—mainly because it has proven so difficult to apply the necessary controls in research. The ideal study of the effects of early bilingualism would be one in which children, matched on relevant variables, were placed at random into groups receiving or not receiving the bilingual experience and were tested longitudinally on appropriate measures of cognitive functioning. Unfortunately, this is not very practical because parents are not likely to accept being told that they should or should not raise their children bilingually. So we are left with studies that do not employ random assignment, most of which have not controlled the relevant variables (especially intelligence), have not been longitudinal, and have not used reliable dependent variables.

Without randomization, researchers must compare children from families that decide to raise their children bilingually with children from families in the same community who do not raise their children bilingually. But as MacNab (1979) pointed out, parents who decide to raise their children bilingually are likely to be different, in important ways, from other parents. The family environment is probably different from that where children are raised monolingually, and it becomes impossible to separate the linguistic and cognitive consequences due to family environment from those due to bilingualism per se.

If parents do decide to raise their children bilingually—either for educational and cultural purposes or because of immigration to a new country—it seems clear that the child must have the opportunity to "negotiate meaning" in both languages. The evidence from research on child language development indicates that the quality of parental contributions to conversation is a strong predictor of the child's language learning. Parents who habitually collaborate in conversations designed to encourage children to express their needs, ideas, and intentions will enrich their children linguistically and cognitively, whether this be in an environment in which a single language is spoken or in a bilingual environment.

8 Conclusion

In the beginning of this book I mentioned that there are a number of common misconceptions about second-language acquisition in children that do not stand up under empirical scrutiny. In concluding, I will look at some of these unproven assertions by way of summarizing what is not known about childhood bilingualism. Once the limits of knowledge have been delineated, I will set down some propositions I feel are warranted on the basis of research on second-language acquisition in childhood.

SOME COMMON MISCONCEPTIONS

There are a number of widely held beliefs about second-language acquisition in children that are unsubstantiated. Of course, there is a sense in which no scientific statement is ever definitively proven. Scientific knowledge consists of an accumulation of probabilistic statements, some more likely to be true that others. To say that a scientific statement is proven is merely to say that the evidence to date leads one to the conclusion that the proposition is likely to be true. The propositions I shall examine here, however, although often accepted as proven, seem as likely to be false as true. I shall restrict the discussion to six such statements.

> *Proposition 1. The young child acquires a language more quickly and easily than an adult because the child is biologically programmed to acquire languages, whereas the adult is not.*

215

This hypothesis is accepted dogma in the writings of many authors discussing second-language acquisition (e.g., Andersson, 1969; Fodor, Bever, & Garrett, 1974; Jakobovits, 1972; Wilkins, 1972). There are two parts to this proposition: first, the statement that children acquire languages more quickly and easily than adults, and second, the statement that the reason for this superiority is biologically based.

Let us consider the second statement first. Advocates of a critical period notion argue that the child's brain possesses a plasticity with respect to language that the adult's brain has lost. Lenneberg (1967) proposed that the reason for this cerebral plasticity relates to the fact that the child's brain is not completely lateralized with respect to language function, whereas the adult's brain is. As evidence he cited research with aphasic adults and children that indicated that damage to the right hemisphere causes more language disturbance in children than in adults and studies that show that adults cannot transfer language functions after left hemispherectomies, whereas children can. He argued from this that it is only before puberty that the brain possesses the plasticity necessary to acquire languages effortlessly through mere exposure.

Reanalysis of the data on which Lenneberg based his conclusion has shown that it is not puberty that is the cutoff point for lateralization of language function but that lateralization is essentially complete by the age of 4 or 5, or even earlier. If this is the case, the critical period has to be revised downward to between the ages of 2 and 4 or 5. This seems to be counter to the views of advocates of the critical period notion and ignores a great deal of evidence that language learning continues during the elementary school years (Palermo & Molfese, 1972).

In addition, the question of the extent to which components of language are functionally and neurologically asymmetrical is a topic of a great deal of contemporary research, some of which suggests that there is more plasticity with respect to language function after childhood than was previously thought to be the case. Research with split-brain patients, for example, suggests that the minor hemisphere can perform certain linguistic tasks. There are also data from normal subjects that point to the same conclusion.

Returning to the first part of the proposition, what evidence is there that children acquire languages more quickly and easily than adults? Some authors have pointed out that the child's first-language acquisition is by no means as quick as is commonly supposed: given the amount of exposure the child has to the language, acquisition appears to be relatively slow. Furthermore, other authors who have had close contact with children feel that first- and second-language learning is not as easy for the child as theorists would have it. The language learning process is by no means automatic for the young child: there are many false starts and often considerable frustration.

The myth of easy and rapid language acquisition by children is reminiscent of the myth of the happy childhood.

Experimental research in which children have been compared to adults in second-language learning has consistently demonstrated the inferiority of young children under controlled conditions. Even when the method of teaching appears to favor learning in children, they perform more poorly than adults. The one area where children have been found to perform better than adults is in pronunciation; otherwise there is little evidence from such studies for their vaunted language-learning talents.

Nonetheless, the literature abounds with anecdotal and impressionistic evidence that children learn faster than adults. Even the United States Supreme Court, in one of its decisions, cited the superiority of the child in language learning (Donoghue, 1968). Is this superiority illusory? One difficulty in answering this question is that of applying the same criteria of language proficiency in the case of the child and the adult. The requirements of communicative competence are quite different in the two cases. The child's constructions are shorter and simpler, and vocabulary is relative small when compared with what is necessary for adults to speak at the same level of competence in a second language as they achieve in their first language. The child does not have to learn as much to acquire communicative competence as the adult.

Furthermore, there are psychological and social factors that favor the child. Children are likely to have fewer inhibitions and to be less embarrassed when they make mistakes than are adults. Children are likely to speak more and receive more feedback. They may be more motivated than are adults: there is probably more incentive in the playground and school to communicate in the second language that there is for the adult on the job or with friends (who may speak the individual's first language anyway). It frequently happens that children are placed in more situations where they are forced to speak the second language than are adults.

In short, even assuming that the same criteria are applied in both cases and that children are found to be superior to adults in acquiring a second language, there is no way of ruling out the possibility that this difference is caused by psychological and social factors, rather than by biological factors. When the same criteria are applied and other factors are controlled in experimental research, children have invariably done poorer than adults in second-language learning tasks. The one exception is pronunciation, and it may be that there is, in this case, a biological critical period. Even here, however, not enough is known about relevant neurological processes.

Proposition 2. The younger the child, the more skilled in acquiring a second language.

Many authors have argued that the brain becomes less flexible with age and that it is therefore best to begin as early as possible with second-language training to utilize this neurological plasticity. Researchers dealing with this question, however, have generally found that older children do better in acquiring a second language than younger children. When appropriate controls are employed for amount of exposure to the language, older children have been found to be superior in all aspects of language acquisition—with the exception of phonology.

A recent variant of the second proposition is the notion that, although older learners acquire morphology and syntax in a second language faster than younger children, younger learners ultimately attain higher levels of proficiency (Krashen, Long, & Scarcella, 1979). That is, *rate* favors older children, but *ultimate attainment* favors younger. As we saw in Chapter 3, however, the evidence in support of this hypothesis is questionable. Even the study by Patkowski (1980), which appears to lend it most support, does not provide unequivocal evidence that younger children (below 12) ultimately learn a second language better than those who start at an older age (beyond 12). At this point any argument that "younger is better" must be regarded with a certain amount of suspicion.

This is not to say that early exposure to a second language is in some way detrimental to the child. The research suggests that younger children do not necessarily have an advantage over older children and, because of their cognitive and experiential limitations vis-à-vis older children, are actually at a disadvantage in learning a language—other things being equal. The apparent superiority of younger children is probably due, once again, to different criteria of communicative competence, different amounts of exposure, and certain social and psychological factors.

In many situations these nonlinguistic factors work to the advantage of the young child. The preschool child, for example, may have more exposure to a second language in play situations than the school child who experiences a second language as one subject among many in the school curriculum. The younger child may be less inhibited, less afraid of making mistakes, and more willing to learn the language than an older counterpart learning in the classroom (Schumann, 1975).

Indeed, a good deal of the case-study literature points to the advantage of beginning second-language training early, if possible in the family environment simultaneous with exposure to the first language. If persons and situations are kept linguistically distinct, the child is likely to acquire both languages with no more difficulty than the monolingual child acquires a single language. Ronjat's (1913) motto of "one person, one language" appears to be an important rule for successful, second-language training of young children.

The success of young children in acquiring two languages under such conditions need not be attributed to superior language learning skills. Given the same amount and quality of exposure, an older child (or an adult) would presumably do just as well, most likely better. This, of course, is not to denigrate the young child's achievement or to downgrade the advantages of early introduction to a second language. Older children and adults do not have the amount of time at their disposal for learning a second language that the young child does. There is no reason not to utilize this advantage.

Proposition 3. Second-language acquisition is a qualitatively different process than first-language acquisition.

This statement can also be viewed as a corollary of the critical period notion. If one assumes that the individual is biologically preprogrammed to acquire a language before puberty and subsequently loses this facility, some way must be provided of accounting for the fact that adults can also learn a second language. This is done by assuming that second-language learning involves radically different processes before and after puberty. Before puberty, the individual has available a language acquisition device that is preprogrammed for optimal linguistic coding. After puberty, a less optimal language acquisition device must be utilized, one based on general cognitive coding ability. This appears to be the position held by Chomsky (1968), who has argued that the mind is divided into faculties and that whereas first-language acquisition takes place through the faculty of language learning, which atrophies at a certain age, subsequent language learning must rely on other faculties of the mind such as the logical or the mathematical.

It is difficult to disprove such a statement, because it does not lend itself readily to empirical testing. What evidence there is, however, does not support Chomsky's view. Research in which adults acquiring a second language were compared to children acquiring the same language as a first language has shown that the adults pass through essentially the same developmental stages as children do in acquiring the target language (Cook, 1973) and that children and adults process language in basically the same ways (Palermo & Howe, 1970). There has not been enough research of this nature, but what work has been done does not support the view that second-language learning in adults and first-language acquisition in children are radically different processes.

Studies of children acquiring a second language have yielded abundant evidence that second-language acquisition involves a developmental sequence that recapitulates the sequence characteristic of the second language rather than that of the child's first language (e.g., Dato, 1971; Milon, 1974; Ravem, 1974). That is, Japanese-, Norwegian-, or Spanish-speaking children learning English do not apply the structures of their first language to English but rather progress through a developmental sequence that is similar to that characteristic of children acquiring English as a first language (although the rate of development varies depending on the age of the child).

Dulay and Burt (1973) argued that Chinese- and Spanish-speaking children acquired English morphemes ("functors") in the same sequence, although the order of acquisition differed greatly in the child's own first language. They concluded that the children were not using the strategies of their first language as the basis for approaching their second. It should be pointed out, however, that there is some disagreement about the implications of the morpheme studies. Longitudinal case studies sometimes show the same results as cross-sectional research (Kessler & Idar, 1977) and sometimes yield very different results (Hakuta, 1974a; Rosansky, 1976). Furthermore, as Rosansky (1976) pointed out, the morpheme order obtained by analyzing spontaneous speech does not always correlate with the morpheme order obtained by elicitation techniques such as the Bilingual Syntax Measure. Indeed, the cross-sectional studies measure the *accuracy* with which morphemes are supplied in obligatory contexts at one point in time, whereas the case studies deal with the *acquisition* of the morphemes as measured by their presence in obligatory contexts at different points in time.

Nonetheless, there is no evidence for the contention that second-language acquisition is radically different from first-language acquisition because second-language acquisition is filtered through the structures of the first language and hence involves different processes (Haugen, 1970; Stern, 1970). The evidence suggests that first-language structures have a minimal effect on the course of second-language development. The child seems in some way to develop strategies that derive from properties of the second language rather than from the child's own first language.

This suggests that there is a unity of process that characterizes all language acquisition, whether of a first or second language, at all ages. In acquiring a second language, the individual uses the same strategies that are employed in acquiring a first language, although these strategies are now adapted to the second language so that the sequence of development reflects this language more than the first language. Although there are differences in input conditions, in ability to store and retrieve information, in linguistic knowledge, and so forth, the adult, the older, and the younger child seem to process language in the same way so that the developmental sequence they pass through is remarkably similar.

Proposition 4. Interference between first and second languages is an inevitable and ubiquitous part of second-language learning.

In a discussion of the differences between first- and second-language acquisition, Prator (1969) mentioned interference between languages as a factor so obviously influencing second-language acquisition as not to require amplification. The case-study literature, however, suggests that under certain conditions interference between languages rarely occurs. Especially in the simultaneous acquisition of two languages, where the input conditions are such as to allow the child to keep the two languages separate, little interference is found. In reviewing his findings concerning his daughter's early language development, for example, Leopold (1949a) reported little evidence for interference in phonology, semantics, or syntax.

Research with children who acquire a second language after a first language has been established also indicates that under certain conditions very little interference occurs. When the larger social milieu provides a supportive context in the sense that the child has peers to communicate with in the second language, interference is minimized. When, on the other hand, the second language is not the language of the child's larger social environment, interference between languages increases. This was proposed as a reason why so much interference between languages is found when a second language is learned in the school and the child has little or no contact with peers who speak the language.

The attempt systematically to identify sources of errors in the speech of second-language learners reveals that relatively few of the errors that second-language learners make can be attributed to interference from their first language. Generally, no more than a third of the errors in a speech corpus can be identified as due to intrusion of first-language structures. The majority of the errors that second-language learners make are the result of generalizing and misapplying the rules of the second language before they are mastered, oversimplifying morphology and syntax in the way that first-language learners oversimplify, and other errors also found in the developmental data for first-language learners of the target language. Some errors are unique in that they do not seem to reflect developmental factors or first-language structures.

One problem in this area is the difficulty of deciding whether a particular mistake is due to developmental features or to intrusions from the first language. When a Spanish-speaking child says *It no cause too much trouble,* does this mistake reflect the influence of Spanish or a developmental stage that native, English-speaking children also pass through? No unequivocal answer seems possible, and such errors are best classified as ambiguous.

Evidence for the predominance of developmental errors in children's speech comes from the study of Dulay and Burt (1974b), in which they found that speech samples of Spanish-, Chinese-, Japanese-, and Norwegian-speaking children learning English as a second language indicated that the types of mistakes made by the children were strikingly similar. If first-language structures were the major source of a second-language learner's errors, one would expect that children with such structurally dissimilar first languages would make very dissimilar mistakes in their English. Apparently, the child is guided more by input than by previous learning experience (Wagner–Gough & Hatch, 1975).

This does not mean that interference or transfer errors are unimportant in second-language acquisition. We have seen that first-language influences do enter into various aspects of second-language performance (Hecht & Mulford, 1982; Keller–Cohen, 1979; Lightbrown, 1980), and that the error-analysis approach is subject to criticism. Again, emphasis should be on where and why transfer errors occur. There is some evidence that such errors are more frequent early in the process of second-language learning and when the particular construction to be mastered proves especially intractable. In such cases, the child second-language learner uses what information is available to solve the linguistic riddle. And since a first language is available, the child will use it.

Proposition 5. There is a single path to acquiring a second language in childhood.

There is a tendency in textbooks to make it appear that language learning is a uniform process. Certainly the evidence for uniformity exists. Studies of first-language learning—especially studies of various syntactic forms such as questions and the negative—indicate that children pass through regular developmental stages (Lindfors, 1980). We have seen that children who learn English as their second language pass through many of these stages, regardless of their first language. This does not imply, however, that children proceed in some lock-step fashion to learn either first or second languages.

The evidence is that children vary greatly in language learning—whether it be a first or a second language. Research on first-language learning has consistently demonstrated that children differ in the rate at which they learn their language. Recent research has shown, in addition, that children differ in the manner in which they learn their first language. Peters (1977) and others have demonstrated that children display different learning styles. Some children seem to take language word by word, analyzing it into its components; other children approach language more globally, seizing on whole phrases or clauses to express early intentions.

There are also differences between children that reflect cultural factors. Children in the black and white communities that Heath (1983) studied in South Carolina differed in the kind of input they received from their parents and the parents differed in the expectations they had concerning their children's language learning. From the beginning children in the white community were seen as conversational partners by their parents. They received the simplified caretaker speech noted in many studies (Snow & Ferguson, 1977). Their early utterances were attended to and rewarded. None of this was true for children in the black community, who grew up in a very rich language environment, but who did not receive as much direct support and tutoring in language. They were not expected to be conversational partners with adults; their speech was not given much attention until they could hold the floor on their own. Children in the black community appeared to learn to speak by imitating the ends of phrases they heard in adult speech. Their learning experience—like that of many children in cultures that differ from the American middle-class culture—was quite different from that typically described in the literature on first-language acquisition.

Evidence also exists for variation in the second-language learning process. Even children in the same family, who learned their second language under very similar conditions, differed in certain aspects of syntactic and phonological development (Wode, 1981). Children adopt different strategies, so that even while progressing through the same developmental stages, their errors differ considerably (Meisel, 1980).

The richest source of information about the way in which individual children differ in their acquisition of a second language is probably Wong Fillmore's (1976) investigation of five Spanish-speaking children acquiring English. As we saw in Chapter 6, Wong Fillmore itemized various social and cognitive strategies that the children employed and showed how the children differed in their utilization of these strategies. She saw these differences to be reflections of personality factors that interact with the requirements of the situation and the strategies that are called for at various points in the learning process.

One especially important contribution of Wong Fillmore's research is the emphasis put on the role of formulaic speech in child second-language learning. Although there were differences between children in the extent to which they experimented with formulas, all of the children used formulas to explore the structural possibilities of the language. Wong Fillmore's research has brought the importance of formulaic speech to the attention of researchers in first- and second-language learning, some of whom have argued that imitated formulas constitute a repertoire of linguistic structures from which children gradually discover information about the rules of the language.

Proposition 6. The experience of early bilingualism positively (or negatively) affects the child's language development, cognitive functioning and/or intellectual development.

A great deal of research has been conducted to determine the consequences of early child bilingualism. Unfortunately, this is a research area where the methodological problems are considerable, and there are very few studies that have succeeded in ruling out extraneous factors so as to assure that the obtained effects can be interpreted as the result of bilingualism and nothing else. In particular, much of the early research failed to rule out socioeconomic factors, so that generalizations based on this research are questionable.

Recent research suggests that bilingualism may delay the lexical and syntactic development of the young child in comparison to monolingual speakers (the "bilingual handicap"). But the delay seems to be of very short duration; bilingual children seem to catch up quickly and investigators have been especially impressed with how little interference there is between the bilingual's two languages, once the languages are differentiated.

Is there a "bilingual advantage" in language development? Some research suggests that the bilingual experience sensitizes children to the formal aspects of language. Thus bilingual children performed better than monolingual children on word substitution tasks that required violations of syntactic selection rules (Ben Zeev, 1977). This may be due to the bilingual child's understanding that the same idea can have different formal means of realization—a consequence of having access to two languages. There has not been sufficient well-controlled research on this topic, however, so that it would be premature to postulate any such bilingual advantage.

The discussion in Chapter 7 of the consequences of early bilingualism on cognitive development led to a similar conclusion. There is not enough evidence to say that early bilingualism produces either a handicap or an advantage. One particular recurrent methodological problem for research showing a positive effect is determining the direction of causality: does bilingualism lead to cognitive advantages or are bilingual children smarter to begin with? Research showing negative consequences usually has failed to control for socioeconomic factors, intelligence, and even facility in understanding instructions.

The effects of bilingualism may be different for early and late bilinguals. That is, children who grow up learning two languages simultaneously may experience cognitive consequences from their bilingualism that are quite different from those experienced by children who learn a second language once the first is established. There is some research that supports this hypothesis, but not enough is known at this point about the effects of different types of bilingual experience.

Finally, the evidence from research concerning the effects of bilingualism on intelligence supports neither the handicap nor the advantage position. Bilingualism seems to have no negative consequences for intellectual development as measured by intelligence on nonverbal IQ tests. When IQ tests with a large verbal component are employed, the bilingual child may be at a disadvantage when compared to a monolingual counterpart and may do more poorly. This is hardly evidence that bilingualism has negative consequences on intellectual development. On the other hand, the evidence that bilingual children do better on tests of intelligence is methodologically suspect.

In short, almost no general statements are warranted by research on the effects of early bilingualism. It has not been demonstrated that early bilingualism has positive or negative consequences for language development, cognitive functioning, or intellectual development. In each of these areas the findings of research are either contradicted by other research or can be questioned on methodological grounds. The one statement that is supported by research findings is that command of a second language makes a difference if the child is tested in that language—a not very surprising finding.

SECOND-LANGUAGE ACQUISITION PROCESSES

It is, unfortunately, easier to point to what is not known or proven than to attempt to spell out what can be said about second-language acquisition in children. Nonetheless, there are some general statements that seem warranted in the light of the evidence considered. These relate to the three central issues discussed in examining the literature: the similarity between first- and second-language developmental processes, interference phenomena in second-language acquisition, and the process of code switching.

Proposition 1. First and second language acquisition involve essentially the same general (perhaps universal) cognitive strategies.

This statement is an elaboration of the argument above that first- and second-language learning involve the same processes. I maintained there that the evidence to date favors the hypothesis that there is a unity of process that characterizes all language acquisition, whether first- or second-language, and that this unity of process reflects the use of similar strategies of language acquisition.

What is known about these strategies? First of all, they relate to all aspects of language acquisition, not just syntactic development. We saw in Chapter 2 that the child, in acquiring a first language, must distinguish sound units, learn phonological rules, and attach sounds to their referents. Furthermore, the child has to develop a dictionary of meanings and give semantic relations grammatical expression. We have evidence that children learn the more simple rules of phonology before the more complex, that they give the meaning of individual words a broad extension, only gradually assigning words roughly the same set of semantic features they have for adults. These findings hold for both first- and second-language learning. In general, however, second-language research has tended to focus on the processes involved in the acquisition of syntax.

We know, for example, that the meanings of words are important, since the syntactic features of sentences such as *John hit the ball* become apparent only after the child understands the meaning of the individual words. Word-order regularities are also an important clue for the child in discovering the rules of syntax. In early sentences the child learning English tends to prefer a subject–verb–object sequence, both as a means of comprehending sentences and in production. There is also evidence that the child generally proceeds from the simple to the more complex in syntactic development, acquiring first forms that are structurally more simple and then advancing to those that are structurally more complex.

Research with children acquiring second languages indicates that the process of second-language acquisition looks much like the process of first-language acquisition. Ervin–Tripp's (1974) research in particular shows that early sentences in a second language are similar in their function, their form, their semantic redundancy, their reliance on short-term memory storage to those of the first language. Simple word-order strategies are preferred, even though the child has learned more complex strategies—e.g., for negative and interrogative constructions—in the first language. Overgeneralization of lexical and of morphological forms occurs in second-language acquisition as in first-language acquisition.

Comparison of children acquiring their first language with adults learning second languages shows that the developmental process, mistakes in imitation and comprehension, strategies for dealing with such irregularities as past-tense inflection, are all similar. When confronted with embedded sentences, adults do not utilize the knowledge of how to deal with these sentences they have from their experience with their first language; instead they approach embedded sentences as the child does and make the same mistakes. The evidence again suggests that there is a similarity of process and strategy.

There is no denying that the child and the adult perform at levels appropriate to their ages. There are vast differences between the 3-year-old child and the 30-year-old adult. Adults have superior memory heuristics at their disposal that enable them to retain longer input and discover meaning more easily. They have the lexicon of their first language to fall back on in attempting to decipher the lexicon of the second language. The adult can process information more quickly and has more experiential knowledge than the child.

The fact that adults make use of acquired knowledge, skills, and tactics does not, however, distinguish their learning process from that of the child. Children also use their acquired knowledge and skills. The essential question is whether differences in cognitive abilities and knowledge of the world and language mean that different processes are involved. It seems unparsimonious to suppose that this is the case. As Kinsbourne (1981) concluded after summarizing the neurological evidence:

> [T]he literature on brain basis of bilingualism teaches us to be as sparing of hypotheses as nature is of organizing principles. In phylogeny, the same mechanism is used over and over again to meet new and different adaptive needs. In language acquisition, matters also appear to be simpler than believed and the following null hypotheses have not been disconfirmed as yet. Second and subsequent languages are acquired much as the first, making allowance only for known differences in cognitive strategies at different stages in the life span. The same brain territories are involved in all language acquisition. The aging of the brain during childhood does not diminish ability to learn the vocabulary, syntax, or pronunciation of a second language, and no period of the life span is critical to such acquisition. The well-documented greater plasticity of the immature than the mature brain relates to the ability to compensate for structural loss of brain tissue; it has not been shown to affect the functioning of the brain while it is intact (p. 56).

Research on speech production supports this conclusion. Longitudinal studies of syntactic development generally show the same developmental sequences for first- and second-language acquisition (e.g., Dato, 1971; Milon, 1974; Ravem, 1968, 1974). There is some evidence—especially with respect to the acquisition of negative constructions—that the second-language learner will deviate from the pattern of acquisition observed in first-language acquisition (Cancino, Rosansky, & Schumann, 1974; Hakuta, 1975; Wode, 1978). The child may indeed revert to first-language structures—e.g., early in the acquisition of the second language or when faced with a linguistic riddle that remains insoluble. In doing so, the child is simply using the strategy of employing what is known to solve the problem— just as the child does in acquiring the first language.

This strategy can be thought of as an abstract cognitive operation that transcends the pecularities of specific languages. Such abstract operations characterize first- and second-language acquisition. They tell the learner to pay attention to word order, to use meaning as a clue to syntax, to simplify, to interpret what is unknown in terms of what is known, to generalize rules, and so on. In addition, the second-language learner uses a strategy of employing formulaic expressions in speech, which are subsequently broken down as the linguistic features of the constituents are mastered (Wong Fillmore, 1976).

Research on discourse analysis also suggests that second-language learners internalize language rules on the basis of patterns acquired in discourse sets (Wagner–Gough, 1978). Evelyn Hatch and her coworkers

(Huang & Hatch, 1978; Peck, 1978; Wagner–Gough, 1978) have found that children acquiring a second language imitate sentences of considerable length and complexity and recall these sentences in the appropriate context. The strategy of analyzing the internal structure of prepackaged routines acquired through imitation may be one of the most important techniques employed in second-language acquisition (Vihman, 1982b).

It should be pointed out that the use of general strategies by second-language learners does not rule out the possibility of individual differences in acquisition. Wong Fillmore's (1976) research showed how individual variation occurs among children employing the same cognitive and social strategies. Psychological and social psychological variables certainly enter into the process of language acquisition. Children and adults who possess the requisite cognitive styles and social skills are at an advantage when compared to those who lack these personality traits and skills.

Proposition 2. Errors of various types are best described in strategy terms.

I argued above that interference between languages is not as inevitable or ubiquitous as was once supposed. Under certain conditions of acquisition, very little interference between languages has been observed. Much of what appears to be interference between languages is actually a result of strategies the learner uses to discover regularities in the target language. In fact, I propose that all errors represent learning strategies.

Dulay and Burt (1974b) found that children of various linguistic backgrounds made the same types of errors in acquiring English as a second language. That Spanish-, Chinese-, Japanese-, and Norwegian-speaking children made the same types of mistakes suggests that the children go through a similar process in acquiring English and use similar strategies. It seems reasonable to argue, as Dulay and Burt did, that children attempt to construct rules for the speech they hear, guided by general cognitive strategies that lead them to formulate certain types of hypotheses about the language system being acquired. There is also considerable evidence from the errors made by adult learners of English as a second language that suggests that they make similar mistakes regardless of their first language and that their mistakes are analyzable as incorrect attempts to discover the rules of the English language.

Certain of the errors that second-language learners make can be clearly categorized as developmental in character. They occur in the same sequence as errors that first-language learners of the target language make. This is especially true of negative and interrogative constructions and modal and auxiliary verbs, where first- and second-language learners of English generally show the same pattern of mistakes. There is, however, some conflicting evidence concerning negative constructions (Cancino, Rosansky, & Schumann, 1974; Wode, 1978).

Another source of errors is simplification. One finds this strategy used by both first- and second-language learners. Both types of learner will tend to prefer simple to more complex constructions, will drop endings, will use the infinitive or imperative verb form for other conjugations, and so forth. The tendency to simplify, in fact, underlies many of the developmental errors observed in first- and second-language learners.

Other mistakes made by second-language learners are more subtle and more difficult to categorize. It seems quite likely, however, that some errors that appear to reflect the influence of first-language structures may reflect instead a strategy of generalizing on the basis of regularities observed in the target language. An example given by Dulay and Burt (1972) is the sentence *I know to do all that* spoken by a child whose first language was Spanish. Although this sentence appears to show the influence of Spanish, it may in fact be an overgeneralization of English verb–complement constructions such as would be the case if *want* were the verb rather than *know*. The child may be overgeneralizing from one English construction to another in an effort to determine the range of application of rules.

In other situations, the child may in fact make errors that show unambiguously the influence of the first language. Such errors, however, can also be interpreted in terms of strategies the learner is using to discover linguistic regularities in the target language. In this case, learners resort to what they know about language as a source of hypotheses for discovering regularities that they do not know. In some language learning situations this strategy may be frequently employed, especially when the second language is learned in the classroom and when the learner has little contact with peers who speak the second language.

This is not to deny that learners make interference or transfer errors. As we have seen, research leads to the conclusion that order of acquisition of phonological, syntactic, and morphological structures in a second language involves the interplay of both developmental and transfer factors (Hakuta & Cancino, 1977; Hecht & Mulford, 1982; Zobl, 1980). The pendulum seems to have swung from an over-emphasis on transfer to an excessive de-emphasis. A more balanced position is to see transfer errors as interesting for what they reveal about learner's strategies.

One of the reasons for preferring a strategy analysis to an analysis based on interference between languages is that an interference analysis rests on a weak theoretical foundation. It derives from a habit theory of learning: interference occurs because old habits have not been extinguished. According to this theory, new learning (of a second language) is only possible when old habits (the first language) have been extinguished. But people obviously do not forget their first language in mastering a second language.

In addition, an analysis of errors in terms of interference has unfortunate pedagogic implications. The teacher and the student tend to regard errors negatively. They are to be exorcised by all possible means; they contribute nothing to the learning process and only retard the student's progress. In contrast, a strategy analysis views errors as a positive source of information about the way in which learners try to make sense out of the second-language input to which they are exposed. It is not so much the error that matters as the strategy that underlies the error. Once the limitations of a particular strategy can be made clear to the student, a whole complex of errors can be avoided.

> *Proposition 3.   There is a single language system that forms the basis for acquisition, storage, and retrieval of first and second languages.*

The evidence from studies of children who acquire two languages simultaneously points to the conclusion that the language acquisition process is the same in each language as it is for the monolingual child. This means that in the bilingual child's language development certain structures in one language will lag behind those of the other language because they are more complex, with the pattern in each language replicating that found in monolingual children.

There is also evidence that the bilingual child does not encode the two languages separately. In the early stages there is syntactic and morphological confusion as a result of the child's attempt to apply a single set of rules to both languages. In time the child learns to keep the separate rules straight. What evidence there is, however, suggests that the child learns the rules of languages as a single set with those specific to a particular code tagged as such through a process of differentiation. Similarly, the lexical systems of the two languages do not seem to be stored separately, but rather together, with some means of tagging used to keep them separate.

The system might be quite complex. There may be, as Paradis (1978) has suggested, a number of different stores within a single extended system. Some elements of both languages may be stored in identical ways in the system, but other elements may form separate networks or subsystems within the larger system. This is somewhat speculative, because at present so little is known about bilingual storage and retrieval, especially of syntactic aspects of language.

Nonetheless, the postulation of a single language system seems to be consistent with available evidence. To suggest that there is a separate system for each language contradicts most evidence from studies of memory processes in adult bilingual subjects. Nor do the data from studies comparing first- and second-language acquisition in children and second-language learning in adults appear to require the postulation of different language acquisition systems before and after puberty.

In addition, the hypothesis of separate language systems is unparsimonious. It is more economical to regard the bilingual's two languages as separate linguistic codes, analogous to the separate codes of a monolingual speaker. There seems to be no reason to argue that the task of switching languages involves additional processes over and above those used to switch codes in a single language.

In some languages—Javanese is the example frequently given—there are a large number of different language codes associated with such variables as age, sex, kinship relation, occupation, wealth, religion, education, and family background. The complexity of code switching in these various communication situations is enormous, relative to what we are used to in European languages. Anthropologists describing the Javanese system report it to be more complex than is bilingualism for Europeans.

Yet we do not usually postulate separate language systems for the various codes of a single language. The ability of the speaker to move from code to code within a language does not seem to require a multiple language system, one system for each code. Each code is part of a single system with some means available for tagging entries or structures as belonging to one code or another.

It seems consistent to hypothesize that the same is true of bilingualism. The bilingual's language system is a single system with some means of discriminating lexical entries and syntactic forms. Switching codes within this system is not any different from switching codes within a single language. Of course, we do not know very much about the mechanisms involved—either in monolingual or bilingual individuals. It may be, however, that research with bilinguals will throw light on the still mysterious process of code switching in monolingual individuals.

In concluding, I should emphasize that the three propositions I have been discussing are not necessarily true. They are merely proposed as being consistent with most research findings to this point, whereas the propositions discussed earlier appear to run counter to what has been learned through research. It may be that future investigations will show that some or all of the statements I feel are warranted are wrong, whereas those that at present seem unwarranted may turn out to be correct. The study of second-language acquisition in children is an exciting area of research precisely because it does not allow apodictic statements.

References

Albert, M. L., & Obler, L. K. *The bilingual brain: Neuropsychological and neurolinguistic aspects of bilingualism.* New York: Academic Press, 1978.

Anastasi, A., & de Jesus, C. Language development and nonverbal I.Q. of Puerto Rican preschool children in New York City. *Journal of Abnormal and Social Psychology,* 1953, *48,* 357–366.

Andersen, E. *Learning to speak with style: A study of the sociolinguistic skills of young children.* Doctoral Dissertation, Stanford University, 1977.

Andersen, R. An implicational model for second language research. *Language Learning,* 1978, *28,* 221–282.

Andersson, T. *Foreign languages in the elementary school.* Austin: University of Texas Press, 1969.

Andersson, T. Children's learning of a second language: Another view. *Modern Language Journal,* 1973, *57,* 254–259.

Anglin, J. M. *The growth of meaning.* Cambridge, MA: MIT Press, 1970.

Arnberg, L. *Early childhood bilingualism in the mixed-lingual family.* Doctoral Dissertation, Linköping University, Linköping, Sweden, 1979.

Arnberg, L. *The effects of bilingualism on development during early childhood: A survey of the literature.* Linköping University: Linköping Studies in Education Reports, No. 5., 1981.

Aronsson, K. Nominal realism and bilingualism: A critical review of the studies on word-referent differentiation. *Osnabrücker Beiträge zur Sprachtheorie,* 1981, *20,* 106–116.

Arsenian, S. *Bilingualism and mental development.* New York: Columbia University Press, 1937.

Asch, J. E., & Nerlove, H. The development of double function terms in children: An exploratory investigation. In B. Kaplan & J. Wapner (Eds.), *Perspectives in psychological theory: Essays in honor of Heinz Werner.* New York: International Universities Press, 1960.

Asher, J. J. The strategy of total physical response: An application to learning Russian. *International Review of Applied Linguistics in Language Teaching,* 1965, *3,* 291–300.

Asher, J. J. The total physical response approach to second language learning. *Modern Language Journal,* 1969, *53,* 3–17.

Asher, J. J., & Garcia, R. The optimal age to learn a foreign language, *Modern Language Journal*, 1969, *53,* 334–341.

Asher, J. J., Kusudo, J. A., & de le Torre, R. Learning a second language through commands: The second field test. *Modern Language Journal,* 1974, *58,* 24–32.

Asher, J. J., & Price, B. S. The learning strategy of a total physical response: Some age differences. *Child Development,* 1967, *38,* 1219–1227.

Baetens Beardsmore, H. *Bilingualism: Basic principles.* Clevedon, England: Tieto Ltd., 1982.

Bailey, N., Madden, C., & Krashen, S. D. Is there a "natural sequence" in adult second language learning? *Language Learning,* 1974, *24,* 235–243.

Bain, B. Verbal regulation of cognitive processes: A replication of Luria's procedures with bilingual and unilingual infants. *Child Development,* 1976, *47,* 543–546.

Bain, B., & Yu, A. Cognitive consequences of raising children bilingually: "One parent, one language." *Canadian Journal of Psychology,* 1980, *34,* 304–313.

Balkan, L. *Les effets du bilingualisme français-anglais sur les aptitudes intellectuelles.* Brussels: AIMAV, 1970.

Barik, H. C., & Swain, M. English-French bilingual education in the early grades: The Elgin study. *Modern Language Journal,* 1974, *58,* 392–403.

Barke, E. M. A study of the comparative intelligence of children in certain bilingual and monoglot schools in South Wales. *British Journal of Educational Psychology,* 1933, *3,* 237–250.

Basser, L. S. Hemiplegia of early onset and the faculty of speech with special reference to the effects of hemispherectomy. *Brain,* 1962, *85,* 427–460.

Bates, E., & MacWhinney, B. Functionalist approaches to grammar. In L. Gleitman & E. Wanner (Eds.), *Language acquisition: The state of the art.* Cambridge, MA: Harvard University Press, 1982.

Bellugi, U. Simplification in children's language. In R. Huxley & E. Ingram (Eds.), *Methods and models in language acquisition.* New York: Academic Press, 1971.

Ben Zeev, S. The influence of bilingualism on cognitive strategy and cognitive development. *Child Development,* 1977, *48,* 1009–1018.

Bergman, C. R. Interference vs. independent development in infant bilingualism. In G. D. Keller, R. V. Teschner, & S. Viera (Eds.), *Bilingualism in the bicentennial and beyond.* New York: Bilingual Press/Editorial Bilingue, 1976.

Berko, J. The child's learning of English morphology. *Word,* 1958, *14,* 150–177.

Berlin, C. S., Lowe-Bell, R., Hughes, L., & Berlin, H. Dichotic right ear advantage in males and females—ages 5 to 13. *Journal of the Acoustical Society of America.* 1972, *53,* 368.

Berman, R. The re-emergence of a bilingual: A case study of a Hebrew-English speaking child. *Working Papers on Bilingualism,* 1979, *19,* 157–180.

Bever, T. G. The cognitive basis for linguistic structures. In J. R. Hayes (Ed.), *Cognition and the development of language.* New York: Wiley, 1970.

Bierwisch, M. Some semantic universals of German adjectives. *Foundations of Language,* 1967, *3,* 1–36.

Bloom, L. *Language development: Form and function in emerging grammars.* Cambridge, MA: MIT Press, 1970.

Bloom, L. *One word at a time: The use of single word utterances before syntax.* The Hague: Mouton, 1973.

Bloom, L., Hood, L., & Lightbown, P. Imitation in language development: If, when and why. *Cognitive Psychology,* 1974, *6,* 380–420.

Bloom, L. M., Lightbown, P., & Hood, L. Structure and variation in child language. *Monographs of the Society for Research in Child Development,* 1975, (No. 160).

Bloomfield, L. *Language.* London: Allen and Unwin, 1935.

Bock, J. K. Toward a cognitive psychology of syntax: Information processing contributions to sentence formation. *Psychological Review,* 1982, *89,* 1–47.

Bowerman, M. *Early syntactic development: A cross-linguistic study with special reference to Finnish.* Cambridge: Cambridge University Press, 1973.

Bowerman, M. Semantic factors in the acquisition of rules for word use and sentence construction. In D. Morehead & A. Morehead (Eds.), *Normal and deficient language.* Baltimore: University Park Press, 1976.

Bradshaw, W. L., & Anderson, H. E. Developmental study of the meaning of adverbial modifiers. *Journal of Educational Psychology,* 1968, *59,* 111–118.

Braine, M. D. S. On two types of models of internalization of grammars. In D. I. Slobin (Ed.), *The ontogenesis of grammar.* New York: Academic Press, 1971. (a)

Braine, M. D. S. The acquisition of language in infant and child. In C. E. Reed (Ed.), *The learning of language.* New York: Appleton-Century-Crofts, 1971. (b)

Braine, M. D. S. Length constraints, reduction rules, and holophrastic processes in children's word combinations. *Journal of Verbal Learning and Verbal Behavior,* 1974, *13,* 448–456.

Bransford, J. D., & Franks, J. J. The abstraction of linguistic ideas: A review. *Cognition,* 1972, *1,* 211–249.

Braun, M. Beobachtungen zur Frage der Mehrsprachigheit. *Göttingische Gelehrte Anzeigen,* 1937, *199,* 115–130.

Bridges, A., Sinha, C., & Walkerdine, V. The development of comprehension. In G. Wells, *Learning through interaction: The study of language development.* Cambridge: Cambridge University Press, 1981.

Brown, A. L., & Scott, M. S. Recognition memory for pictures for preschool children. *Journal of Experimental Child Psychology,* 1971, 11, 401–412.

Brown, H. D. *Principles of language learning and teaching.* Englewood Cliffs, NJ: Prentice-1980, *14,* 157–164. (a)

Brown, H. D. *Principles of language learning and teaching.* Englewood Cliffs, N.J.: Prentice-Hall, 1980. (b)

Brown, R. The development of Wh-questions in child speech. *Journal of Verbal Learning and Verbal Behavior,* 1968, *1,* 279–290.

Brown, R. *A first language: The early stages.* Cambridge, MA: Harvard University Press, 1973 (a)

Brown, R. Development of the first language in the human species. *American Psychologist,* 1973, *28,* 97–106. (b)

Brown, R., & Bellugi, U. Three processes in the acquisition of syntax. *Harvard Educational Review,* 1964, *34,* 133–151.

Brown, R., & Fraser, C. The acquisition of syntax. In C. N. Cofer & B. Musgrave (Eds.), *Verbal behavior and learning.* New York: McGraw-Hill, 1963.

Brown, R., & Hanlon, C. Derivational complexity and order of acquisition in child speech. In J. Hayes (Ed.), *Cognition and the development of language.* New York: Wiley, 1970.

Bruck, M., Lambert, W. E., & Tucker, G. R. Bilingual schooling through the elementary grades: The St. Lambert Project at grade seven. *Language Learning,* 1974, *24,* 183–204.

Brudhiprabha, P. *Error analysis: A psycholinguistic study of Thai English compositions.* Masters Thesis, McGill University, 1972.

Bubenik, V. The acquisition of Czech in the English environment. In M. Paradis (Ed.), *Aspects of bilingualism.* Columbia, SC: Hornbeam Press, 1978.

Buddenhagen, R. G. *Establishing vocal verbalizations in mute mongoloid children.* Champaign, IL: Research Press, 1971.

Bühler, K. *The mental development of the child.* London, 1930 (translated from 5th German edition).

Bühler, U. B. *Empirische und lernpsychologische Beiträge zur Wahl des Zeitpunktes für den*

Fremdsprachenunterrichtsbeginn: Lernpsychologischinterpretierte Leistungsmessungen im Frage Französischunterricht an Primärschulen des Kantons Zürich. Zürich: Orell Füssli, 1972.

Burke, S. J. Language acquisition, language learning, and language teaching. *International Review of Applied Linguistics in Language Teaching,* 1974, *12,* 53–68.

Burling, R. Language development of a Garo and English speaking child. *Word,* 1959, *15,* 45–68.

Burt, M. K., Dulay, H. C., & Hernández–Chavez, E. *Bilingual syntax measure.* New York: Harcourt Brace Jovanovitch, 1975.

Burt, M. K., & Kiparsky, C. *The gooficon: A repair manual for English.* Rowley, MA: Newbury House, 1972.

Cambon, J., & Sinclair, E. Relations between syntax and semantics: Are they "easy to see"? *British Journal of Psychology,* 1974, *65,* 133–140.

Canale, M., & Swain, M. Theoretical bases of communicative approaches to second language teaching and testing. *Applied Linguistics,* 1980, *1,* 1–47.

Cancino, H., Rosansky, E. J., & Schumann, J. H. Testing hypotheses about second language acquisition: The copula and the negative in three subjects. *Working Papers in Bilingualism,* 1974, *3,* 80–96.

Cancino, H., Rosansky, E. J., & Schumann, J. H. The acquisition of the English auxiliary by native Spanish speakers. *TESOL Quarterly,* 1975, *9,* 421–430.

Carey, S. The child as word learner. In M. Halle, J. Bresnan, & G. A. Miller (Eds.), *Linguistic theory and psychological reality.* Cambridge, MA: MIT Press, 1978.

Carroll, J. B. Development of native language skills beyond the early years. In C. E. Reed (Ed.) *The learning of language.* New York: Appleton-Century-Crofts, 1971.

Carrow, M. A. (E) Linguistic functioning of bilingual and monolingual children. *Journal of Speech and Hearing Disorders,* 1957, *22,* 371–380.

Carrow, E. Comprehension of English and Spanish by preschool Mexican-American children. *Modern Language Journal,* 1971, *55,* 299–307.

Casagrande, J. B. Comanche baby language. *International Journal of American Linguistics,* 1948, *14,* 11–14.

Cazden, C. The acquisition of noun and verb inflections. *Child Development,* 1968, *39,* 433–438.

Celci–Murcia, M. The simultaneous acquisition of English and French in a two-year-old child. In E. Hatch (Ed.), *Second language acquisition: A book of readings.* Rowley, MA: Newbury House, 1978.

Chi, M. T. H. Short-term memory limitations in children: Capacity or processing deficits? *Memory and Cognition,* 1976, *4,* 559–572.

Child, I. L. *Italian or American? The second generation in conflict.* New Haven, CT: Yale University Press, 1943.

Chomsky, C. *The acquisition of syntax in children from 5 to 10.* Cambridge, MA: MIT Press, 1969.

Chomsky, N. *Syntactic structures.* The Hague: Mouton, 1957.

Chomsky, N. Review of B. F. Skinner, *Verbal Behavior. Language,* 1959, *35,* 26–58.

Chomsky, N. Noam Chomsky and Stuart Hampshire discuss the study of language. *The Listener,* 1968, *79,* No. 2044.

Chomsky, N. A., & Halle, M. *The sound pattern of English.* New York: Harper & Row, 1968.

Christian, C. C., & Sharp, J. M. Bilingualism in a pluralistic society. In D. L. Lange & C. J. James (Eds.), *Foreign language education: A reappraisal.* Skokie, IL: National Textbook Co., 1972.

Christophersen, P. *Second-language learning: Myth and reality.* Baltimore: Penguin, 1973.

Clahsen, H. Psycholinguistic aspects of L2 acquisition: Word order phenomena in foreign workers' interlanguage. In S. Felix (Ed.), *Second language development: Trends and issues.* Tübingen: Narr, 1980.

Clark, E. V. What's in a word? On the child's acquisition of semantics in his first language. In T. E. Moore (Ed.), *Cognitive development and the acquisition of language.* New York: Academic Press, 1973.

Clark, E. V. Some aspects of the conceptual basis for first language acquisition. In R. L. Schiefelbusch & L. L. Lloyd (Eds.), *Language perspectives: Acquisition, retardation, and intervention.* New York: Macmillan, 1974.

Clark, H. H. The primitive nature of children's relational concepts. In J. R. Hayes (Ed.), *Cognition and the development of language.* New York: Wiley, 1970.

Clark, H. H. Space, time, semantics, and the child. In T. E. Moore (Ed.), *Cognitive development and the acquisition of language.* New York: Academic Press, 1973.

Clark, H. H., & Chase, W. G. On the process of comparing sentences against pictures. *Cognitive Psychology,* 1972, *3,* 472-517.

Clark, H. H., & Clark, E. V. *Psychology and language.* New York: Harcourt, Brace and Jovanovich, 1977.

Clark, H. H., & Haviland, S. E. Psychological processes as linguistic explanation. In D. Cohen (Ed.), *Explaining linguistic phenomena.* Washington, DC: Hemisphere, 1974.

Clark, R. Performing without competence. *Journal of Child Language,* 1974, *1,* 1-10.

Clark, R. Some even simpler ways to learn to talk. In N. Waterson & C. Snow (Eds.), *The development of communication.* New York: Wiley, 1978

Cook, V. J. The comparison of language development in native children and foreign adults. *International Review of Applied Linguistics in Language Teaching,* 1973, *11,* 13-29.

Cooper, R. L. What do we learn when we learn a language? *TESOL Quarterly,* 1970, *4,* 312-320.

Corder, S. P. The significance of learner's errors. *International Review of Applied Linguistics in Language Teaching,* 1967, *5,* 161-170.

Corder, S. P. Error analysis, interlanguage, and second language acquisition. *Language Teaching and Linguistics,* 1975, *8,* 201-217.

Cornejo, R. J. The acquisition of lexicon in the speech of bilingual children. In P. R. Turner (Ed.), *Bilingualism in the Southwest.* Tucson: University of Arizona Press, 1973.

Cromer, R. F. Children are nice to understand: Surface structure clues for the recovery of a deep structure. *British Journal of Psychology,* 1970, *61,* 397-408.

Cross, T. G. Mothers' speech and its association with linguistic development in young children. In N. Waterson & C. Snow (Eds.), *The development of communication.* New York: Wiley, 1978.

Cukovsky, L. *From two to five.* Berkeley: University of California Press, 1965.

Cummins, J. The influence of bilingualism on cognitive growth: A synthesis of research findings and explanatory hypotheses. *Working Papers on Bilingualism,* 1976, *9,* 1-9.

Cummins, J. Bilingualism and the development of metalinguistic awareness. *Journal of Cross-Cultural Psychology,* 1978, *9,* 139-149. (a)

Cummins, J. Educational implications of mother tongue maintenance in minority-language groups. *Canadian Modern Language Review,* 1978, *34,* 395-416. (b)

Cummins, J. Linguistic interdependence and the educational development of bilingual children. *Review of Educational Research,* 1979, *49,* 222-251.

Cummins, J. Age on arrival and immigrant second language learning: A reassessment. *Applied Linguistics,* 1981, *2,* 132-149.

Curran, C. A. Counselling skills adapted to the learning of foreign languages. *Bulletin of the Menninger Clinic,* 1961, *25,* 79-83.

Curtiss, S. *Genie: A psycholinguistic study of a modern-day "Wild Child."* New York: Academic Press, 1977.

d'Anglejan, A., & Tucker, G. R. The acquisition of complex English structures by adult learners. *Language Learning,* 1975, *25,* 281–293.

Darcy, N. T. A review of the literature on the effects of bilingualism upon the measurement of intelligence. *Journal of Genetic Psychology,* 1953, *82,* 21–58.

Darcy, N. T. Bilingualism and the measurement of intelligence: A review of a decade of research. *Journal of Genetic Psychology,* 1963, *103,* 259–282.

Dato, D. P. *American children's acquisition of Spanish syntax in the Madrid environment. Preliminary edition.* U.S. Office of Education. Institute of International Studies. Project No. 3036. Contract No. OEC 2-7-002637, May, 1970.

Dato, D. P. The development of the Spanish verb phrase in children's second-language learning. In P. Pinsleur & T. Quinn (Eds.), *The psychology of second-language learning.* Cambridge: Cambridge University Press, 1971.

De Avila, E. A., & Duncan, S. E. Definition and measurement of bilingual students. In *Bilingual program, policy, and assessment issues.* Sacramento, CA: California State Department of Education, 1980.

Della Corte, M., Benedict, H., & Klein, D. The relationship of pragmatic dimensions of mothers' speech to the referential-expressive distinction. *Journal of Child Language,* 1983, *10,* 35–43.

Dempster, F. N. Memory span and short-term memory capacity: A developmental study. *Journal of Experimental Child Psychology,* 1978, *26,* 419–431.

De Villiers, P. A., & De Villiers, J. G. Early judgments of semantic and syntactic acceptability by children. *Journal of Psycholinguistic Research,* 1972, *1,* 299–310.

Diller, K. C. "Compound" and "coordinate" bilingualism: A conceptual artifact. *Word,* 1970, *26,* 254–261.

Dimitrijevic, N. R. A bilingual child. *English Language Teaching,* 1965, *20,* 23–28.

Donaldson, M., & Balfour, G. Less is more: A study of language comprehension in children. *British Journal of Psychology,* 1968, *59,* 461–472.

Donaldson, M., & Wales, R. On the acquisition of relational terms. In J. R. Hayes (Ed.), *Cognitive and the development of knowledge.* New York: Wiley, 1970.

Donoghue, M. R. *Foreign languages and the elementary school child.* Dubuque, Iowa: Brown, 1968.

Dore, J. A pragmatic description of early language development. *Journal of Psycholinguistic Research,* 1974, *3,* 343–350.

Dornic, S. Information processing in bilinguals: Some selected issues. *Psychological Research,* 1979, *40,* 329–348.

Doyle, A. B., Champagne, M., & Segalowitz, N. Some issues in the assessment of the consequences of early bilingualism. In M. Paradis (Ed.), *Aspects of bilingualism.* Columbia, SC: Hornbeam Press, 1978.

Dulay, H. C., & Burt, M. K. Goofing: An indication of children's second language learning strategies. *Language Learning,* 1972, *22,* 299–307.

Dulay, H. C., & Burt, M. K. Should we teach children syntax? *Language Learning,* 1973, *23,* 245–258.

Dulay, H., & Burt, M. K. A new perspective on the creative construction processes in child second language acquisition. *Language Learning,* 1974, *24,* 253–278. (a)

Dulay, H. C., & Burt, M. K. Errors and strategies in child second language acquisition. *TESOL Quarterly,* 1974, *8,* 129–136. (b)

Dulay, H. C., & Burt, M. K. Natural sequences in child second language acquisition. *Language Learning,* 1974, *24,* 37–53. (c)

Dulay, H., Burt, M. K., & Krashen, S. *Language two.* New York: Oxford University Press, 1982.

Duncan, S. E., & De Avila, E. A. Bilingualism and cognition: Some recent findings. *NABE Journal,* 1979, *4,* 15–50.

Echeverría, M. S. On needed research in second-language learning in the light of contemporary developments in linguistic theory. *International Review of Applied Linguistics in Language Teaching*, 1974, *12*, 69–77.

Eckman, F. R. Markedness and the contrastive analysis hypothesis. *Language Learning*, 1977, *27*, 315–330.

Eimas, P. D., Siqueland, E. R., Jusczyk, P., & Vigorito, J. Speech perception in infants. *Science*, 1971, *171*, 303–306.

Ekstrand, L. H. Age and length of residence as variables related to the adjustment of immigrant children, with special reference to second language learning. In G. Nickel (Ed.), *Proceedings of the Fourth International Congress of Applied Linguistics*. Stuttgart: Hochschul-Verlag, 1976.

Ekstrand, L. H. Replacing the critical period and optimum age theories of second language acquisition with a theory of ontogenetic development beyond puberty. *Educational and Psychological Interactions*. Department of Educational and Psychological Research, Malmo School of Education, 1979.

Elwert, W. T. *Das zweisprachige Individuum: Ein Selbstzeugnis*. Wiesbaden: Steiner, 1960.

Emrich, L. Beobachtungen über Zweisprachigkeit in ihrem Anfangsstadium. *Deutschtum im Ausland*, 1938, *21*, 419–424.

Engel, W. von R. Del bilinguismo infantile. *Archivio Glottologico Italiano*, 1965, *50*, 175–180.

Engel, W. von R. Linguaggio attivo e linguaggio passivo. *Orientamenti Pedagogici*, 1966, *13*, 893–894.

Ervin-Tripp, S. M. Language development. In L. W. Hoffman & M. L. Hoffman (Eds.), *Review of child development research*. New York: Russell Sage Foundation, 1966.

Ervin-Tripp, S. An Issei learns English. *Journal of Social Issues*, 1967, *23*, 78–90.

Ervin-Tripp, S. Commentary on a paper by R. M. Jones. In L. G. Kelley (Ed.), *Description and measurement of bilingualism: An international seminar*. Toronto: University of Toronto Press, 1969.

Ervin-Tripp, S. Discourse agreement: How children answer questions. In J. R. Hayes (Ed.), *Cognition and the development of language*. New York: Wiley, 1970. (a)

Ervin-Tripp, S. Structure and process in language acquisition. *Monograph Series on Language and Linguistics*, 1970, *23*, 313–344. (b)

Ervin-Tripp, S. Some strategies for the first two years. In T. E. Moore (Ed.), *Cognitive development and the acquisition of language*. New York: Academic Press, 1973. (a)

Ervin-Tripp, S. The structure of communicative choice. In S. Ervin-Tripp, *Language acquisition and communicative choice*. Edited by A.D.I. Dil. Stanford: Stanford University Press, 1973. (b)

Ervin-Tripp, S. Is second language learning like the first? *TESOL Quarterly*, 1974, *8*, 111–127.

Ervin-Tripp, S. Social process in first- and second-language learning. In H. Winitz (Ed.), *Native language and foreign language acquisition*. New York: The New York Academy of Sciences, 1981.

Ervin, S. M., & Osgood, S. E. Second language learning and bilingualism. *Journal of Abnormal and Social Psychology*, 1954, *49*, 139–146.

Fantini, A. E. *Language acquisition of a bilingual child: A sociolinguistic perspective (to age 5)*. Brattleboro, VT: The Experiment Press, 1974.

Fathman, A. The relationship between age and second language productive ability. *Language Learning*, 1975, *25*, 245–253.

Feldman, C., & Shen, M. Some language-related cognitive advantages of bilingual 5-year-olds. *Journal of Genetic Psychology*, 1971, *118*, 235–244.

Felix, S. W. Some differences between first and second language acquisition. In C. Waterson & C. Snow (Eds.), *The development of communication*. New York: Wiley, 1978.

Ferguson, C. A. Diglossia. *Word,* 1959, *15,* 325–340.

Fischer, J. L. Social influences on the choice of a linguistic variant. *Word,* 1958, *14,* 47–56.

Fishman, J. A. Language maintenance and language shift as fields of inquiry. *Linguistics,* 1964, *9,* 32–70.

Fishman, J. A. *Language loyalty in the United States.* The Hague: Mouton, 1966.

Fishman, J. A. *Sociolinguistics: A brief introduction.* Rowley, MA: Newbury House, 1970.

Fishman, J. Bilingual education in the United States under ethnic community auspices. In J. E. Alatis (Ed.), *Georgetown University round table on languages and linguistics 1980.* Washington, DC: Georgetown University Press, 1980.

Flavell, H. H. Developmental studies of mediated memory. In H. W. Reese & L. P. Lipsitt (Eds.), *Advances in child development and behavior.* Vol. 5. New York: Academic Press, 1970.

Fodor, J. A., Bever, T. G., & Garrett, M. F. *The psychology of language.* New York: McGraw-Hill, 1974.

Francescato, G. Appunti teorico-pratici sul bilinguismo infantile. *Lingua e Stile,* 1969, *4,* 445–458.

Fraser, C., Bellugi, V., & Brown, R. Control of grammar in imitation, comprehension, and production. *Journal of Verbal Learning and Verbal Behavior,* 1963, *2,* 121–135.

Fromkin, V., Krashen, S., Curtiss, S., Rigler, D., & Rigler, M. The development of language in Genie: A case of language acquisition beyond the critical period. *Brain and Language,* 1974, *1,* 81–107.

Furrow, D., Nelson, K., & Benedict, H. Mothers' speech to children and syntactic development: Some simple relationships. *Journal of Child Language,* 1979, *6,* 423–442.

Gaer, E. P. Children's understanding and production of sentences. *Journal of Verbal Learning and Verbal Behavior,* 1969, *8,* 289–294.

Garcia, E. E. The function of language switching during bilingual mother-child interactions. *Journal of Multilingual and Multicultural Development,* 1980, *1,* 243–252.

Gardner, R., Smythe, P., Clement, R., & Gliksman, L. Second language learning: A social psychological perspective. *The Canadian Modern Language Review,* 1976, *32,* 198–213.

Garrett, M., & Fodor, J. Psychological theories and linguistic constructs. In T. R. Dixon & D. L. Horton (Eds.), *Verbal behavior and general behavior theory.* Englewood Cliffs, NJ: Prentice-Hall, 1968.

Gazzaniga, M. S. *The bisected brain.* New York: Appleton-Century-Crofts, 1970.

Geertz, C. *The religion of Java.* New York: The Free Press, 1960.

Geissler, H. *Zweisprachigheit deutscher Kinder im Ausland.* Stuttgart: Kohlhammer, 1938.

George, H. V. *Common errors in language learning.* Rowley, MA: Newbury House, 1972.

Gerald, J. A. *The sea dreamer.* Hamden, CT: Archon Books, 1967.

Gerullis, G. Muttersprache und Zweisprachigheit in einem preussisch-litauischen Dorf. *Studi Baltici,* 1932, *2,* 59–67.

Gleason, J. B. Code switching in children's language. In T. E. Moore (Ed.), *Cognitive development and the acquisition of language.* New York: Academic Press, 1973.

Goldman–Eisler, F. *Psycholinguistics: Experiments in spontaneous speech.* New York: Academic Press, 1968.

Gordon, D., & Lakoff, G. Conversational postulates. *Papers from the 7th Regional Meeting, Chicago Linguistic Society,* 1971.

Grégoire, A. *L'apprentissage tu langage: les deux premières années.* Liège: Bibliothèque de la Faculté de Philosophie et Lettres, 1937.

Grider, R. E., Otomo, A., & Toyota, W. *Comparison between second, third, and fourth grade children in the audio lingual learning of Japanese as a second language.* Research report, Honolulu; University of Hawaii, 1961.

Grimm, H. *Analysis of short-term dialogues in 5-7 year olds: Encoding of intentions and modifications of speech acts as a function of negative feedback.* Paper presented at the Third International Child Language Symposium, London, Sept. 1975.

Grosjean, F. *Life with two languages: An introduction to bilingualism.* Cambridge, MA: Harvard University Press, 1982.

Gumperz, J. J. Types of linguistic communities. *Anthropological Linguistics,* 1962, *4,* 28–40.

Gumperz, J. J. Verbal strategies in multilingual communication. *Monograph Series on Languages and Linguistics,* 1970, *23,* 129–143.

Gumperz, J. J., & Hernández-Chavez, E. Bilingualism, bidialectalism, and classroom interaction. In C. B. Cazden, V. P. John, & D. Hymes (Eds.), *Functions of language in the classroom.* New York: Teacher College Press, 1972.

Hakuta, K. A preliminary report on the development of grammatical morphemes in a Japanese girl learning English as a second language. *Working Papers in Bilingualism,* 1974, *3,* 18–38. (a)

Hakuta, K. Prefabricated patterns and the emergence of structure in second language acquisition. *Language Learning,* 1974, *24,* 287–297. (b)

Hakuta, K. Learning to speak a second language: What exactly does the child learn? In D. P. Dato (Ed.), *Georgetown University round table on languages and linguistics 1975.* Washington, DC: Georgetown University Press, 1975.

Hakuta, K. Becoming bilingual: A case study of a Japanese child learning English. *Language Learning,* 1976, *26,* 321–351.

Hakuta, K. English language acquisition by speakers of Asian languages. In M. Chu Chang (Ed.), *Comparative research in bilingual education.* New York: Teachers College Press, 1983.

Hakuta, K., & Cancino, H. Trends in second-language acquisition research. *Harvard Educational Review,* 1977, *47,* 294–316.

Hakuta, K., & Diaz, M. The relationship between degree of bilingualism and cognitive ability. In K. E. Nelson (Ed.), *Children's Language.* Vol. 6. In press.

Halle, M. Phonology in a generative grammar. *Word,* 1962, *18,* 54–72.

Halliday, M. A. K., McIntosh, A., & Stevens, P. *The linguistic sciences and language teaching.* London: Longman, 1964.

Harshman, R., & Krashen, S. An "unbiased" procedure for comparing degree of laterization of dichotically presented stimuli. *Journal of the Acoustical Society of America,* 1972, *52,* 174.

Hatch, E. *A historical overview of second language acquisition research.* Paper presented at the Los Angeles Second Language Research Forum, Feb., 1977.

Hatch, E. (Ed.) *Second language acquisition: A book of readings.* Rowley, MA: Newbury House, 1978.

Hatch, E. *Psycholinguistics: A second language perspective.* Rowley, MA: Newbury House, 1983.

Haugen, E. *The Norwegian language in America.* Philadelphia: University of Pennsylvania Press, 1953.

Haugen, E. Problems of bilingual description. *General Linguistics,* 1955, *1,* 1–9.

Haugen, E. *Bilingualism in the Americas.* University of Alabama: University of Alabama Press, 1956.

Haugen, E. Linguistics and dialinguistics. *Georgetown Monograph Series on Languages and Linguistics,* 1970, *23,* 1–7.

Heath, S. B. *Ways with words: Language, life and work in communities and classrooms.* Cambridge: Cambridge University Press, 1983.

Hecht, B. F., & Mulford, R. The acquisition of a second language phonology: Interaction of transfer and developmental factors. *Applied Psycholinguistics,* 1982, *3,* 313–328.

Heilenman, L. K. Do morphemes mature? The relationship between cognitive maturation and linguistic development in children and adults. *Language Learning,* 1981, *31,* 51–65.

Hill, J. Foreign accents, language acquisition and cerebral dominance revisited. *Language Learning,* 1970, *20,* 237–248.

Hoff–Ginsberg, E., & Shatz, M. Linguistic input and the child's acquisition of language: A critical review. *Psychological Bulletin,* 1982, *92,* 3–26.

Horgan, D. Nouns: Love 'em or leave 'em. In V. Teller & S. J. White (Eds.), *Studies in child language and multilingualism.* New York: Annals of the New York Academy of Sciences, 1980.

Horton, M., & Markman, E. Developmental differences in the acquisition of basic and super-ordinate categories. *Child Development,* 1980, *51,* 708–719.

Hoyer, A. E., & Hoyer, G. Über die Lallsprache eines Kindes. *Zeitschrift für angewandte Psychologie,* 1924, *24,* 363–384.

Huang, J., & Hatch, E. A Chinese child's acquisition of English. In E. Hatch (Ed.), *Second language acquisition.* Rowley, MA: Newbury House, 1978.

Huebner, T. Order of acquisition vs. dynamic paradigm: A comparison of methods in inter-language research. *TESOL Quarterly,* 1979, *13,* 21–28.

Huerta, A. The acquisition of bilingualism: A code-switching approach. *Sociolinguistic Working Paper, No. 39.* Austin, TX: Southwest Education Development Laboraotory, 1977.

Huntsberry, R. *Second language acquisition in childhood.* Manuscript, Language Acquisition Laboratory, University of Connecticut, 1972.

Hymes, D. *Language in culture and society.* New York: Harper & Row, 1964.

Ianco–Worrall, A. D. Bilingualism and cognitive development. *Child Development,* 1972, *43,* 1390–1400.

Imedadze, N. V. K psikhologicheskoy prirode rannego dvuyazychiya. *Voprosy Psikhologii,* 1960, *6,* 60–68.

Imedadze, N. V. On the psychological nature of child speech formation under conditions of exposure to two languages. *International Journal of Psychology,* 1967, *2,* 129–132.

Ingram, D. Phonological rules in young children. *Journal of Child Language,* 1974, *1,* 49–64.

Itard, J. *The wild boy of Aveyron.* New York: Appleton-Century-Crofts, 1962.

Itoh, H., & Hatch, E. Second language acquisition: A case study. In E. Hatch (Ed.), *Second language acquisition.* Rowley, MA: Newbury House, 1978.

Jakobovits, L. A. *Foreign language learning: A psycholinguistic analysis of the issues.* Rowley, MA: Newbury House, 1970.

Jakobovits, L. The physiology and psychology of second language learning. In E. M. Birk-maier (Ed.), *Foreign language education: An overview.* Skokie, IL: National Textbook Co., 1972.

Jakobson, R. *Kindersprache, Aphasie, und allgemeine Lautgesetze.* Uppsala: Almquist und Wiksell, 1941.

Jakobson, R. Why "mama" and "papa"? In B. Kaplan & S. Wapner (Eds.), *Perspectives in psychological theory.* New York: Wiley, 1960.

James, C. The exculpation of contrastive linguistics. In G. Nickel (Ed.), *Papers in contrastive linguistics.* London: Cambridge University Press, 1971.

James, C. *Contrastive analysis.* London: Laongman, 1980.

Jensen, J. V. The effects of childhood bilingualism. *Elementary English,* 1962, *39,* 132–143, 358–366.

Jones, W. R. The language handicap of Welsh-speaking children. *British Journal of Education,* 1952, *22,* 114–123.

Jones, W. R. *Bilingualism in Welsh education.* Cardiff: University of Wales Press, 1966.

Katz, J. J. *The philosophy of language.* New York: Harper, 1966.

Keller–Cohen, D. Systematicity and variation in the nonnative child's acquisition of conversational skills. *Language Learning,* 1979, *29,* 27–44.

Kelley, K. L. *Early syntactic acquisition.* P-3719, The Rand Corporation, Santa Monica, CA, 1967.

Kenyeres, A. Comment une petite Hongroise de sept ans apprend le français. *Archives de Psychologie,* 1938, *26,* 321–366.

Kessler, C. *The acquisition of syntax in bilingual children.* Washington, DC: Georgetown University Press, 1971.

Kessler, C. Syntactic contrasts in child bilingualism. *Language Learning,* 1972, *22,* 221–223.

Kessler, C., & Idar, I. *The acquisition of English syntactic structures by a Vietnamese child.* Paper presented at the Second Language Research Forum, UCLA, February, 1977.

Kessler, C., & Idar, I. Acquisition of English by a Vietnamese mother and child. *Working Papers on Bilingualism,* 1979, *18,* 65–79.

King, R. D. *Historical linguistics and generative grammar.* Englewood Cliffs, N.J.: Prentice-Hall, 1969.

Kinsbourne, M. Neurolinguistic aspects of bilingualism. In H. Winitz (Ed.), *Native language and foreign language acquisition.* New York: The New York Academy of Sciences, 1981.

Kirstein, B., & de Vincenz, A. A note on bilingualism and generative grammar. *Praxis des neusprachlichen Unterrichts,* 1974, *12,* 159–161.

Klein, D. *Expressive and referential communication in children's early language development: The relationship to mothers' communicative styles.* Doctoral Dissertation, Michigan State University, 1980.

Klima, E. S., & Bellugi, U. Syntactic regularities in the speech of children. In J. Lyons & R. J. Wales (Eds.), *Psycholinguistic papers.* Edinburgh: Edinburgh University Press, 1966.

Kobrick, J. W. The compelling case for bilingual education. *Saturday Review,* 1972, *55,* 54–58. No. 18.

Krashen, S. D. Lateralization, language learning, and the critical period: Some new evidence. *Language Learning,* 1973, *23,* 63–74.

Krashen, S. The development of cerebral dominance and language learning: More new evidence. In D. P. Dato. (Ed.), *Georgetown University round table on language and linguistics.* Washington, DC: Georgetown University Press, 1975.

Krashen, S. *Second language acquisition and second language learning.* Elmsford, NY: Pergamon Press, 1981.

Krashen, S. Accounting for child-adult differences in second language rate and attainment. In S. D. Krashen, R. C. Scarcella, & M. H. Long (Eds.), *Child-adult differences in second language acquisition.* Rowley, MA: Newbury House, 1982.

Krashen, S., Long, M., & Scarcella, R. Age, rate, and eventual attainment in second language acquisition. *TESOL Quarterly,* 1979, *13,* 573–582.

Krashen, S., & Scarcella, R. On routines and patterns in language acquisition and performance. *Language Learning,* 1978, *28,* 283–300.

Krashen, S., Sferlazza, V., Feldman, L., & Fathman, A. Adult performance on the SLOPE test: More evidence for a natural sequence in adult second language acquisition. *Language Learning,* 1976, *26,* 145–151.

Kuczaj, S. A. Acquisition of word meaning in the context of the development of the semantic system. In C. J. Brainerd & M. Pressley (Eds.), *Progress in cognitive development research: Verbal processes in children.* Berlin: Springer, 1982.

Kuo, E. C. The family and bilingual socialization: A sociolinguistic study of a sample of Chinese children in the United States. *Journal of Social Psychology,* 1974, *92,* 181–191.

Lado, R. *Language teaching: A scientific approach.* New York: McGraw-Hill, 1964.

Lambert, R., & Freed, B. (Eds.) *The loss of language skills.* Rowley, MA: Newbury House, 1982.

Lambert, W. A social psychology of bilingualism. *Journal of Social Issues,* 1967, *23,* 91–109.

Lambert, W. E. The effects of bilingualism on the individual: Cognitive and sociocultural consequences. In P. A. Hornby (Ed.), *Bilingualism: Psychological, social, and educational implications.* New York: Academic Press, 1977.

Lambert, W. E., & Rawlings, C. Bilingual processing of mixed-language associative networks. *Journal of Verbal Learning and Verbal Behavior,* 1969, *8,* 604–609.

Lambert, W. E., & Tucker, G. R. *Bilingual education of children: The St. Lambert experiment.* Rowley, MA: Newbury House, 1972.

Lance, D. *A brief study of Spanish-English bilingualism: Final report.* Research Project Orr-Liberal Arts-15504. College Station, TX, Texas A and M, 1969.

Landry, R. G. A comparison of second-language learners and monolinguals on divergent thinking tasks at the elementary school level. *Modern Language Journal,* 1974, *58,* 10–15.

Larsen–Freeman, D. An explanation for the morpheme acquisition order of second language learners. *Language Learning,* 1976, *26,* 125–134. (a)

Larsen–Freeman, D. ESL teacher speech as input to ESL learner. *Workpapers in Teaching English as a Second Language,* 1976, *10,* 45–50. (b)

Lee, L. L., & Canter, S. M. Developmental sentence scoring: A clinical procedure for estimating syntactic development in children's spontaneous speech. *Journal of Speech and Hearing Disorders,* 1971, *50,* 315–339.

Lee, W. R. Language, experience, and the language teacher. *English Language Teaching Journal,* 1973, *27,* 234–245.

Lenneberg, E. Understanding language without ability to speak: A case report. *Journal of Abnormal and Social Psychology,* 1962, *65,* 419–425.

Lenneberg, E. H. *Biological foundations of language.* New York: Wiley, 1967.

Leopold, W. F. *Speech development of a bilingual child: A linguist's record.* Vol. 1.: *Vocabulary growth in the first two years.* Vol. 2.: *Sound learning in the first two years.* Vol. 3: *Grammar and general problems in the first two years.* Vol. 4.: *Diary from age two.* Evanston, IL: Northwestern University Press, 1939, 1947, 1949a, 1949b.

Leopold, W. F. Patterning in children's language learning. *Language Learning,* 1953, *5,* 1–14.

Liepmann, D., & Saegert, J. Language tagging in bilingual free recall. *Journal of Experimental Psychology,* 1974, *103,* 1137–1141.

Lightbown, P. French second-language learners: What they're talking about. *Language Learning,* 1977, *27,* 371–381.

Lightbown, P. The acquisition and use of questions by French L2 learners. In S. Felix (Ed.), *Second language development: Trends and issues.* Tübingen: Narr, 1980.

Limber, J. The genesis of complex sentences. In T. E. Moore (Ed.), *Cognitive development and the acquisition of knowledge.* New York: Academic Press, 1973.

Limber, J. Language in child and chimp? *American Psychologist,* 1977, *33,* 280–295.

Lindfors, J. W. *Children's language and learning.* Englewood Cliffs, NJ: Prentice-Hall, 1980.

Lindholm, K. J., & Padilla, A. M. Language mixing in bilingual children. *Journal of Child Language,* 1977, *5,* 327–335.

Lindholm, K. J., & Padilla, A. M. Child bilingualism: Report on language mixing, switching, and translations. *Linguistics,* 1978, *16,* 23–44.

Littlewood, W. T. A comparison of first-language acquisition and second language learning. *Praxis des neusprachlichen Unterrichts,* 1973, *20,* 343–348.

Lopez, M., Hicks, R. E., & Young, R. K. Retroactive inhibition in a bilingual A-B, A-B' paradigm. *Journal of Experimental Psychology,* 1974, *103,* 85–90.

Luria, A. R. *The working brain.* Baltimore, MD: Penguin, 1973.

Mackey, W. F. Bilingual interference: Its analysis and measurement. *Journal of Communication,* 1965, *15,* 239–249.

MacNab, G. L. Cognition and bilingualism: A reanalysis of studies. *Linguistics,* 1979, *17,* 231–255.

Macnamara, J. *Bilingualism and primary education.* Edinburgh: Edinburgh University Press, 1966.

Macnamara, J. Bilingualism in the modern world. *Journal of Social Issues,* 1967, *23,* 1–7. (a)

Macnamara, J. (Ed.), The bilingual's linguistic performance: A psychological overview. *Journal of Social Issues,* 1967, *23,* 58–77.(b)

Macnamara, J. Cognitive basis of language learning in infants. *Psychological Review,* 1972, *79,* 1–14.

Macnamara, J. Nurseries, streets, & classrooms. *Modern Language Journal,* 1973, *57,* 250–254.

Major, R. C. Phonological differentiation of a bilingual child. *Ohio State University Working Papers in Linguistics,* 1976, *22,* 88–122.

Malmberg, B. Drag ur en fy råarig finsk flichas språkliga utvectling. *Nordisk Tidskrift för Vetenskap.* 1945, *21,* 170–181.

Manuel, H. T., & Wright, C. E. The language difficulty of Mexican children. *Journal of Genetic Psychology,* 1929, *36,* 458–466.

McCarthy, D. Language development in children. In L. Carmichael (Ed.), *Manual of child psychology.* New York: Wiley, 1946.

McLaughlin, B. *Learning and social behavior.* New York: The Free Press, 1971.

McLaughlin, B. Second-language learning in children. *Psychological Bulletin,* 1977, *84,* 438–459.

McLaughlin, B. The monitor model: Some methodological considerations. *Language Learning,* 1978, *28,* 309–332.

McLaughlin, B. Theory and research in second-language learning· An emerging paradigm. *Language Learning,* 1980, *30,* 331–350.

McLaughlin, B. Differences and similarities between first and second language learning. In H. Winitz (Ed.), *Native language and foreign language acquisition.* New York: The New York Academy of Sciences, 1981.

McLaughlin, B. Early bilingualism: Methodological and theoretical issues. In M. Paradis (Ed.), *Early bilingualism and child development.* Amsterdam: Swets and Zeitlinger, in press.

McNeill, D. Developmental psycholinguistics. In F. Smith & G. A. Miller (Eds.), *The genesis of language.* Cambridge, MA: MIT Press, 1966.

McNeill, D. *The acquisition of language: The study of developmental psycholinguistics.* New York: Harper & Row, 1970.

Meertens, P. J. Sprachforschung im Noordoostpolder der Zuidersee. *Zeitschrift für Mundartforschung,* 1959, *26,* 239–256.

Meisel, J. Linguistic simplification. In S. Felix (Ed.), *Second language development: Trends and issues.* Tübingen: Narr, 1980.

Meisel, J., Clahsen, H., & Peinemann, M. On determining the developmental stages in natural second-language acquisition. *Wuppertaler Arbeitspapier zur Sprachwissenschaft.* 1979, No. 2. 1–37.

Menn, L. Towards a psychology of phonology: Child phonology as a first step. In *Applications of linguistic theory in the human sciences.* Lansing, MI: Michigan State University, 1979.

Menyuk, P. *The acquisition and development of language.* Englewood Cliffs, NJ: Prentice-Hall, 1971.

Metraux, R. W. Study of bilingualism among children of U.S.-French parents. *French Review,* 1965, *38,* 650–665.

Mikeš, M. Acquisition des catégoires grammaticales dan le langage de l'enfant. *Enfance,* 1967, *20,* 289–298.

Mikeš, M., & Vlahović, P. Razvoj gramatickik kategorija u decjem govoru. *Prilozi Proucavanjy jezika,* 1966, *II.* Novi Sad, Yugoslavia.

Miller, N. E., & Dollard, J. *Social learning and imitation.* New Haven, CT: Yale University, 1941.

Milon, J. P. The development of negation in English by a second language learner. *TESOL*

Quarterly, 1974, *8,* 137–143.

Mitchell, A. J. The effect of bilingualism in the measurement of intelligence. *Elementary School Journal,* 1937, *38,* 29–37.

Mitchell, P. M. Tresprogethed. *Berlingske Tidends Kronik,* 1954, 30/7.

Moerk, E., & Moerk, C. Quotations, imitations, and generalizations: Factual and methodological analyses. *International Journal of Behavioral Development.* 1979, *2,* 43–72.

Montessori, M. *Education for a new world.* Adyas, Madras, India: Kalakshetra Publications, 1959.

Morrison, J. R. Bilingualism: Some psychological aspects. *The Advancement of Science,* 1958, *56,* 287–290.

Moscovitch, M. Language and the cerebral hemisphere. Reaction-time studies and their implications for models of cerebral dominance. In P. Pliner, L. Krames, & T. Alloway (Eds.), *Communication and affect: Language and thought.* New York: Academic Press, 1973.

Moscovitch, M. On the representation of language in the right hemisphere of right-handed people. *Brain and Language,* 1976, *3,* 47–71.

Moskowitz, A. I. The two-year-old stage in the acquisition of English phonology. *Language,* 1970, *46,*426–441.

Mowrer, O. H. *Learning theory and behavior.* New York: Wiley, 1960.

Murrell, M. Language acquisition in a trilingual environment: Notes from a case study. *Studia Linguistica,* 1966, *20,* 9–35.

Naiman, N. The use of elicited imitation in second language acquisition research. *Working Papers in Bilingualism,* 1974, *3,* 1–37.

Natalicio, D. S., & Natalicio, L. F. S. A comparative study of English pluralization by native and non-native speakers. *Child Development,* 1971, *42,* 1302–1306.

Nelson, K. Structure and strategy in learning to talk. *Monographs of the Society for Research on Child Development,* 1973, *38.* No. 149.

Nelson, K. Individual differences in language development: Implications for development and language. *Developmental Psychology,* 1981, *17,* 225–287.

Newmark, L., & Reibel, D. Necessity and sufficiency in language learning. *International Review of Applied Linguistics in Language Teaching,* 1968, *6,* 145–161.

Nygren–Junken, L. *The interaction between French and English in the speech of four bilingual children.* Masters Thesis, Ontario Institute for Studies in Education, Toronto, Ont., 1977.

O'Donnell, R. C., Griffin, W. J., & Norris, R. C. *Syntax of kindergarten and elementary children: A transformational analysis.* (Research Report #8). Champaign, IL: National Council of Teachers of English, 1967.

Ochs, E. *Talking to children in Western Samoa.* Manuscript. Linguistics Department, University of Southern California, 1980, 15–119.

Oksaar, E. Besprechung vom V. Rūķe-Draviņa *Mehrsprachigheit im Vorschulalter. Die Sprache,* 1969, *15,* 187–190.

Oksaar, E. Zum Spracherwerb des Kindes in Zweisprachiger Umgebung. *Folia Linguistica,* 1970, *4,* 330–358.

Oller, J. Research on the measurement of affective variables: Some remaining questions. In R. W. Andersen (Ed.), *New dimensions in research on the acquisition and use of a second language.* Rowley, MA: Newbury House, 1981.

Olson, G. M. Developmental changes in memory and the acquisition of language. In T. E. Moore (Ed.), *Cognitive development and the acquisition of language.* New York: Academic Press, 1973.

Oyama, S. A sensitive period for the acquisition of nonnative phonological system. *Journal of Psycholinguistic Research,* 1976, *5,* 261–284.

Padilla, A. M., & Liebman, E. Language acquisition in a bilingual child. *Bilingual Review,* 1975, *2,* 34–55.

Palermo, D. S., & Howe, H. E. Jr. An experimental analogy to the learning of past tense inflection rules. *Journal of Verbal Learning and Verbal Behavior,* 1970, *9,* 410–416.

Palermo, D. S., & Molfese, D. L. Language acquisition from age five onwards. *Psychological Bulletin,* 1972, *78,* 409–428.

Paradis, M. *Bilingual linguistic memory: Neurolinguistic considerations.* Paper presented to the Linguistic Society of America, Boston, 1978.

Paradis, M. Language and thought in bilinguals. In *The sixth LACUS forum.* Columbia, SC: Hornbeam Press, 1980.

Patkowski, M. The sensitive period for the acquisition of syntax in a second language. *Language Learning,* 1980, *30,* 449–472.

Pavlovitch, M. *Le langage enfantin: Acquisition du serbe et du francais par un enfant serbe.* Paris: Champion, 1920.

Peal, E., & Lambert, W. E. The relation of bilingualism to intelligence. *Psychological Monographs,* 1962, *76,* 1–23 (No. 546).

Peck, S. Child-child discourse in second language acquisition. In E. Hatch (Ed.), *Second language acquisition: A book of readings.* Rowley, MA: Newbury House, 1978.

Peddie, R. *Par Erruer: Error analysis and the early stages of adolescent foreign language learning.* Doctoral Dissertation, University of Auckland, 1982.

Penfield, W., & Roberts, L. *Speech and brain-mechanisms.* Princeton, NJ: Princeton University Press, 1959.

Perren, G. New languages and young children. *English Language Teaching,* 1972, *26,* 229–238.

Peters, A. Language learning strategies: Does the whole equal the sum of the parts? *Language,* 1977, *53,* 560–573.

Peters, A. M. *The units of language acquisition.* Cambridge: Cambridge University Press, 1983.

Pienemann, M. The second language acquisition of immigrant children. In S. Felix (Ed.), *Second language development: Trends and issues.* Tübingen: Narr, 1980.

Politzer, R. L. *Foreign language learning: A linguistic introduction.* Englewood Cliffs, NJ: Prentice-Hall, 1965.

Politzer, R. L. Developmental sentence scoring as a method of measuring second language acquisition. *Modern Language Journal,* 1974, *58,* 245–250.

Politzer, R. L., & Ramirez, A. G. An error analysis of the spoken English of Mexican-American pupils in a bilingual school and a monolingual school. *Language Learning,* 1973, *23,* 39–61.

Politzer, R. L., & Weiss, L. Developmental aspects of auditory discrimination, echo response, and recall. *Modern Language Journal,* 1969, *53,* 75–85.

Porsché, D. Urteile und Vorurteile über Zweisprachigheit in Kinderalter. *Linguistik und Didaktik,* 1975, *23,* 179–189.

Prator, C. H. Adding a second language. *TESOL Quarterly,* 1969, *3,* 95–104.

Preyer, W. *Die Seele des Kindes: Beobchtungen über die geistige Entwichlung des Menschens in den ersten Lebensjahren.* Leipzig: Schaefer, 1882.

Price, E. Early bilingualism. In C. J. Dodson, E. Price, & L. T. Williams (Eds.), *Toward bilingualism.* Cardiff: University of Wales Press, 1968.

Ramsey, C. A., & Wright E. N. Age and second language learning. *Journal of Social Psychology,* 1974, *94,* 115–121.

Ravem, R. Language acquisition in a second language environment. *International Review of Applied Linguistics in Language Teaching,* 1968, *6,* 175–185.

Ravem, R. The development of Wh-questions in first and second language learners. In J. C. Richards (Ed.), *Error analysis: Perspectives on second language acquisition.* London: Longman, 1974.

Redlinger, W. E. Early developmental bilingualism: A review of the literature. *The Bilingual*

Review/Le Revista Bingue, 1979, *6,* 11–30.

Redlinger, W. E., & Park, T. Language mixing in young bilinguals. *Journal of Child Language,* 1980, *7,* 337–352.

Richards, J. Error analysis and second language strategies. *Language Sciences,* 1971, *17,* 12–22.

Richards, J. C. Social factors, interlanguage, and language learning. *Language Learning,* 1972, *22,* 159–188.

Rigg, M. Some further data on the language handicap, *Journal of Educational Psychology,* 1928,*19,* 252–256.

Riley, C. *The role of transfer in child second language acquisition.* Senior thesis. University of California, Santa Cruz, 1977.

Rivers, W. *The psychologist and the foreign-language teacher.* Chicago: University of Chicago Press, 1964.

Roberts, J. T. The LAD hypothesis and L2 acquisition: The relevance of the former for the latter. *Audio-Visual Language Journal,* 1973, 11, 97–112.

Roeper, T. Connecting children's language and linguistic theory. In T. E. Moore (Ed.), *Cognitive development and the acquisition of language.* New York: Academic Press, 1973.

Ronjat, J. *Le développement du langage observé chez un enfant bilingue.* Paris: Champion, 1913.

Rosansky, E. J. Methods and morphemes in second language acquisition research. *Language Learning,* 1976, *26,* 409–425.

Rosch, E. H. On the internal structure of perceptual and semantic categories. In T. E. Moore (Ed.), *Cognitive development and the acquisition of language.* New York: Academic Press, 1973.

Rūķe-Draviņa, V. The process of acquisition of apical /r/ and uvular /R/ in the speech of children. *Linguistics,* 1965, *17,* 56–68.

Rūķe-Draviņa, V. *Mehrsprachigheit im Vorschulalter.* Lund: Gleerup, 1967.

Rumelhart, D. E., Lindsay, P. H., & Norman, D. A. *A process model for long-term memory.* New York: Academic Press, 1972.

Russell, W. R., & Espir, M. L. E. *Traumic aphasia.* Oxford: Oxford University Press, 1961.

Saer, D. J. The effect of bilingualism on intelligence. *British Journal of Psychology,* 1923, *14,* 25–38.

Saporta, S. Applied linguistics and generative grammar. In A. Valdman (Ed.), *Trends in language teaching.* New York: McGraw-Hill, 1966.

Schachter, J. An error in error analysis. *Language Learning,* 1974, *24,* 205–214.

Schachter, J., & Celce-Murcia, M. Some reservations concerning error analysis. *TESOL Quarterly,* 1977, *11,* 441–451.

Schank, R. C. Cognitive dependency: A theory of natural language understanding. *Cognitive Psychology,* 1972, *3,* 552–631.

Schieffelin, B. B. *How Kaluli children learn what to say, what to do, and how to feel: An ethnographic study of the development of communicative competence.* Doctoral Dissertation, Columbia University, 1979.

Schlesinger, I. M. Production of utterances and language acquisition. In D. Slobin (Ed.), *The ontogenesis of grammar.* New York: Academic Press, 1971.

Schmidt-Rohr, G. *Muttersprache.* Jena: Amt der Sprache bei der Volkwerdung, 1933.

Schumann, J. H. The implications of interlanguage, pidginization, and creolization for the study of adult second language acquisition. *TESOL Quarterly,* 1974, *8,* 145–152.

Schumann, J. H. Affective factors and the problem of age in second language acquisition. *Language Learning,* 1975, *25,* 209–235.

Scovel, T. Foreign accents, language acquisition, and cerebral dominance. *Language Learning,* 1969, *19,* 245–254.

Seidl, J. C. G. *The effect of bilingualism on the measurement of intelligence.* Doctoral Dissertation, Fordham University, 1937.

Seliger, H. W. Implications of a multiple critical-periods hypothesis for second language learning. In W. C. Ritchie (Ed.), *Second language acquisition research.* New York: Academic Press, 1978.

Seliger, H. W. Exceptions to critical period predictions: A sinister plot. In R. Andersen (Ed.), *New dimensions in second language acquisition research.* Rowley, MA: Newbury House, 1981.

Selinker, L. Interlanguage. *International Review of Applied Linguistics,* 1972, *10,* 209–231.

Selinker, L., Swain, M., & Dumas, G. The interlanguage hypothesis extended to children. *Language Learning,* 1975, *25,* 139–152.

Senn, A. Einiges aus der Sprache. *Studi Baltici,* 1932, *2,* 35–58.

Shatz, M. How to do things by asking: Form-function pairings in mothers' questions and their relation to children's responses. *Child Development,* 1979, *50,* 1093–1099.

Sinclair-deZwart, H. Language acquisition and cognitive development. In T. E. Moore (Ed.), *Cognitive development and the acquisition of language.* New York: Academic Press, 1973.

Singh, J. A. L., & Zingg, R. M. *Wolf-children and feral man.* Hamden, CT: Archon Books, 1966.

Skinner, B. F. *Verbal behavior.* New York: Appleton-Century-Crofts, 1957.

Skutnabb–Kangas, T. Semilingualism and the education of migrant children as a means of reproducing the caste of assembly line workers. In N. Dittmar, H. Haberland, T. Skutnabb-Kangas, & V. Teleman (Eds.), *Papers from the first Scandinavian-German symposium on the language of immigrant workers and their children.* Roshilde, Denmark, Universitetscenter, 1978.

SkutnabbzKangas, T., & Toukomaa, P. *Teaching migrant children's mother tongue and learning the language of the host country in the context of the socio-cultural situation of the migrant family.* Helsinki, Finland: The Finnish National Commission for UNESCO, 1976.

Slobin, D. I. The acquisition of Russian as a native language. In E. Smith & G. A. Miller (Eds.), *The genesis of language.* Cambridge, MA: MIT Press, 1966. (a)

Slobin, D. I. Grammatical transformations and sentence comprehension in childhood and adulthood. *Journal of Verbal Learning and Verbal Behavior,* 1966, *5,* 219–227. (b)

Slobin, D. I. Developmental psycholinguistics In W, O. Dingwall (Ed.), *A survey of linguistic science.* College Park, MD.: University of Maryland Linguistics Program, 1971.

Slobin, D. I. Cognitive prerequisites for the development of grammar. In C. Ferguson & D. Slobin, (Eds.), *Studies of child language development.* New York: Holt, Rinehart & Winston, 1973.

Slobin, D. I. Language change in childhood and in history. In J. Macnamara (Ed.), *Language learning and thought.* New York: Academic Press, 1977.

Slobin, D. I. A case study of early language awareness. In A. Sinclair, R. Jarvella, & W. J. M. Levelt (Eds.), *The child's conception of language.* Berlin: Springer–Verlag, 1978.

Slobin, D. I. *Psycholinguistics.* (2nd ed.) Glenview, IL: Scott, Foresman, 1979.

Slobin, D. I., & Welsh, C. A. Elicited imitation as a research tool in developmental psycholinguistics. In C. A. Ferguson & D. I. Slobin (Eds.), *Readings in child language acquisition.* New York: Holt, Rinehart, Winston, 1973.

Smith, M. E. A study of language development in bilingual children in Hawaii. *Psychological Bulletin,* 1933, *30,* 629.

Smith, M. E. A study of the speech of eight bilingual children of the same family. *Child Development,* 1935, *6,* 19–25.

Smith, M. E. Some light on the problem of bilingualism as found from a study of the progress in mastery of English among preschool children of non-American ancestry in Hawaii. *Genetic Psychology Monographs* 1939, *21,* 121–284.

Smith, M. Measurement of vocabularies of young bilingual children in both of the languages used. *Journal of Genetic Psychology,* 1949, *74,* 305-310.

Smith, M. Word variety as a measure of bilingualism in preschool children. *Journal of Genetic Psychology,* 1957, *90,* 143-150.

Snow, C. F. The uses of imitation. *Journal of Child Language,* 1981, *8,* 205-212.

Snow, C., & Ferguson, C. A. (Eds.), *Talking to children: Language input and acquisition.* Cambridge: Cambridge University Press, 1977.

Snow, C., & Hoefnagel-Höhle, M. Age differences in the pronunciation of foreign sounds. *Language and Speech,* 1977, *20,* 357-365.

Snow, C., & Hoefnagel-Höhle, M. The critical period for language acquisition: Evidence from second language learning. *Child Development,* 1978, *49,* 1114-1118.

Snow, C. E., & Hoefnagel-Höhle, M. Individual differences in second-language ability: A factor-analytic study. *Language and Speech,* 1979, *22,* 151-162.

Snow, K. A comparative study of sound substitutions by "normal" first grade children. *Speech Monographs,* 1964, *31,* 135-142.

Sperry, R. W., Gazzaniga, M. S., & Bogen, J. E. Interhemispheric relationships: The neo- *90,* 131-148.

Sperry, R. W., Gazzaniga, M. S., & Bogen, J. E. Interhemispheric relationships: The neo cortical commisures; syndromes of hemispheric disconnection. In P. J. Vinken & G. W. Bruyn (Eds.), *Handbook of clinical neurology.* Vol. 4. Amsterdam: North Holland Publishers, 1969.

Spoerl, D. T. The academic and verbal adjustment of college age bilingual students. *Journal of Genetic Psychology,* 1944, *64,* 139-157.

Staats, A. W. *Learning, language, and cognition.* New York: Holt, Rinehart, & Winston, 1968.

Stern, C., & Stern, W. *Die Kindersprache: Eine psychologische und sprachtheoretische Untersuchung.* Leipzig: Barth, 1907.

Stern, H. H. *Perspectives on second language teaching.* Toronto: Ontario Institute for Studies in Education, 1970.

Stewart, W. A. Facts and issues concerning Black dialect. *English Record,* 1971, 21 (4).

Stolz, W., & Tiffany, J. The production of "child-like" word associations by adults to unfamiliar adjectives. *Journal of Verbal Learning and Verbal Behavior,* 1972, *11,* 38-46.

Strong, M. *Social styles and the second language acquisition of Spanish-speaking kindergartners.* Doctoral Dissertation, University of California, Berkeley, 1982.

Swain, M. *Bilingualism as a first language.* Doctoral Dissertation. University of California, Irvine, 1972.

Swain, M. Child bilingual language learning and linguistic interdependence. In S. Carey (Ed.), *Bilingualism, biculturalism and education.* Edmonton: University of Alberta Press, 1974.

Swain, M., & Wesche, M. Linguistic interaction: Case study of a bilingual child. *Language Sciences,* 1975, *37,* 17-22.

Tabouret-Keller, A. L'acquisition du langage parlé chez un petit enfant en milieu bilingue. *Problemes de Psycholinguistique,* 1962, *8,* 205-219.

Taylor, B. Toward a theory of language acquisition. *Language Learning,* 1974, *24,* 23-35.

Taylor, B. P. The use of overgeneralization and transfer learning strategies by elementary and intermediate students of ESL. *Language Learning,* 1975, *25,* 73-108.

Taylor, M. Speculations on bilingualism and the cognitive network. *Working Papers on Bilingualism,* 1974, *2,* 68-124.

Thurstone, L. *The differential growth of mental abilities.* Chapel Hill, NC: University of North Carolina Press, 1955.

Titone, R. Some factors underlying second-language learning. *English Language Teaching,* 1973, *27,* 110-120.

Tits, D. *Le mécanisme de l'acquisition d'une langue se substituent à le langue maternelle chez une enfant espagnole âgée de six ans.* Brussels: Veldeman, 1948.

Totten, G. O. Bringing up children bilingually. *American Scandinavian Review,* 1960, *48,* 42–50.

Tremaine, R. V. *Syntax and Piagetian operational thought.* Washington, DC: Georgetown University Press, 1975.

Tulving, E., & Colotla, V. A. Free recall of trilingual lists. *Cognitive Psychology,* 1970, *1,* 86–98.

Tulving, E., & Madigan, S. A. Memory and verbal learning. *Annual Review of Psychology,* 1970, *24,* 437–484.

Turner, E. A., & Rommetveit, R. Experimental manipulation in the production of active and passive voice in children. *Language and Speech,* 1967, *10,* 169–180.

Ulibarri, H. Bilingualism. In E. M. Birkmaier (Ed.), *Foreign language education: An overview.* Skokie, IL: National Textbook Co., 1972.

Vaid, J. Visual, phonetic and semantic processing in early and late bilinguals. In M. Paradis (Ed.), *Early bilingualism and child development.* Amsterdam: Swets and Zeitlinger, in press.

Valette, R. M. Some reflections on second-language learning in young children. *Language Learning,* 1964, *14,* 91–98.

Velten, H. V. The growth of phonemic and lexical pattern in infant language. *Language,* 1943, *19,* 281–292.

Vey, M. Le vocabulaire tchèque en Grande-Bretagne pendant la guerre. *Revue des Études Slaves,* 1946, *22,* 117–127.

Vihman, M. M. Phonology and the development of the lexicon: Evidence from children's errors. *Journal of Child Language,* 1981, *8,* 239–264.

Vihman, M. M. The acquisition of morphology by a bilingual child: The whole-word approach. *Applied Psycholinguistics,* 1982, *3,* 141–160. (a)

Vihman, M. M. Formulas in first and second language acquisition. In L. Obler & L. Menn (Eds.), *Exceptional language and linguistics.* New York: Academic Press, 1982. (b)

Vihman, M. M. *Language differentiation by the bilingual infant.* Manuscript, Stanford University, 1983.

Vihman, M. M., & McLaughlin, B. Bilingualism and second language acquisition in preschool children. In C. J. Brainerd & M. Pressley (Eds.), *Progress in cognitive development research: Verbal processes in children.* Berlin: Springer, 1982.

Vildomec, V. *Multilingualism: General linguistics and psychology of speech.* Leyden: Sijthoff, 1963.

Volterra, V., & Taeschner, T. The acquisition and development of language by a bilingual child. *Journal of Child Language,* 1978, *5,* 311–326.

Vygotsky, L. S. *Thought and language.* Cambridge, MA: MIT Press, 1962.

Waggoner, D. Non-English language background persons: Three U.S. Surveys. *TESOL Quarterly,* 1978, *12,* 247–262.

Wagner-Gough, J. Excerpts from *Comparative studies in second-language learning.* In E. Hatch (Ed.), *Second language acquisition: A book of readings.* Rowley, MA: Newbury House, 1978.

Wagner-Gough, J., & Hatch, E. The importance of input data in second language acquisition studies. *Language Learning,* 1975, *25,* 297–308.

Walsh, T. M., & Diller, K. C. Neurolinguistic considerations on the optimum age for second language learning. In K. Diller (Ed.), *Individual differences and universals in language learning aptitude.* Rowley, MA: Newbury House, 1981.

Weinreich, W. *Languages in contact.* The Hague: Mouton, 1953.

Weir, R. H. *Language in the crib.* The Hague: Mouton, 1962.

Weisgerber, L. *Deutsches Volk und deutsche Sprache.* Frankfurt/Main, 1935.

Wells, G. *Learning through interaction: The study of language development*. Cambridge: Cambridge University Press, 1981.

Werner, H., & Kaplan, B. *Symbol formation*. New York: Wiley, 1964.

Whitaker, H. A., Bub, D., & Leventer, S. Neurolinguistic aspects of language acquisition and bilingualism. In H. Winitz (Ed.), *Native language and foreign language acquisition*. New York: The New York Academy of Sciences, 1981.

Wilkins, D. A. *Linguistics in language teaching*. Cambridge, MA: MIT Press, 1972.

Wilkins, D. A. *Second-language learning and teaching*. London: Arnold, 1974.

Winograd, T. *Understanding natural languages*. Edinburgh: University Press, 1972.

Wode, H. Developmental principles in naturalistic L2 acquisition. In E. Hatch (Ed.), *Second language acquisition: A book of readings*. Rowley, MA: Newbury House Press, 1978.

Wode, H. *Learning a second language: 1. An integrated view of language acquisition*. Tübingen: Narr, 1981.

Wode, H., Bahns, J., Bedey, H., & Frank, W. Developmental sequence: An alternative approach to morpheme order. *Language Learning, 1978, 28,* 175–186.

Wong Fillmore, L. *The second time around: Cognitive and social strategies in second language acquisition. Doctoral Dissertation, Stanford University, 1976.*

Zaręba, A. Język polski w szwecji. *Język Polski,* 1953, *33,* 29–37, 98–111.

Zedlitz, G. W. von. *The search for a country*. Wellington, New Zealand: Paul's Book Arcade, 1963.

Zobl, H. Systems of verb classification and cohesion of verb-complement relations as structural conditions on interference in a child's L2 development. *Working Papers on Bilingualism, 1979, 18,* 25–74.

Zobl, H. The formal and developmental selectivity of L1 influence on L2 acquisition. *Language Learning,* 1980, *30,* 43–57.

Zobl, H. A direction for contrastive analysis: The comparative study of developmental sequences. *TESOL Quarterly,* 1982, *16,* 169–183.

Author Index

Subject Index